The Scramble for Asia

Total War
New Perspectives on World War II

Series Editors
MICHAEL B. BARRETT, The Citadel

The Second World War, a conflict that literally spanned the globe, has spawned the publication of thousands of books. In fact, it seems that new ones appear almost daily. Why, then, another series on this subject? Because there is a need for brief, accessible, and affordable books that synthesize the best of recent scholarship on World War II. Marked by tightly focused studies on vital aspects of the conflict, from the war against Japan to the Anglo-American alliance to the rise of the Red Army, the books in this provocative series will compel World War II scholars, students, and buffs to consider old questions in new terms. Covering significant topics—battles and campaigns, world leaders, and political and social dimensions—*Total War* intends to be lively, engaging, and instructive.

Volumes Published

H. P. Willmott, *The War with Japan: The Period of Balance, May 1942–October 1943* (2002).

Thomas W. Zeiler, *Unconditional Defeat: Japan, America, and the End of World War II* (2003).

Haruo Tohmatsu and H. P. Willmott, *A Gathering Darkness: The Coming of War to the Far East and the Pacific, 1921–1942* (2004).

Geoffrey Megargee, *War of Annihilation: Combat and Genocide on the Eastern Front, 1941* (2006).

Marc Gallicchio, *The Scramble for Asia: U.S. Military Power in the Aftermath of the Pacific War* (2008).

The Scramble for Asia

U.S. Military Power in the Aftermath of the Pacific War

MARC GALLICCHIO

ROWMAN & LITTLEFIELD PUBLISHERS, INC.
Lanham • Boulder • New York • Toronto • Plymouth, UK

ROWMAN & LITTLEFIELD PUBLISHERS, INC.

Published in the United States of America
by Rowman & Littlefield Publishers, Inc.
A wholly owned subsidiary of The Rowman & Littlefield Publishing Group, Inc.
4501 Forbes Boulevard, Suite 200, Lanham, Maryland 20706
www.rowmanlittlefield.com

Estover Road
Plymouth PL6 7PY
United Kingdom

British Library Cataloguing in Publication Information Available

Library of Congress Cataloging-in-Publication Data:

Gallicchio, Marc S., 1954–
  The scramble for Asia : U.S. military power in the aftermath of the Pacific War / Marc
Gallicchio.
      p. cm. — (Total War: New Perspectives on World War II)
  Includes bibliographical references and index.
  ISBN-13: 978-0-7425-4437-6 (cloth : alk. paper)
  ISBN-10: 0-7425-4437-0 (cloth : alk. paper)
  eISBN-13: 978-0-7425-6481-7
  eISBN-10: 0-7425-6481-9
  1. East Asia—Relations—Foreign countries. 2. Southeast Asia—Relations—Foreign
countries. I. Title. II. Title: U.S. military power in the aftermath of the Pacific War.
  DS518.1.G34 2008
  355'.0330509045—dc22   2008020290

To Paul J. Gallicchio

Contents

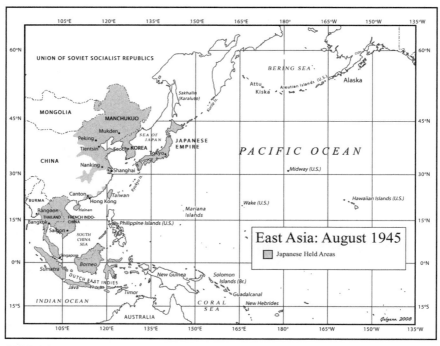

EAST ASIA MAP

East Asia—and Japanese-held areas at the time of the surrender.

Francis Galgano

Preface

Victory over Japan Day was August 15, 1945. Yet that day was not the end of hostilities across Asia. Japan's defeat was solemnized in tightly choreographed ceremonies designed to signal the transfer of power and the dawn of a new era. But as American generals and diplomats moved toward the official surrender on the deck of the USS *Missouri* at the beginning of September, the allied combatants wrestled for power in the new postwar world. There was no clean break with the past. Japan's rampage through Asia had shattered old empires and abetted the growth of revolutionary movements throughout the region. Total war had produced Japan's defeat but at the time of Japan's surrender, more than three million undefeated Japanese troops remained at their posts or in the field. As a force in being, the Japanese Imperial Army held its ground in a political no-man's-land, standing somewhere between restoration of the prewar order and the forces of revolution. Taking the surrender of Japanese troops was a military operation fraught with political implications. The decisions made to effect Japan's surrender entangled U.S. forces on the mainland of Asia for the next two years and helped to shape the next several decades of international relations in Asia.

The main purpose of this book is to show how American officials sought to translate victory over Japan into a lasting peace in Asia. It is primarily concerned with the interaction between military planning, operations, and foreign policy. The American position in postwar East Asia resulted from a series of ad hoc decisions and improvised responses to the chaos that followed in the wake of Japan's collapse. The United States was an East Asian power before World War II by virtue of its treaty rights in China and possession of the Philippine islands. Nevertheless, East Asia rarely held the attention of Americans. In the decade before the war, as Japanese forces invaded and conquered large portions of China, neither President Herbert Hoover nor President Franklin D. Roosevelt deemed American interests in the region worth the risks of war. Europe more readily commanded American attention. By 1940, Germany's conquest of the Low Countries and France and its isolation of Great Britain posed a more immediate threat to American security. The United States registered its objections to Japanese aggression and restricted trade with Tokyo but avoided confrontation until 1941 when Japan's widening campaigns linked the Asian and European wars into a single global struggle. Following Japan's attack on Pearl Harbor on December 7, 1941, the Roosevelt administration adopted a policy of aiding China militarily but that assistance took the forms of Lend Lease aid controlled by the United States and often unwelcome advice provided by American military advisors. Instead of armies, Roosevelt sent envoys to China. In place of unrestricted military assistance, the United States offered gestures of political support.

Expressions of solidarity with the peoples confronting Japanese imperialism led to more explicitly anti-colonial measures. Militarily the United States treated China as a second-class ally. Politically, however, the Roosevelt administration removed the legal trappings of China's international inferiority. In 1943, the United States negotiated away its claims to extraterritoriality, the legal privilege that shielded foreigners from Chinese law. The same year, Congress repealed the Chinese exclusion provision in American immigration law. Also in 1943, the United States and Great Britain pledged to restore to China the territories conquered by Japan and liberate Korea from Japan's empire. In 1944 Roosevelt and Congress agreed to grant the Philippines independence and designated 1946 as the year in which the United States would relinquish sovereignty over the islands. These changes signaled American support for a transformation of international relationships in Asia. But it remained unclear what role the United States would play in constructing a new system. Indeed, for much of the war American ambitions toward the mainland remained limited and ill defined. The pursuit of victory over Japan was the overriding concern. China's deteriorating situation in the final year of the war reinforced the thinking of policy makers that American resources were best employed in driving toward Japan from across the Pacific. China would have to hold on until the United States could defeat Japan, an outcome that was expected some time in 1946.[1]

The sudden collapse of Japanese resistance in August 1945 created an unexpected opportunity to influence events on the mainland and possibly check Soviet power in the region. In seeking to shape events on the mainland, the administration of President Harry S. Truman confronted the anomalous nature of American power. Its amassed invasion forces, armadas of planes and ships and, of course, its nuclear monopoly gave the United States the appearance of irresistible might. But the American public, which had brought that juggernaut into being, and the soldiers, sailors, and marines who wielded it against the enemy, had a voice in how it would be used. In the final months of the conflict the Americans had begun debating the purposes of the war and the price they were prepared to pay to achieve those ends. The abrupt end of the conflict provided only a brief interlude in that debate. In the aftermath of Japan's defeat, public debate over American aims in Asia resumed in an atmosphere of growing dissatisfaction with the disposition of American forces overseas. Eventually, protest replaced debate as Americans voiced their contending views on the meaning of victory and the obligations of world leadership.

American officials were not prepared for this democratic outburst. Some feared a resurgence of prewar isolationism. Others worried about Communist subversion at a time of growing anxiety over Soviet intentions. All understood that American power had reached its high water mark in the weeks after Japan's surrender. New limits on the use of American forces appeared. Time worked against any attempt to sustain an American presence on the mainland and undercut efforts to control the future there. The American people were calling their forces home.

The withdrawal of American forces did not wipe the slate clean. The military operations undertaken by the United States in the early days of peace affected developments in Asia in unexpected ways. Disengagement from the mainland proved more difficult than imagined. Americans would soon find that the scramble for Asia had set the stage for future conflict.

Although they strive for objectivity, historians are always subject to a variety of influences. Professional fashion, personal experiences, and contemporary events often combine to shape how the historian thinks about the past. During the last several years in which I have worked on this book the United States has struggled to build peace in the aftermath of another overwhelming military victory. The issues in Iraq were, of course, quite different from the ones faced by American policymakers in Asia after Japan's surrender. Nevertheless, comparisons seemed unavoidable. Before launching Operation Iraqi Freedom, advocates of the invasion invoked the lessons of the American occupation of Japan to assure doubters that the United States could bring democracy to the Middle East. Military victory came quickly but supporters of the war were perplexed when a stubborn insurgency grew out of the rubble of Saddam Hussein's regime. British military historian Sir John Keegan sought to chastise the war's critics by reminding them that wars often produced messy outcomes. "Peace never really came to Japanese-occupied Asia," Keegan noted. "In China, Vietnam, Indonesia and Burma, the Second World War became several wars of national liberation, lasting years and killing hundreds of thousands."[2]

I did not find those attempts to draw comparisons between the aftermath of World War II and the Iraq War historically useful or persuasive. Instead, I saw the manpower problems the American armed forces faced and the ensuing public debates over the meaning of victory in Iraq as more relevant to the concerns I wished to address. In this respect, my attention to those subjects owes something to the daily reports coming out of Baghdad and Washington while I was writing this book.

When I first wrote about the aftermath of the Pacific War nearly two decades ago I was interested in joining the scholarly debate over the origins of the Cold War in Asia. It is probably only natural for that debate to seem less important to me now than it did twenty years ago. When I returned to write about this period it was with other questions in mind. As mentioned, those questions were raised, in part, by current events. But in rethinking my approach to the aftermath of Japan's defeat I was also influenced by two of my mentors. As a graduate student at Temple University in the 1980s I had the good fortune to study diplomatic history with Waldo Heinrichs and military history with the late Russell Weigley. In that era, students in Russ's classes were always required to think about how Americans sought to reconcile the existence of professional military forces with republican institutions. Weigley's *Towards an American Army, History of the United States Army,* and his classic text *The American Way of War* were foundational works on this subject. In the late 1990s, Weigley revived discussion of this crucial issue with two important articles on the history of civil-military relations in the United States.[3] The opportunity to teach a graduate course in American military history in the summer of 2003 gave me a chance to explore these subjects again, this time with the aid of my Villanova University students.

Coincidentally, as I began thinking about this book my former graduate school adviser, Waldo Heinrichs, was beginning a project that would eventually lead him to a book-length study of American preparations for the invasion of Japan. In the course of our many discussions about our work, Waldo generously shared with me a remarkable collection of letters he wrote home while an infantryman in the 86th Division. The letters begin shortly before he sailed from the West Coast in August 1945 and continue through the period of the GI "mutiny" of January 1946. They end that spring when he returned home. Waldo also kindly loaned me a copy of the *Tandem Times*, the regimental newspaper for which he was a correspondent, and shared his memories of being one of the many GIs who languished in Asia as they waited for the ship home that would let them restart their lives.

In the course of writing this book personal experience and professional interest mingled in another, more intimate way. This book is dedicated to my father. Drafted in 1942, he spent nearly three years overseas in an anti-aircraft unit. His sojourn traced the route of the allied advance in Europe: North Africa, Corsica, Italy, and toward the end of the campaign France and finally Germany. By the time Germany surrendered he had been overseas long enough and earned enough points to be designated for discharge from the army. After V-E Day, the army concluded that for at least some GIs, one war was enough. The public was increasingly of the same mind. Following Germany's defeat, which is where this book begins, the Pacific War had entered a brief lull, an interlude of nervous anticipation that most observers thought was only an intermission before the dreaded invasion of Japan.

As noted above, I owe a special debt of thanks to Waldo Heinrichs for his contributions to this book. In addition to loaning me his letters he helpfully read and corrected the entire manuscript. He has been unfailingly generous in providing me with help and guidance for more than twenty years. Sam Gallicchio also read the entire manuscript and offered helpful comments. I also want to thank Michael Barnhart for inviting me to write this book and Tom Zeiler for offering commentary on various parts of it along the way. Dennis Giangreco kindly let me read drafts of *Hell to Pay*, his forthcoming carefully researched book on the summer of 1945. I wrote the first three chapters while teaching at the University of the Ryukyus, Okinawa, Japan as a Fulbright Visiting Lecturer in 2004–2005. I especially wish to thank Dr. Francis Galgano of Villanova University's Department of Geography and the Environment for creating the map of East Asia used here. Frank Shirer and David Hogan at the United States Center of Military History generously reproduced the photos from the Gallagher collection for me. Tom Prescott used his considerable talents to touch up some of the images reproduced for the book. Portions of chapter one were presented to a colloquium at Temple University's Center for Force and Diplomacy and the faculty forum of Villanova University Department of History. Supplementary research trips to the United States Army Center of Military History, Washington, D.C., and the Herbert Hoover Presidential Library and Museum in West Branch, Iowa were funded by a Villanova University special research grant and a grant from the Department of History's Faculty Research Fund.

Finally, I am very grateful to Michael B. Barrett, the editor of the series in which this book appears, Elizabeth Bortka, who copyedited the manuscript, and Niels Aaboe, Catherine Forrest Getzie, Asa Johnson, and Michael McGandy at Rowman & Littlefield for tolerating my delays, providing encouragement, and otherwise coaxing this book to completion.

NOTES

1. For a discussion of American wartime policy toward China that emphasizes the limited nature of American assistance see Warren I. Cohen, *America's Response to China: A History of Sino-American Relations,* 3rd edition (New York: Columbia University Press, 1990), 126–134.

2. John Keegan, "History tells us that most conflicts end in chaos," *Telegraph.Co.Uk,* 1 June 2004, http://www.telegraph.co.uk/opinion/main.jhtml?xml=/opinion/2004/06/01/do0101.xml

3. Russell F. Weigley, *Towards an American Army: Military Thought from Washington to Marshall* (New York: Columbia University Press, 1962); Weigley, *History of the United States Army,* Enlarged edition (Bloomington, IN: Indiana University Press, 1984); Weigley, *The American Way of War: A History of United States Military Strategy and Policy* (New York: Macmillan, 1973); Weigley, "The American Military and the Principle of Civilian Control from McClellan to Powell," *Journal of Military History* 57 (Special issue, October, 1993), 5: 27–58. Weigley, "The Soldier, The Statesman, and the Military Historian," *Journal of Military History* 63 (October 1999), 4: 807–822.

1

Intermission

The summer of 1945 is one of those hinges of history that seems to connect eras without possessing any clearly defined identity of its own. Germany surrendered in May, the battle for Okinawa ended in June. The American conquest of Okinawa had breached Japan's inner ring of defenses, but no new military campaigns were scheduled until autumn. For the moment much of Asia existed somewhere between war and its aftermath. Beneath the apparent calm, preparations were underway for the next stage in the struggle against Japan's battered empire. The Allied forces, Americans, British, and Chinese would soon be joined by the Soviet Union's Far Eastern forces in the final push against Japan. In anticipation of a coordinated assault the Allied armies replenished their supplies and redeployed to new fronts where they waited, coiled for the next battles.

TRUMAN'S DIPLOMATIC INHERITANCE

In mid-July, the summit meeting between President Harry S. Truman, Prime Minister Winston Churchill, and Soviet Premier Marshall Joseph Stalin in the Berlin suburb of Potsdam added to the sense of anticipation. The Allied leaders and their military staffs gathered near the blasted ruins of Hitler's capital to discuss postwar plans for the reconstruction of Europe and to coordinate diplomatic policies and military planning for the last stages in the war against Japan.

Concerning Europe, a host of problems awaited the Big Three as World War II drew to a close. The Nazis had ravaged Soviet territory and inflicted casualties numbering in the tens of millions. Soviet leader Joseph Stalin pressured his allies for the promise of significant aid in rebuilding Russia. The British, led by Winston Churchill, worried that Soviet control of Eastern Europe, including a portion of Germany, would pose as great a danger to Great Britain's security as Nazi Germany had.

The postwar disposition of Germany loomed as the most difficult problem of all. The Soviets' main concern was to ensure that Germany never again became strong enough to threaten them. Stalin wanted Germany militarily and economically enfeebled. The British and Americans worried that the Soviets would fill the void left by Germany, but they also believed that an economically devastated Germany would impede Europe's overall economic recovery, as had been the case after World War I. These issues reminded Allied leaders of the fragile nature of their wartime cooperation. The Grand Alliance had been a marriage of convenience. Could the relationship forged in war continue after Germany's defeat?

By the time he arrived in Potsdam, Truman knew it would be difficult to maintain a policy of cooperation with Stalin. Soviet actions in Eastern Europe, particularly Stalin's unilateral action in redrawing the Polish border, put the president on his guard. Thrust into a position of leadership by the death of Franklin D. Roosevelt, Truman felt the surest course would be to continue the policies of his predecessor. That was no easy task, given Roosevelt's penchant for keeping his own counsel. Truman recognized that Roosevelt had sought to continue the wartime cooperation with the Soviet Union into the postwar era. Truman also knew, however, that Roosevelt had begun to take a stronger line with Stalin weeks before his death. Roosevelt's public optimism regarding the alliance could be justified as necessary to maintain solidarity in the final stages of the war against Germany. But the late president's sunny view hid a cluster of disputes that could not be kept from the public after Germany's defeat. By July the contentious nature of the alliance was on full display.

Nevertheless, Truman came to Potsdam determined to cooperate, if for no other reason than to secure Soviet assistance in defeating Japan. As with Europe, Truman faced the unpleasant task of unraveling Roosevelt's tangle of public pronouncements and private agreements concerning the future of Asia. In February, Roosevelt, Stalin and Churchill had met at Yalta in the Crimea to sketch out a comprehensive plan for dealing with the aftermath of Japan's defeat. Roosevelt, at the urging of the Joint Chiefs of Staff (JCS), came seeking a commitment from Stalin to bring Russia into the war against Japan in a timely fashion. As expected, Stalin sought American and British support for the return of czarist concessions in Manchuria that had been lost to Japan earlier in the century. Roosevelt and Churchill agreed, even though the concessions contradicted a previous promise to recognize Chinese sovereignty in Manchuria.

When finished, the secret Yalta Far Eastern protocol called for joint Soviet-Chinese ownership of the Eastern and South Manchurian railways, a Soviet-leased naval base at Port Arthur, Soviet control of the port of Dairen, and the return of South Sakhalin Island to the Russians. The agreement also provided for Soviet acquisition of the Kurile Islands, although Japan had obtained these through peaceful negotiation in the nineteenth century.

With the exception of the Kurile Islands, the Far Eastern protocol gave to the Soviet Union little that it could not take by force. In return, Roosevelt received a pledge of timely assistance against Japan. The agreements regarding Manchuria would not please the Chinese. But Roosevelt had obtained Stalin's promise to recognize and deal only with the Nationalist Chinese government of Jiang Jieshi (Chiang Kai-shek). Roosevelt hoped that Stalin's pledge to deal only with Jiang's government, as opposed to his Communist rivals, would mollify the Nationalist leader. Although some historians have interpreted this part of the Yalta agreement as an attempt to contain the Chinese Communists, the president's goals were more modest. The war's end seemed likely to see China further divided and on the verge of civil war. By conceding to Stalin what he could take by force, Roosevelt hoped to avoid a scramble for influence after the war. The Soviet leader might try to seize more territory after the war, but in doing so he would lose international approval for the substantial gains made at Yalta. Roosevelt gambled that Stalin would not take that risk; but with American forces scattered throughout the Pacific and with the first stage of the invasion of Japan half a year off, he saw few alternatives.

Given these choices, Roosevelt found it easy to pay for Soviet cooperation with Chinese territory. He had once hoped for Chinese-American partnership in Asia, but the Nationalists' corruption, inefficiency, and military weakness shattered those plans. China seemed destined to sink into civil war and a resumption of warlord politics seemed possible. The best that Roosevelt could do was obtain Stalin's agreement that the Great Powers would not seek additional advantages at China's expense. He and Stalin would stand outside the ring while the Communists and the Guomindang (Nationalists) wrestled for the Mandate of Heaven.

When Truman succeeded Roosevelt, he turned to the State Department for guidance regarding his predecessor's policies. The State Department interpretation only served to confound the new president. In the matter of China, Truman was told that American policy strongly supported Jiang as the leader most likely to build a unified and democratic China friendly to the United States. As Truman knew, that was America's publicly stated policy. It was difficult, however, to square that public policy with Roosevelt's secret agreements. Other issues were equally perplexing. In the case of European imperialism in Asia, especially in French Indochina, Truman was told that despite Roosevelt's numerous anticolonial pronouncements during the war, he had never challenged the right of France or the other European powers to regain their lost colonies.

The status of Japan's Korean colony was a problem of a different sort. In the Cairo Declaration of October 1943, the Allies had announced that Korea would be liberated from Japan and become independent "in due course." No one had taken the trouble to explain what in due course meant but it was clear to observers, especially outraged Korean patriots, that the Cairo Declaration did not imply immediate independence for Korea. In fact, the State Department had proposed plans for the creation of a four power trusteeship consisting of the United States, Britain, the Soviet Union, and China to guide the former colony toward independence. In part this proposal rested on the assumption that after more than forty years of Japanese domination, Koreans lacked the necessary experience to govern themselves. But the plan also appealed to Roosevelt as a means of controlling any potential Chinese-Soviet rivalry over the peninsula. By the time Truman arrived in Potsdam nothing had been done to obtain Allied approval for the trusteeship plan. To remedy this situation, the State Department's planners urged Truman and Secretary of State James Byrnes to reach a final agreement on Korea during the conference.

UNCONDITIONAL SURRENDER, DOMESTIC POLITICS, AND MILITARY NECESSITY

While Truman prepared for the myriad of postwar issues that awaited his attention at Potsdam, the apparent intermission in the Pacific campaigns invited politicians, diplomats, and military planners to reexamine familiar policies and speculate about the future. In particular, the policy of unconditional surrender, a bold assertion of America's single-minded pursuit of victory, received new scrutiny. Did unconditional surrender apply to the Japanese government or just its armed forces? What if an invasion of Japan could be avoided by allowing Japan to keep the emperor? Supporters of unconditional surrender asserted that preservation of the throne would produce an incomplete victory and jeopardize the democratization of Japan. Critics of unconditional surrender doubted the necessity or efficacy of democratic reform in Japan and questioned if the war should be continued to achieve those ends. In the summer of 1945 the controversy over unconditional surrender became the medium through which the goals of the war and the very meaning of victory were debated.

That debate took place under circumstances unfamiliar to us today. Most of the participants did not know about the atomic bomb. Few Americans believed that a democratic Japan could be created under the auspices of the emperor. Fewer still could imagine that the United States and Soviet Union were headed toward a fifty-year confrontation. Given what we know about the war's end it is easy to lose sight of the uncertainty that prevailed that summer. It would help if we recognized that the summer of 1945 was an anxious time for New Dealers. Their leader was dead and his legacy seemed in doubt. Republicans and Southern conservatives in Congress had fought the New Deal to a standstill. In 1945 business leaders began an extensive advertising and lobbying campaign to refurbish the image of the free market system and inveigh against regulation, unionization, and taxes. As the end of the European conflict drew near they prepared to remove the remaining economic regulations put in place during the war and begin the process of restoring the country to normalcy.

Democratic control of the executive branch provided little comfort to those who worried about the New Deal's dimming prospects. For much of the war a coalition government presided in Washington. Prominent Republicans and business leaders like Secretary of War Henry Stimson and assistant secretary John J. McCloy, and undersecretary Robert Patterson, had been brought into the War and Navy Departments to manage the wartime economy and oversee military production. Often during the war they had circumvented New Deal policies in the name of efficiency. Now, as the war ended, many conservative politicians, as well as officials like Stimson and McCloy, questioned the necessity of demanding an unconditional surrender so that they could impose on Japan the same programs they wished to dismantle at home.

A reading of the American press during the final months of the war reveals the outlines of ideological struggle then underway. In the summer of 1945 Republican outlets such as the *Army and Navy Journal, Time, Wall Street Journal,* and the Hearst press appealed for modification of the surrender terms and ridiculed the "New Dealers" who sought to conduct their social engineering experiments in Japan. Henry Luce, the Republican publisher of *Time, Life,* and *Fortune* magazines, sought a meeting with Truman during which he hoped to persuade the new president to modify unconditional surrender. During the same period seven Republican senators spoke in favor of modifying unconditional surrender. This press and congressional commentary was aided by former Republican president Herbert Hoover, who regularly and covertly received reports on American military planning from the War Department, and William Castle, a former diplomat who retained extensive contacts in the government.

In May, Hoover took advantage of a meeting with Truman to push his ideas about unconditional surrender. Truman had invited Hoover to the White House to solicit the former president's views on rehabilitation and relief programs for war ravaged territories. During their meeting Hoover shifted the discussion to the topic of how to best end the war currently underway. According to his memorandum prepared after the meeting, Hoover warned the president that an invasion of Japan could cost upwards of 500,000 lives. To avoid such a bloodbath, Hoover recommended that Truman modify unconditional surrender by letting the Japanese know that they could keep the emperor. Hoover also thought that it was advisable to let Japan maintain control over Korea and Formosa, areas he considered to have been much improved by Japanese colonialism. He ended by reminding Truman that the Soviets would only enter the war with Japan during the "last five minutes."

While in Washington the former president also met with nine Republican senators at the home of William R. Castle, an arch-conservative who had served as Hoover's undersecretary of state and, briefly, ambassador to Japan. According to Castle, Hoover's advocacy of a negotiated settlement with Japan was well received by the senators. Shortly afterward, Castle discussed the matter with Hugh Wilson, another former diplomat who was serving as foreign policy advisor to the Republican Party. Wilson welcomed Hoover's recommendations on Japan, calling them "an opportunity for the minority party to take the lead." Wilson recognized, however, that the subject had to be approached cautiously so as to avoid accusations of appeasement. By the summer of 1945 conservative politicians and publicists had joined with Republican officials and even some professional military officers to challenge the policy of unconditional surrender and redefine the meaning of victory.[1]

Modification of unconditional surrender appealed to some Republicans for a variety of reasons; opposition to New Deal reforms abroad and economic restrictions at home as well as a growing concern over the prospect of Soviet expansion in Asia brought together prewar isolationist Republicans like Hoover and more internationalist-minded members of the party like Henry Luce. As Hugh Wilson implied, the Republicans might also gain political advantage by contributing constructively to ending the war on terms satisfactory to the public. But proponents of a negotiated settlement could also point to sound military reasons for modifying unconditional surrender. Throughout Japan's vast empire largely intact armies remained at their posts, undersupplied and ill equipped, but undefeated nonetheless. Enforcing their surrender posed a daunting challenge for Allied commanders. In assessing that situation, American military planners grew increasingly convinced that the safest course would be to preserve the emperor so that he could order the surrender of his loyal troops. Once they reached that conclusion it seemed only logical that the Japanese be informed of American willingness to define unconditional surrender so as to leave the emperor Hirohito on his throne.

The Joint Chiefs' growing concern over the state of American morale after V-E Day created further interest in seeing if it would be possible to negotiate an end to the war on terms that would satisfy American requirements for postwar security. During the previous year Americans had ridden an emotional roller coaster as expectations rose and fell in reaction to events in the European theater. The breakout in Normandy in July 1944, and the sudden dash across France encouraged hopes that the war would be ended by Christmas. In September an ill-planned attempt to leap the Rhine and plunge into Germany from the north ended in failure. The next few months were a period of resupply, forming up, and steady progress. In December, Hitler's rash gamble in the Ardennes offensive inflicted heavy casualties and strained American manpower. By early January 1945, Anglo-American forces began the difficult task of regaining lost ground. The next few weeks were characterized by steady but slow movement across a broad front. The future seemed to hold only hard fighting as whole German armies escaped encirclement and took up new defensive positions. In January, the Office of War Mobilization sought to remind the public of the struggle that lay ahead by imposing new restrictions on the domestic economy. The austerity program halted the reconversion of war plants, closed race tracks, set curfews for saloons and otherwise riled a public that chafed under these constraints and resented being scolded for supposedly immoral behavior.

Events soon made additional belt-tightening seem unnecessary. In April, American forces unexpectedly captured a bridge across the Rhine. Allied troops poured into the German interior bagging thousands of enemy troops along the way. The Americans linked up with the Red Army along the Elbe River in May. The remains of the German Reich surrendered on May 8. The war in Europe was over.

Believing that one war was enough for any soldier, the parents and wives of combat veterans in the European theater began to clamor for the return of their loved ones. Many of the veterans were likewise willing to consider their job done. Sensing the flagging enthusiasm among his troops, General Maxwell Taylor tried to fire up the men of his crack 101st Airborne Division with visions of "new worlds to conquer." "We've licked the best that Hitler had in France and Holland and Germany. Now where do we want to go?" To a man the Screaming Eagles shouted back, "Home."[2]

The Joint Chiefs had other plans. Many of the victorious divisions were designated for reassignment to the Pacific. In acknowledgement of the public's mood, however, the army instituted a demobilization system based on such factors as combat experience and length of service overseas. Planning for demobilization had begun during the war and was based on a system in which discharge would be tied to points accumulated through a variety of circumstances including length of service, combat experience, health, and number of dependents. Under this program, soldiers who accumulated eighty-five points would be discharged. Timetables adopted in 1944 estimated that V-E Day would be July 1, 1945. V-J day would be at least a year later. In the interim, partial demobilization would begin.

V-E Day arrived two months early, however, and by late May an impatient public was already pressuring the War Department for swift action. Following

Germany's surrender, 450,000 men earned their release from the service. In fairness to those who had been fighting the Japanese, the War Department extended the point system to Pacific theater veterans as well. Thirty thousand soldiers from the theater were separated from their divisions in June pending their release from service. Army Chief of Staff General George C. Marshall, who was already worried that troop morale would be undermined by the domestic disquiet, grew concerned that the army was losing its "first team," as the most experienced veterans and noncommissioned officers shipped off for home. Depleted units needed more time to train raw recruits. That raised the possibility that major operations would have to be delayed which would, in turn, fuel public dissatisfaction even more. The loss of experienced leadership also raised the very real possibility that the Americans would suffer even higher casualties in combat than previously anticipated. In short, the point system played havoc with the buildup for the invasion of Japan. Here then was another argument for seeking a negotiated settlement with Japan.

Deputy Chief of Staff General Thomas Handy captured the mood in Washington when he informed General Dwight Eisenhower that "From all indications it is going to be one hell of a job to keep the war in any priority."[3] That prediction proved accurate. As the buildup for the invasion of Japan gained momentum, Congress, industry, and organized labor pounded the army and War Department for what they viewed as the unnecessarily slow pace of reconversion and demobilization. Industry groups flayed the War Department for hoarding materials that could be used for domestic production and accused Undersecretary of War Robert Patterson of seeking to stockpile materials for the postwar era. Stung by these and other charges, Patterson complained that every organized group imaginable including dentists and ministers was insisting on the early release of its own members. Everyone, it seemed, believed they had already done their bit for the war effort.

Even the stoical General Marshall contemplated an escape to civilian life after Germany surrendered. After six grueling years as chief of staff, Marshall had earned a break. He explained to John Callan O'Laughlin, a Republican insider and publisher of *The Army and Navy Journal*, Germany's defeat created an opportune moment to bow out gracefully. As he poured out his thoughts to the surprised O'Laughlin, the normally laconic Marshall confessed that he was concerned by the "dwindling of public confidence in his conduct of the military features of the war." According to O'Laughlin, the general was also frustrated by what he saw as Congress's tendency to "criticize everything he did and recommends."[4]

Marshall was personally frustrated in his dealings with Congress but he made it clear to O'Laughlin that he was more concerned by how restiveness at home was affecting the conduct of the war. The general explained that there were two groups vying for control of the Japanese government, the "Manchurian Gang" which remained committed to fighting to the bitter end, and a peace faction that hoped to negotiate a surrender that would salvage some elements of the empire. According to O'Laughlin, Marshall predicted that the peace party would "win out in a short time," but for that to happen there could be no let up in "our attacks or the preparations we are making for a long war."[5] For Marshall, personal pique and professional responsibilities converged at this point. Marshall worried that divisiveness at home, which included congressional criticism of the War Department, army, and Marshall, would be viewed as signs of weakness by the "Manchurian Gang." To prevent that from happening, the United States needed to apply unrelenting pressure on Japan while also offering the peace party some hope that unconditional surrender could be modified in substance if not in name.

Geopolitical concerns also seemed weighted toward finding a substitute for the orgy of destruction required to compel Japan's unconditional surrender. Rear Admiral Charles "Savvy" Cooke, the head of the Navy's Strategic Plans Division, worried about the vacuum that would be created by the wholesale destruction of Japanese power. Cooke advised Chief of Naval Operations Admiral Ernest King that the best way to end the war would be with a "strengthened CHINA and a JAPAN thrown back to her homeland, incapable of aggression, on the one hand, but, at the same time not completely eliminated as a party to the stabilization in EASTERN ASIA and the WESTERN PACIFIC."[6] Cooke's concern about the cost of an invasion, not only to American forces, but to Japan as well, was shared by other officials in the administration who urged the new president to modify American demands for unconditional surrender. Navy secretary James Forrestal, Secretary of War Henry Stimson, and former ambassador to Japan Joseph Grew privately voiced concerns about Soviet expansion in East Asia at the end of the war. These presidential advisers also feared that the ashes of Japanese cities would provide fertile ground for the growth of Japanese radicalism. Such thinking colored their advice to Truman although in their formal recommendations Grew and Stimson limited themselves to assessing the prospects for obtaining American aims through modification of unconditional surrender.

Public opinion provided little guidance to Truman. On the one hand, as noted, a growing segment of the public appeared tired of war. In addition to calling for demobilization, a majority of Americans, 70 percent in one poll, demanded an immediate end to rationing. On the other hand, a similar majority insisted on unconditional surrender and complete victory over Japan. When asked about how to treat Hirohito, only 3 percent of respondents thought the United States should keep the emperor in place and govern Japan through him. Complicating the picture was a Cantril Poll in June 1945, in which 58 percent of respondents preferred to see the Japanese brought to the brink of starvation by the Navy and American airpower before any invasion. Only 27 percent called for a prompt invasion. Unconditional surrender was deemed essential, it seemed, but Americans wanted the administration to achieve that goal with a minimal loss of life. In keeping with that outlook, concerned citizens were writing their congressmen, the State Department, and the White House in increasing numbers urging a public statement clarifying unconditional surrender in the hopes that it might shorten the war.

Americans, according to the polls, wanted unconditional surrender but they also wanted to avoid an invasion of Japan if at all possible. Such contradictory impulses only confirmed the long held suspicions of elite public servants like Grew and Stimson. Public opinion was emotional and uninformed, they believed. Truly public-spirited men disregarded the polls and acted on the best information available. As long as they defended the nation's interest and explained their decisions accordingly, the public would support them. *New York Times* columnist Arthur Krock gave his approval to such an outlook. Reviewing the debate over unconditional surrender, Krock noted that those who wished to preserve Hirohito did not believe the public had the information necessary to make the right decision. Krock agreed saying that the fate of the emperor involved questions that could only be answered by those in "high authority on the basis of expert judgment, to which popular opinion can offer no useful contribution."[7]

But what would happen if the public did not agree with a change in unconditional surrender? Grew or Stimson, and presumably Krock, would have said that was always a chance one took in a republic. Perhaps that was so, but Harry Truman was not likely to find much comfort in such political fatalism.

Truman's highly developed sense of personal responsibility inclined him to carry out Roosevelt's policies. The American people had not elected him, he explained. In his first speech to Congress on April 15, Truman had pledged his fealty to his predecessor's policies. His use of the phrase "unconditional surrender" drew the most enthusiastic applause. On May 8, V-E Day, Truman repeated his commitment to unconditional surrender. But he refined that pledge by declaring that "Our blows will not cease until the Japanese *military and naval forces* lay down their arms in unconditional surrender." Truman explained further that unconditional surrender did not mean the "extermination or enslavement" of the Japanese people. By seeming to confine unconditional surrender to Japanese armed forces, Truman's statement appeared to leave the way open for negotiations on other issues, most notably the future of the imperial institution. That was certainly how Truman meant his speech to be heard.[8] The president's address evoked no response from Japan nor did it quiet public debate over unconditional surrender. Nevertheless, for the time being, this was as far as Truman was prepared to go on the matter.

But what were Roosevelt's plans for Japan? As with much else, Roosevelt's pronouncements on unconditional surrender revealed little about his ultimate intentions for Japan. Advice from trusted mentors provided some insight and reinforced Truman's inclination to avoid softening war aims against Japan. James Byrnes, Truman's former senate colleague and newly appointed secretary of state, and Cordell Hull, who had held the same post under Roosevelt for twelve years, opposed any tampering with unconditional surrender. At a time when Republican legislators and publishers were calling for modification of unconditional surrender, these two prominent Democrats, both of whom could claim special knowledge of Roosevelt's intentions, urged Truman to avoid compromise. Hull drove the point home by declaring that he saw no reason why the United States should "appease" Japan. Hull's meaning was unmistakable. Truman should stick to Roosevelt's policy unless he wanted to be compared to Neville Chamberlain, the British Prime Minister who was condemned for appeasing Hitler at Munich in 1938.

Intelligence information available to American officials through the code breaking operation known as MAGIC gave Hull's warning a special resonance. During the summer American intelligence officials watched intently as Japanese diplomats in Europe sent out peace feelers in an attempt to soften unconditional surrender. These efforts went nowhere. The militarists in Tokyo renounced the "peace entrepreneurs" and ordered them to cease immediately. According to Japan's military authorities, American interest in negotiations proved that the enemy's morale was cracking. The best way to end the war on terms favorable to Japan would be to "prosecute the Greater East Asia War to the end."[9]

In July, Tokyo authorized efforts to end the war through Soviet mediation, but this Moscow gambit only demonstrated the militarists' capacity for self-delusion. Once again American code breakers looked on intently as frustrated Japanese diplomats tried to accomplish the impossible. Tokyo offered the Soviets territorial concessions in return for the Russians' help in ending the war. Stalin brushed aside these entreaties and headed for Potsdam. The Moscow venture amply illustrated the emptiness of Japanese diplomacy and the determination of the militarists in Tokyo to gain acceptable terms through battle. Maintenance of the institution of the emperor was only the starting point of Japanese demands. The military authorities in Tokyo also insisted on their right to disarm their own troops, try their own war criminals, and restrict any occupation to a few small enclaves in the home islands. In keeping with that outlook, the Japanese government even refused to consider its own emissary's suggestion that Japan should accept unconditional surrender if it provided for the continuation of the imperial household.

Tokyo's belligerence gave Truman little reason to believe that an Allied promise to preserve the emperor would bring about a prompt end to the war. It was more likely that such an offer would be met with more demands from Japan. To put it simply, Truman was in a tight spot. He knew that the militarists were prepared to make the United States pay the highest price possible for an invasion of the home islands. He also knew that the demobilization schedule was weakening the army on the eve of its biggest test in the Pacific War. As historian Michael Pearlman has noted, "America, like a Greek melodrama, needed a *deus ex machina* to solve its insoluble dilemma. . . ."[10]

Truman no doubt thought he had found one. Shortly after he arrived in Potsdam the president was greatly relieved to learn of the first successful test of an atomic device in the New Mexico desert. At first Truman received only a brief report. The news, however, was good. The report indicated that the test went better than hoped. Truman needed additional information, but it most likely occurred to him that if the bomb proved to be even more powerful than predicted the new weapon might well give the United States the means to compel Japan's unconditional surrender without an invasion.

MILITARY PLANNING FOR UNCONDITIONAL VICTORY

Much to the dismay of those hoping to avoid an invasion of Japan, the militarists in Tokyo remained convinced that if they inflicted enough casualties on the invaders they could force the Allies into ending the war on acceptable terms. The final weeks of the war found the Japanese high command practically lusting for the final struggle. How can one explain the militarists' willingness to risk the very survival of millions of their countrymen in the face of such overwhelming odds? The Allies would have command of the air and sea. They also enjoyed substantial advantages in manpower and material. Conversely, terrain and shorter lines of communication favored the defenders. Allied air and naval superiority could not be negated, but it might be diminished by the thousands of young pilots ready to launch suicide missions against the invaders. Most importantly, Japanese strategists felt supremely confident that they knew where the enemy landings would take place. As events were to show, they were correct.

American military plans for the invasion of Japan envisioned a two-stage campaign designed to minimize logistical obstacles and maximize the force that could be brought to bear against the enemy. The first stage, code-named OLYMPIC, would launch fourteen divisions and two regiments against Kyushu, Japan's southernmost home island. The attackers would land on three separate beaches at the southern tip of the island as well as on several smaller islands off the southern coast of Kyushu. Once the invading force had consolidated control of the southern part of Kyushu, the buildup for the second stage of the invasion would begin. Stage two, code-named CORONET, would send twenty-five divisions against Honshu, Japan's main island. The attackers would land in the vicinity of Tokyo and drive into the heartland region of the Kanto Plain. The tentative date for OLYMPIC, which would employ units already in the Pacific, was November 1, 1945. The assault on Honshu, which depended on the transfer of divisions from the European theater, was not expected to take place before March 1, 1946. Before leaving for Potsdam, Truman had approved plans for the invasion of Kyushu, but he withheld final assent on CORONET, preferring to "decide as to the final action later."[11] Knowledge gained from battling the Americans in the Pacific, particularly the

enemy's preference for shortened lines of communication and assault landings covered by land-based air power, convinced the Japanese Imperial Headquarters that Kyushu would be the first battleground in the defense of the
home islands. The geographical determinants of Kyushu allowed Japanese
strategists to accurately predict the most likely sites for the invasion. Seasonal
weather patterns, in this case the approaching typhoon season, suggested an
invasion date sometime in fall. Imperial Headquarters issued specific instructions for combating the invasion directly behind the beaches, as opposed to a
protracted campaign anchored on defensive positions deeper inland. To repel
the invaders, the Japanese would have nearly 900,000 men in fourteen divisions, nine of which would be deployed directly against the invasion sites in
the south. If OLYMPIC came off as expected the Americans would be committing 650,000 troops to the invasion.[12]

To prepare for the decisive battle for the home islands, Imperial Headquarters consolidated its forces in China and dug into defensive positions in
Manchuria. The Manchurian force, the notorious Kwantung army, was only a
shadow of the renegade army that launched Japan's aggression in China with
the conquest of Manchuria in 1931. On paper, the Kwantung army in
Manchuria still looked formidable. But over the course of the war Imperial
Headquarters had siphoned off nineteen infantry and two armored divisions
for combat in the Pacific. These losses were made good with inexperienced
and ill-equipped recruits.[13]

In the event of war with the Soviet Union, an increasingly likely possibility,
Japanese commanders planned to defend only a small portion of southeastern
Manchuria. This decision was poorly communicated to the Kwantung army's
field commanders and not at all to the million and a half Japanese civilians living in Manchuria. Implementation of this new defense plan did not begin until June. Even then preparations commenced in desultory fashion owing to the
widespread belief among the defenders that the Red Army's offensive would
not commence until after the American invasion, and perhaps as late as spring
1946. As a result, Japanese preparations were woefully inadequate. Imperial
Headquarters had shown uncanny perceptiveness in anticipating the location
of America's next campaign. A comparable insight into Russian intentions was
utterly lacking.

The Soviets planned their offensive with exemplary skill. The Red Army's
campaign would draw on one and a half million men, five and a half thousand

tanks, and an equally impressive number of artillery pieces and self-propelled guns. In the three months after Germany's surrender more than thirty divisions redeployed from the European theater. During the summer, over 1,000 trains rolled across Siberia carrying 700,000 battle tested troops and the supplies they would need for the invasion of Manchuria. To conduct the campaign, Stalin created a special High Command for the Far East headed by former Chief of the General Staff Marshall Aleksandr Vasilevsky. Employing deception and camouflage to mask its intentions, the High Command assembled troops well behind their designated jumping off points and moved most often at night. In his instructions to the general staff, Stalin emphasized the need for a swift decisive campaign. A quick victory would serve his political objectives by bringing the maximum amount of territory under Soviet control before Japan surrendered. Speed became even more imperative once Stalin learned that the United States had added the atomic bomb to its arsenal. The initial plans for operation AUGUST STORM anticipated that it would take two months of fighting to defeat the Japanese. The final timetable aimed for victory in thirty days.

South, below the Great Wall, military conditions in China posed little difficulty for the Japanese. For most of the war the Imperial Army had held China's coastal areas and moved at will into the interior. In many parts of the so-called front, Nationalist troops established truces with their Japanese counterparts and traded goods across the supposedly active battle lines. In 1944 the Japanese mounted their last major offensive of the war and brought Jiang Jieshi's government to the brink of defeat before ceasing operations. Jiang's regime recovered from this near-death experience and with American aid slowly rebuilt its armies under the tutelage of Lieutenant General Albert C. Wedemeyer. The Japanese became increasingly aware of the improving quality of the American trained Chinese troops but the Nationalists did little to disturb what was already a planned withdrawal to the coast.

For some Americans, including Wedemeyer's predecessor Lieutenant General Joseph Stilwell, Nationalist corruption and inefficiency made aid to the Communists seem like a tantalizing prospect, especially in the event of American landings along the China coast. The Communists, led by Mao Zedong (Mao Tse-tung), moved easily behind Japanese lines conducting raids and recruiting peasants to their cause. American observers saw in the Communists a level of integrity and concern for the welfare of peasants that seemed absent from the upper echelons of the Nationalist regime. Jiang, of course, would not permit precious American supplies to be redirected to his mortal enemies. In retrospect, it is doubtful that American aid could have done much to improve the offensive capabilities of the Communists. Like their Nationalist rivals, the Communists arranged de facto truces with the Japanese and marshaled their resources for the civil war that both sides knew would follow Japan's defeat.

By the summer of 1945, Nationalist troops had cleared northern Burma and reopened land communications between southwestern China and India and were readying for a move against the south China coast. Operation RASHNESS, as the offensive was called, aimed at opening a port along the coast to facilitate the supply and reorganization of thirty-nine divisions along American lines. Another offensive, tentatively dubbed CARBONADO, would bring Nationalist troops into the vicinity of Hong Kong, Britain's colonial bastion. Jiang had made no secret of his intention to reclaim Hong Kong for China "at the proper moment." The British were even more adamant about retaking control of the colony when the Japanese were driven out. The Americans hoped to finesse the whole problem. American policy recognized Hong Kong as a British colony but also hoped for its eventual return to China. That fence-straddling might suffice if the United States did not become directly involved in the dispute. By early summer, however, Chinese troops, trained, armed, and advised by Americans began preparing for operations in the Hong Kong area. Thus it seemed possible that China's first major offensive of the war might embroil the United States in a showdown over Britain's most important colony in East Asia.

Despite the imperialist tensions that afflicted Anglo-Chinese relations, the two allies had managed to coordinate their efforts in Burma during 1944 and 1945. There, the Japanese were solidly beaten by Chinese and American troops operating in the north and British forces in the south. Success in Burma set the stage for future British operations to the south. Together, southern Burma, Thailand, Malaya, Sumatra, and Singapore formed the area of operations for the Southeast Asian theater, commanded by the young British admiral, Lord Louis Mountbatten. Southeast Asia Command (SEAC) was created in 1943 to clarify command responsibilities among the Americans, Chinese, and British operating in Asia. The political implications of the reorganization were obvious. American critics drew attention to these by sarcastically insisting that the theater acronym really stood for "Save England's Asian Colonies."

As operations in Burma neared completion, Mountbatten planned for Operation ZIPPER, an assault on the Port Sweetenham–Dickson area on the west coast of the Malaya peninsula in the fall. ZIPPER would be followed by an attack on Singapore in December, and the recapture of Hong Kong a few months after that. Japan's smashing victories over the British, French, and Dutch at the start of the war had done much to shatter the Europeans' aura of invincibility in Asia. Now, after a four-year hiatus in European rule, Mountbatten hoped to retake Southeast Asia gradually, in stages, so that the British could restore order and impress the inhabitants with the awesome power of the returning Europeans.

MILITARY PLANNING AND POSTWAR GOALS

Apart from the Soviet Union, none of the major belligerents premised their impending campaigns on the assumption that the war would be over in the next several weeks. And although the Soviets expected to seize their main objectives in two months, they planned for additional operations against Sakhalin Island, the Kuriles and possibly Hokkaido, Japan's northernmost home island, once Manchuria was in their control. Lord Mountbatten counted on a gradual restoration of the colonial order in Southeast Asia. Jiang and his American adviser General Wedemeyer concentrated on gaining access to the coast and the steady flow of supplies needed to continue the retraining and reorganization of the Nationalist army. His sites set on future combat with the Japanese, Wedemeyer even sent the War Department a list of general officers he wanted reassigned to China. Wedemeyer's list, which included Lucian Truscott and George Patton, read like a dream team comprised of the most successful commanders from the European theater. But General Marshall and Secretary of War Stimson had already agreed that as long as Japan remained defiant, an increase in the American presence in China was out of the question. In the meantime, preparing for OLYMPIC would consume all of the army's assets and energy. If all went as planned, American forces would converge on Japan's home islands, leaving to Russia the task of defeating Japanese armies in Manchuria.

Preparations for the invasion of Japan forced the JCS to think in terms of limits and restraint. Wartime strategy imposed the same linear trajectory and sequential logic on postwar plans. Japan came first, China trailed behind a distant second. American military planners understood the controversial implications of their priorities. Nevertheless, the army strategists remained confident that the invasion and occupation of Japan would provide for American security in the future. On the eve of the Potsdam conference, planners in the army's Strategy and Policy group (S&P) reminded General Marshall that "The U.S., as a matter of public will, positively supports the integrity of China as a nation. U.S. formal policy at present formally supports the integrity of China as a nation." The planners cautioned, however, that "Whether the future will bring a different definition of what constitutes China proper cannot now be said with certainty."[14]

A plainer warning followed. Referring to the Yalta Far Eastern Agreement, S&P informed Marshall that if Soviet demands exceeded China's willingness to meet them, it was not believed that "U.S. military force could be effectively employed to further our objective."[15] Similar admonitions appeared in other papers dealing with Asian problems. "With reference to the cleanup of the Asiatic mainland," read another, "our objectives should be to get the Russians to deal with the Jap[anese] in Manchuria (and Korea if necessary) and to vitalize the Chinese to a point where, with assistance of American air power and some supplies, they can mop out their own country."[16] With the defeat of Japan at least a year away, there was little else the United States could do.

As these planning papers indicate, the officers in S&P realized that there might be some contradiction between public policy and American strategy in the Pacific. In short, they sensed what historian Ernest May later described as the difference between "calculated policy" and "axiomatic policy." S&P produced the former. They assessed the means at their disposal and identified an attainable goal: "to keep the rest of the world militarily out of the Pacific, rather than to commit us irrevocably and in perpetuity to affairs in the Sea of Japan."[17] This could be achieved by taking and holding Japan. But the axiomatic policy was never far from their thoughts. The American public favored a unified China, they noted. Official American policy supported Jiang for that purpose. Failure to achieve a unified China under the Nationalists after Japan's surrender might well lead to criticism of American wartime strategy. American strategists could plead necessity and argue that America remained secure even as China fell into chaos. But the partitioning of China and defeat of Jiang might well cast a pall over the peace.

Despite the tension between military strategy and public policy, Marshall and Stimson refused to disperse American power onto the Asian mainland.

Political as well as military reasons accounted for their determination on this score. Militarily, it was clear that the defeat of Japanese forces in China would not compel Japan's surrender. Only a devastating strike at the Japanese heartland seemed likely to do that. Politically, Marshall and Stimson suspected that Jiang really wanted to lure the Americans onto the mainland as an ally in the impending civil war with the Communists. Marshall, who was already acutely aware of the American public's growing war weariness, recoiled at the thought of entangling the United States in China's fratricidal strife.

Operational boundaries agreed upon at Potsdam reaffirmed Marshall's single-minded emphasis on the invasion of Japan. To prepare for the Soviet Union's entry into the war the American Joint Chiefs and their Soviet counterparts established an operational boundary to prevent clashes between the converging forces. The line ran through the Kurile Islands below Paramushir and bisected Korea at the forty-first parallel. The area south of the line fell into the American zone of operations. This boundary was for air and sea operations only, as the JCS did not contemplate landing troops on the Kuriles or the Korean peninsula.

In order to further pare down American responsibilities in Asia, the Americans and British agreed to expand the boundaries of the Southeast Asian Command so as to include Indochina below the sixteenth parallel, all of Thailand, Java, the Celebes islands, and Borneo. This agreement added one-half million square miles to Mountbatten's command. Generally speaking, the new boundaries were created to facilitate American and British access to those areas each country felt were in its own interest. The Americans could concentrate on Japan; the British could busy themselves with regaining their empire. The British area of interest now consisted of one and a half million square miles, much of it occupied by undefeated Japanese armies. It was with this situation in mind that Mountbatten later remarked that the decision to enlarge SEAC "was not as flattering as it may sound."[18]

Although Mountbatten felt overwhelmed by this abrupt increase in his responsibilities, he and other members of the British staff made a pitch for adding more territory to the new theater. Specifically the British requested that all of Indochina be placed in their zone. The British knew that the French would object to any agreement that allowed the Chinese to operate in their colony. As the big brother of the European colonial fraternity, the British sought to look after French interests, and by extension their own, until French troops could arrive from the European theater. The JCS declined to alter the boundary. They countered that the Chinese needed operational control of northern Indochina so that General Wedemeyer could have better control over his right flank during his forthcoming offensive. Mountbatten relented, but he pointed out that the French would not be pleased by the new boundary. The Americans were not completely unsympathetic. The final agreement included an important provision stating that all or part of Indochina might come under British control at a later date.

With that additional compromise, the military staffs of the Allies had completed the work that brought them to Potsdam. The operational boundaries were agreed upon and the plans for the new campaign season fleshed out. Everything was settled.

It stayed that way for less than twenty-four hours.

A CHANGE OF PLANS

The guiding assumption of Allied planning, that the war would continue for at least several months, possibly a year, was overthrown with surprising swiftness. On July 25, the day after the Combined Chiefs of Staff had agreed to the final arrangements for Southeast Asia, President Truman met with Marshall and Mountbatten to discuss "the tactical and political situation." Following the meeting, Marshall sent a message to General Douglas MacArthur, the commander of the invasion force assembling in the Pacific, requesting his plans for the rapid occupation of Japan *and* Korea. Similarly, Churchill instructed Mountbatten to notify his staff to be prepared for an early Japanese surrender. The prime minister forbade Mountbatten from saying anything about the reason for this sudden change of plan. As the admiral recalled "my SEAC staff had to rush forward all our plans for landing in Malaya and Singapore, and just take my word for it that there would be no opposition."[19]

The reason for this sudden change of plans was, of course, the atomic bomb. Truman had first received word of the successful test of the new weapon on July 16. During the next several days more details of the test became available. On July 22 Stimson told Truman that the next bomb would be ready sooner than expected. Truman subsequently asked Stimson to find out if General Marshall thought the Soviets were still needed in the war. The general was circumspect in responding, but Stimson kept his own answer simple and told Truman the Russians were no longer needed. He also informed the president that the bomb would be ready sometime during the period of August 1–6. The next morning Truman met with Marshall and Mountbatten. Shortly after that session Marshall fired off the message inquiring into MacArthur's capabilities to respond to an early Japanese surrender.

Historians disagree over how to interpret these developments. It is particularly difficult to be certain how seriously Marshall, Mountbatten, Truman, or Stimson took the possibility of Japan's surrender. By his own account, when Mountbatten learned of the atomic bomb, he said that the war would be over in a matter of days, or the next few weeks at the most. Marshall was less certain but he conceded that it would not last beyond the current year.

More telling were the new instructions issued as a result of Marshall's and Mountbatten's meeting with the president. Of course military staffs always prepare contingency plans. It is their job to be ready for almost any eventuality. Indeed, before the Potsdam Conference began, the JCS had asked MacArthur and his Navy counterpart, Admiral Chester Nimitz, to work up plans for the occupation in the event Japanese resistance collapsed before OLYMPIC. MacArthur's preliminary plan was code-named BLACKLIST, Nimitz's was CAMPUS. The difference between those preparations, which appear to have fit the category of being typical precautionary measures, and the more recent requests issued by Mountbatten and Marshall, was that the latter were issued at the instigation of the president and prime minister. Equally significant, Marshall's message on July 25 asked MacArthur to include Korea in his plans. That would seem to indicate that either Truman or Marshall believed that Japan might surrender before Russia entered the war, or so soon afterward that the Red Army would not have advanced far enough to be in a position to take the Japanese surrender in Korea. The Russians had given August 15 as the earliest starting date for AUGUST STORM. American intelligence estimates expected the Russians to need about thirty days after that before they broke through the Kwantung Army's defenses and began to "roll." Given the information available to the Americans, that put the new planning date for the surrender somewhere between the first week of August and September 15. That was well before OLYMPIC and ZIPPER would be underway and quite early enough to create a new set of challenges for the British, Americans, and Chinese.

Stimson's report to Truman on the bomb's readiness provided the president with his cue for issuing a final public demand for Japan's surrender.

The Potsdam Proclamation, as the ultimatum was called, had been prepared by a committee chaired by Assistant Secretary of War John McCloy.
The committee's draft reflected McCloy's view that the Allies should modify unconditional surrender; specifically it stated that unconditional surrender would not preclude the maintenance of a constitutional monarchy
under the present dynasty. This was not an explicit guarantee of Hirohito's
position but it was still farther than Truman wished to go. The president
heeded Byrnes's advice and struck out the offending provision. In other respects, however, the warning constituted a modification of unconditional
surrender.

The preamble referred to the "terms" the Japanese must accept, which suggested that there were limits to what the Allies demanded. This was a point
that Japanese diplomats readily understood. The proclamation stated that
Japan would be demilitarized and those who "deceived and misled the Japanese people" into following the path of aggression would be removed from authority. Japan would be deprived of the areas it took by force and subjected to
a military occupation. But the proclamation also explained that the Japanese
would not be enslaved and the nation would not be destroyed. It also promised Japan "access to, as distinguished from control of, raw materials" and
called only for the unconditional surrender of "all of Japanese armed forces"
as opposed to the state itself. Regarding the future of Japan's government, the
Allies declared that the occupation would end once the terms of the proclamation had been met and "and there has been established in accord with the
freely expressed will of the Japanese people a peacefully inclined and responsible government."[20]

Presumably, that included a constitutional monarchy if the Japanese desired one. Truman declined to be more specific than that. Byrnes's warning
about the political fallout from any pledge regarding Hirohito was probably
enough to convince Truman not to take that risk. If he had any doubts, however, the bellicosity of the Japanese government, which was on full display in
the messages the Americans intercepted and deciphered, would have been
enough to convince him that the Japanese would not budge until they had
been shocked into seeing the futility of further resistance.

Possession of the atomic bomb provided Truman a way to escape his
dilemma. He could avoid the political risks of making a promise about the emperor and still end the war well before OLYMPIC started. Truman and Byrnes

expected the power of the atomic bomb to make Japan see the reasonableness of the Allies' terms. Despite its opaqueness regarding the emperor, the Potsdam Proclamation substantially softened the unconditional surrender doctrine. As one War Department analysis subsequently explained, the proclamation amounted to a contractual arrangement which included an American pledge to preserve Japan's sovereignty over the home islands and, among other guarantees, permit Japanese troops to return to their homes in return for their surrender. No such offer had been made to Germany.[21]

Truman approved the use of the atomic bomb to force Japan's surrender as quickly as possible without having to invade the home islands. The increasing unrest at home made it clear that the longer the war persisted the higher the probability that the United States would end up settling for a negotiated surrender on terms that fell short of what American officials thought necessary to prevent a future war. As American code breakers knew, the Japanese government staked its entire policy and even its existence on the belief that American morale was cracking.

Possession of the atomic bomb also improved the American position in East Asia at a crucial moment in the life of the Grand Alliance. Stalin's uncooperativeness in Eastern Europe, particularly in Poland, offered the president a foretaste of what he could expect from a Soviet occupation of Manchuria and Korea. While at Potsdam, Truman also received disquieting reports on the status of negotiations between the Russians and Jiang's government to implement the Yalta Far Eastern accords. As Soviet entry into the war neared, Stalin began to insist on concessions from the Chinese concerning control of railroads and the port of Dairen that exceeded American interpretations of the agreement. Jiang was resisting and seeking American support, but it seemed likely that he would decide that it would be better to meet Stalin's new demands than to watch the Russians enter Manchuria unrestrained by any formal treaty with China.

Truman and Byrnes encouraged Jiang to reach an agreement with Stalin, but they also urged him not to go beyond the terms of the protocol signed at Yalta. The Americans had no desire to further abet Soviet aggrandizement at China's expense. Nor did they want to see Jiang make concessions that would interfere with the traditional American principle of the Open Door in Manchuria. Truman and Byrnes would not want to have to explain to Congress why they surrendered a long-standing American principle in order to obtain Russian assistance in the war, especially now that it was no longer needed. For the moment, however, the best that Truman could do was insist that Stalin stick to the original agreements and make sure Jiang did not compromise American rights in a rush to conclude a treaty.

As long as preparations for the invasion of Japan consumed American military resources there was little the United States could do to balance Soviet power in Northeast Asia. The atomic bomb had the potential to change that equation. The United States could not prevent Russia from entering the war, but if the atomic bomb compelled a timely surrender from Japan, American forces would be in a better position to resist Soviet pressure in Northeast Asia. According to one of Byrnes's advisers, the secretary was hoping for time "believing that after atomic bomb Japan will surrender and Russia will not get in so much on the kill, thereby being in a position to press for claims against China."[22] Such thinking owed more to impulse than strategy. But it helps to explain Marshall's instruction to MacArthur requesting his views on the forces needed to occupy Japan and Korea in the event of a sudden collapse of Japanese resistance. It also helps to explain why, despite the earlier urgings of their diplomatic and military advisers, Truman and Byrnes left Potsdam without establishing a trusteeship formula for Korea or discussing long term occupation responsibilities with the Russians.

As the Potsdam conference ended and the Allied delegations headed home, the postwar political arrangements in Asia were suddenly up for grabs.

NOTES

1. William R. Castle to Herbert Hoover, 2 June 1945, Post-Presidential Individual Files, Herbert Hoover Papers, Herbert Hoover Presidential Library, West Branch, Iowa (Hereafter cited as HHL); D. M Giangrecco, "'A Score of Okinawas': President Truman and Casualty Estimates for the Invasion of Japan," *Pacific Historical Review* 73 (February 2003): 93–132.

2. Quoted in Michael D. Pearlman, *Unconditional Surrender, Demobilization, and the Atomic Bomb* (Fort Leavenworth, Kan. Combat Studies Institute, United States Army Command and General Staff College, 1996). http://www.cgsc.army.mil/carl/resources/csi/Pearlman/pearlman.asp#contents

3. Thomas Handy to Dwight Eisenhower, 27 May 1945, Eisenhower Correspondence, Pre-Presidential Papers, Dwight D. Eisenhower Library, Abiline Kansas.

4. Marshall's remarkable meeting with O'Laughlin is related in John Callan O'Laughlin to Herbert Hoover, 9 June 1945, O'Laughlin Correspondence, Post-Presidential Individual Files, Herbert Hoover Papers, HHL.

5. Ibid.

6. Arthur Krock, "Our Policy toward the Emperor of Japan," *New York Times*, 5 July 1945, 12

7. Ibid.

8. Makoto Iokibe, "American Policy Towards 'Unconditional Surrender,'" *Japanese Journal of American Studies* 1 (1981): 48.

9. Marc S. Gallicchio, *The Cold War Begins in Asia: American East Asian Policy and the Fall of the Japanese Empire* (New York: Columbia University Press, 1988), 50.

10. Pearlman, *Unconditional Surrender*.

11. "Basic Military Objectives, Strategy, and Policies in the War against Japan," 18 June 1945, United States Department of State, *Foreign Relations of the United States: The Conference of Berlin (the Potsdam Conference), 1945*, Volume I, 909.

12. Estimates of the attacking force vary slightly. Edward Drea places the number at about 650,000. Richard Frank estimates the total at 693,295. Edward J. Drea, *MacArthur's Ultra: Codebreaking and the War against Japan, 1942–1945* (Lawrence: University Press of Kansas, 1992), 217. Richard B. Frank, *Downfall: The End of the Imperial Japanese Empire* (New York: Random House, 1999), 119.

13. Frank, *Downfall*, 280.

14. United States Postwar Military Policy in the Far East, n.d., OPD Executive Files, Exec. 5, Item 21a, RG 165, Modern Military Reference Branch, National Archives, Suitland, Maryland. (Hereafter cited as MMRB, NARA.)

15. Ibid.

16. Memorandum for the Chief of Staff, n.d., CCS 334 JCS (2-2-45) RG218, MMRB, NARA.

17. United States Postwar Military Policy in the Far East, n.d., OPD Executive Files, Exec. 5, Item 21a, RG 165, MMRB, NARA.

18. John Terraine, *The Life and Times of Lord Mountbatten* (London: Hutchinson, 1968), 124.

19. Mountbatten, *Supreme Allied Commander, South-East Asia, 1943–1946* (London: Collins, 1988), 231–232.

20. Proclamation Defining Terms for Japanese, *Department of State Bulletin* 13, 29 July 1945: 137–138.

21. Robert P. Newman, *Truman and the Hiroshima Cult* (East Lansing: Michigan State University Press, 1995), 70.

22. Gallicchio, *Cold War Begins in Asia*, 46.

2

The Politics of Surrender

By the end of the Potsdam Conference the great powers had yet to pierce the core of Japan's wartime empire. The successful test of the atomic bomb and the impending entry of the Soviet Union into the war introduced the strong possibility that the war might suddenly end without further advance by the British and the Americans. When Lord Mountbatten learned about the atomic bomb he promptly concluded that the sudden need to swing into action to take Japan's surrender "was going to present the wretched commanders with extremely difficult problems." The rapid movement of hundreds of thousands of widely dispersed troops was a daunting operational challenge. American staff officers working at Potsdam estimated that the redeployment of troops for various occupation duties would tie up available shipping for nearly a month. Shipping requirements increased when one factored in the need to transport Allied occupation troops to Japan and repatriate the nearly three million Japanese outside the home islands. Demobilization, a pressing political concern recognized by army planners, added to the burden. High point men would have to be brought home from Europe even as soldiers with lower scores from the same divisions deployed for occupation duties in the Pacific theater.

Complicating this situation were the unsettled conditions throughout the area occupied by Japanese troops. In much of Asia, Japan's defeat would ignite a scramble for control of the areas formerly held by imperial troops. In Southeast

Asia, local anticolonial groups prepared to proclaim their independence and re-sist the return of the Europeans. In China, Mao's Communists would seek to fill any vacuum created by Japan's surrender. The introduction of Soviet forces into northeast Asia created an additional element of unpredictability in the transition from war to peace. Sizing up these problems, American planners turned their at-tention to the daunting task of determining the best way to deploy American forces so as to secure the fruits of victory.

THE ARMY-NAVY GAME

Under the circumstances, it appeared doubtful that MacArthur could move enough divisions quickly enough to secure key points in Japan if Tokyo sud-denly threw in the towel. Thus even before they received MacArthur's actual plans, the JCS tentatively decided that Admiral Nimitz's CAMPUS plan, which envisioned a naval show of force in Tokyo Bay and marine landings at key points along the shore, offered the quickest means of enforcing the surrender. The JCS also informed MacArthur and Nimitz that they desired additional operations on the CAMPUS model to occupy key areas along the coast of China and Manchuria in order to facilitate the reoccupation of central and north China by Nationalist troops. The Chiefs also called for similar opera-tions at Pusan on the Korean peninsula.

According to the JCS, these preparations were now a pressing necessity. MacArthur and Nimitz were designated jointly to receive the Japanese sur-render and coordinate their operations in dealing with the Imperial Head-quarters until MacArthur went ashore and assumed personal responsibility for his forces. MacArthur and Nimitz were further informed that the above arrangements would "not be allowed to interfere with the conduct of local surrenders by naval or other U.S. commanders concerned."[1]

That last provision forbidding any interference with naval commanders re-quires some explanation. After all, obtaining the surrender of Japanese forces is what the war was about, was it not? It was. However, the JCS recognized that the rapidly changing situation in the Pacific was likely to rekindle the long smoldering dispute between MacArthur and Nimitz for preeminence in the Pacific. Inter-service rivalry was especially acute in the Pacific where MacArthur's large scale land campaigns in New Guinea and the Philippines competed for resources and headlines with the navy's fast carriers and island hopping strategy. Ordinarily sympathetic to the navy, Roosevelt had treated

MacArthur with kid gloves owing to the general's popularity and Republican Party connections. As a consequence, the president approved a divided command in the Pacific, thereby fully satisfying neither service and, as one historian has noted, creating command relationships for individual operations "that verged on the bizarre."[2]

In mid-1944 and again in early 1945, MacArthur had fended off challenges from the navy and the JCS to redirect operations against Japan away from his Southwest Pacific Theater. MacArthur had prevailed on both occasions, winning approval for the liberation of the Philippines and the assault on Kyushu. Now, in his moment of triumph, MacArthur was being informed that the early surrender operations would be under Nimitz's direction and that other navy commanders would take surrenders outside of Japan as the opportunity presented itself.

It was not surprising, therefore, that MacArthur opposed the Joint Chiefs' recommendations. The navy, he insisted, was not suited for the dangerous job of initiating the occupation of Japan. He also questioned the use of marines on the China coast. MacArthur took issue with the JCS's delicate parsing of responsibilities between him and Nimitz. The general argued that there should be a single coordinating authority for all of the surrender operations. Command and control of those operations should follow the principals of the OLYMPIC directive which, of course, would put them under MacArthur's overall direction. MacArthur made his case on the basis of sound military procedure but he found it impossible to disguise his preoccupation with service prestige. "[I]t would be psychologically offensive to ground and air forces of the Pacific Theater," he told the Chiefs, "to be relegated from their proper missions at the hour of victory."[3]

If MacArthur's complaints seemed petty, Nimitz was probably not blameless either. According to an army report, earlier efforts to reconcile the BLACKLIST and CAMPUS plans during a conference at Guam broke down when the navy refused to discuss the surrender with MacArthur. This unseemly bickering provoked a sharp response from Marshall. The chief of staff was determined to keep the pressure on Japan for fear that an opportunity to compel the enemy's surrender would slip through the Americans' grasp. Facing mounting political pressure to end the war and aware that Japan sought to take advantage of America's slackening commitment to unconditional surrender, Marshall was more alert to the political explosiveness of the situation than

MacArthur. What would happen if Tokyo announced its willingness to sur-render and then qualified that announcement making it contingent of several conditions? Would the American public still wish to prosecute the war, even if meant an invasion of the home islands? Marshall did not wish to find out.

Marshall told MacArthur that the navy's plan was designed to meet an emergency. If Japan surrendered, American forces would need to arrive before the Japanese could reconsider their actions. Marshall cited previous experi-ence with Germany, when individual commanders decided not to obey sur-render orders, as the primary reason for entering Japan promptly. The solution seemed obvious. What was needed, Marshall explained, was some variation on MacArthur's BLACKLIST which would also provide for the rapid movement of naval forces into key areas during the period between capitula-tion and the arrival of MacArthur's main force. Marshall also expressed be-wilderment at MacArthur's opposition to marine landings in China. By his own admission MacArthur did not have enough troops for occupation duties in Japan and Korea. The marines seemed the logical choice. Frustrated by MacArthur's stubborn parochialism, Marshall ended his message on a rare note of sarcasm. "We are trying to end the war with Japan," he reminded MacArthur.[4]

Before MacArthur and Nimitz could sort out their differences, the first atomic bomb was exploded over Hiroshima on August 6. Two days later the Soviet Union declared war on Japan. At 1:00 a.m. on the ninth Red Army forces invaded Manchuria. On the same day, August 9, a second atomic bomb destroyed Nagasaki. In the midst of these world-shattering events, MacArthur found himself defending his control over OLYMPIC for one last time.

During June and July, American signals intelligence had begun to detect an unexpectedly high buildup of forces on Kyushu. The JCS had predicted some reinforcement of the island but this new information revealed a far more con-certed effort on the part of the Japanese than the Chiefs had thought possible. By the start of August they confirmed the existence of eleven divisions, one regiment, and a brigade on the island. At that point the Americans counted approximately 630,000 Japanese troops on Kyushu, well over the 350,000 they expected to encounter. American military intelligence had counted on meet-ing a force less than half that size when it began planning for OLYMPIC. (Eventually, the Americans learned that Imperial Headquarters had posi-tioned 900,000 men on Kyushu.) Alarmed by this new information, the Joint

Chiefs' planners recommended that Nimitz and MacArthur be asked for their views on alternative plans. In the meantime, the options for a direct assault on Honshu were being explored by army and navy planners in the Pentagon. On August 7, Marshall sought MacArthur's reaction to this new information and asked for his opinion on scrubbing OLYMPIC in favor of a direct assault on Honshu, a revised version of CORONET.

While Marshall waited for a reply, the navy prepared a two-pronged challenge to MacArthur's leadership in the Pacific. On August 8, Secretary of the Navy James Forrestal wrote to President Truman recommending that the uncooperative MacArthur be removed in favor of Nimitz, Marshall, or General Dwight Eisenhower.[5] The following day, MacArthur's reply to Marshall arrived in Washington. MacArthur dismissed the recent intelligence estimates of Japanese forces on Kyushu and opposed any reconsideration of OLYMPIC. MacArthur's assessment was disingenuous and self-serving.[6] In this case, it was imperative that nothing be done to change OLYMPIC. MacArthur was in charge of that operation, but a change in plans would reopen the question of command and control, especially since naval air power would play a larger role in an assault of Honshu if Kyushu were bypassed. It is probably only a slight exaggeration to say that at this point, MacArthur feared the navy more than the Japanese.

The navy apparently sensed MacArthur's vulnerability. Forrestal's extraordinary recommendation that MacArthur be removed is one indication of that awareness. On August 9, the day after Forrestal's letter to Truman, Admiral Ernest King, commander-in-chief of the United States Navy and, as chief of naval operations, Marshall's counterpart, asked Nimitz his views on OLYMPIC in light of the new intelligence available. Since Nimitz had already told King in May that he opposed OLYMPIC, King could expect that Nimitz's opposition could have only gotten stronger. In other words, King was preparing to overturn the previous Army-Navy agreement on the invasion strategy.[7]

With the navy preparing to challenge OLYMPIC, and with it MacArthur's command of the next operations against Japan, a confrontation was brewing. That clash was averted by the event everyone fervently desired, the surrender of Japan. One can well imagine, however, the lingering sense of uneasiness felt by Marshall, Forrestal, and others when they learned that the head of the Allied occupation of Japan would be the general who had displayed such a grim determination to protect his prerogatives.

GENERAL ORDER NUMBER ONE: PARTITIONING ASIA

On August 10, the day after the second atomic bomb exploded over Nagasaki, the Japanese government issued a message to the Allies stating its readiness to surrender according to the terms of the Potsdam Declaration providing they did not prejudice the prerogatives of the emperor as a sovereign ruler. The militarists had finally abandoned their insistence on the right to disarm their own troops and try their own war criminals but, incredibly, after two atomic bombs, the Japanese were still holding out for a promise on the emperor. As the Americans pondered a response, Truman halted the further use of atomic bombs without his express permission. On the afternoon of the tenth, the United States replied to the Japanese offer with a carefully worded compromise implying the continuation of the dynasty but circumscribing its political authority. The critical sentence stipulated that "the authority of the Emperor and the Japanese Government to rule the state shall be subject to the Supreme Commander of the Allied Powers."

While the Americans waited for a response, Marshall issued a stop order on the shipment of fissionable material to the Pacific. Over the next several days Marshall explored an alternative use for the atomic bomb. One possibility was the use of as many as twelve stockpiled nuclear weapons in a pre-invasion bombardment in the vicinity of the projected landing areas on Kyushu. For most American officials the attacks on Hiroshima and Nagasaki inspired a variety of emotions ranging from elation to awe. Celebrations among American GIs in the Pacific had already begun. Others pondered the terrible power of the new weapon. "The killing power of it frightens me," wrote one soldier slated for CORONET. "Shortsightedly one can say it will save many American lives, maybe mine, but God knows how it will be used in the future."[8]

Marshall no doubt experienced some of those emotions, but Japan's insistence on terms forced his thinking in a different direction. Tokyo's stalling revived Marshall's dread that Japan would have to be invaded before it submitted. Marshall concluded that if Tokyo did not surrender after Nagasaki it was doubtful that additional atomic attacks spread out over a period of weeks would shock Japan into accepting defeat. Thus he began to explore the feasibility of using the bombs in support of the American landings.[9] Fortunately, for the attackers, who would be subjected to the radioactive contamination of the invasion area, as well as the defenders on Kyushu or possibly

FIGURE 2.1
Reporters scrambling around a table at the White House evidently picking up press releases announcing the Japanese surrender.
National Park Serviceman Abbie Rowe, courtesy of the Harry S. Truman Library

Honshu, Japan accepted the American clarification of the Potsdam Declaration on August 14. The war was finally over.

The president declared a two-day holiday to commemorate the long-awaited end of hostilities but there was no slackening in the pace of work in the Pentagon. The war had been won, but the officers and civilians who oversaw American military operations knew all too well that much of what had been achieved in war could be lost or jeopardized in the first days of peace. Of immediate concern was the delineation of responsibilities for taking the surrender of Japanese throughout Asia. Accepting the surrender of Japanese troops was a military operation fraught with political implications. Whoever took the surrender of enemy forces in a given area, Manchuria for example, would gain immediate control of that territory by virtue of having the only armed forces on the ground. The Americans had learned that lesson the hard way after watching Soviet troops move into Poland. One potential solution was to reach agreements on postwar occupation duties as a way of mitigating the political advantages of taking the surrender in a given area. This was done in the case of Germany. American forces withdrew from the Elbe River as previously agreed and, in keeping with previous agreements, the British, French, and Americans occupied zones in Berlin, even though the Russians had paid a terrible price in conquering the city by themselves.

The division of Germany into zones worked well as a means of breaking up the country, but it was already becoming clear that it would be more difficult to put the pieces back together again. The Americans, having carried the brunt of the war against Japan for four years were not inclined to see their postwar authority in Japan diluted by a zonal division of the home islands. Although the Americans worried what Russia would do if it conquered all of Korea and Manchuria, they were unwilling to discuss postwar occupation arrangements in those places lest the Russians counter with a demand for their own zone in Japan. While at Potsdam, Truman and the Joint Chiefs had pondered a way out of this dilemma. Their solution, admittedly imperfect, was to try to rush troops onto the mainland of Asia ahead of the Russians. This gambit might work if, as expected, it took the Russians approximately thirty days after the start of AUGUST STORM to break through Japan's defenses. Thus, even though the Red Army might eventually control much of Manchuria and Korea, the Americans would have established a military presence on the mainland.

When the Allies had met at Potsdam they had agreed only upon operational boundaries for the purpose of preventing clashes between the different armies and navies. These operational arrangements were premised on the assumption that the war would not end soon. There had been no discussion of postwar occupation responsibilities. Now it looked as though the war would be over in days instead of months. The problem of who would take the Japanese surrender in different parts of the empire required immediate attention.

Primary responsibility for addressing the politico-military issues arising for the surrender belonged to the State-War-Navy Coordinating Committee (SWNCC), comprised of assistant secretaries from each department, and the Joint Staff Planners, which consisted of uniformed representatives from each of the services. These officials set to work once it appeared possible that Japan would surrender. On the night of August 10–11 the two committees met in adjoining rooms in the Pentagon to draft the documents that would spell out the steps to be taken by Japan in order to complete the surrender. Key among those documents was General Order Number One, a directive to be issued by the Imperial Headquarters to Japanese field commanders telling them to whom they should surrender their arms.

As the committees began their work, they were informed that Secretary of State Byrnes wanted the United States to accept the surrender of Japanese troops in Korea as far north as possible. Aided only by a National Geographic wall map of Asia, Colonel Charles Bonesteel and Colonel Dean Rusk decided upon the thirty-eighth parallel, north latitude as the surrender boundary on the peninsula. The area below that line, which would become the American zone, contained Seoul, the capital, two ports, Inchon and Pusan, and at least one prisoner of war camp known to be holding Americans. When Bonesteel and Rusk submitted their handiwork to the larger committee, discussion ensued regarding the desirability of moving the line to the thirty-ninth parallel. The navy's representative favored this adjustment because the line, if continued onto the mainland, would place the ports of Dairen and Port Arthur in the American zone. The army, with the support of the State Department vetoed this change fearing that the Russians would reject the entire General Order and put American chances of entering Korea at risk.

By morning August 11, the territorial provisions of the General Order were completed. According to the draft, all Japanese troops in China (excluding Manchuria), Formosa, and Indochina north of the sixteenth parallel were to surrender to the representatives of Generalissimo Jiang Jieshi. The Russians would take the surrender of Japanese forces in Manchuria, Korea, north of the thirty-eighth parallel, and Karafuto (southern Sakhalin). Mountbatten was designated to take the surrender in Southeast Asia including Burma, Thailand, Malaya, Borneo, the Netherlands Indies, and French Indochina south of the sixteenth parallel. Nimitz and MacArthur would divide the remainder of Japan's empire between their two commands. Nimitz would take the surrender in the bypassed areas of the Central and Western Pacific, as well as unspecified "other Pacific Islands." MacArthur would take control of "the main islands of Japan, minor islands adjacent thereto, Korea south of the thirty-eighth parallel north latitude and the Philippine Islands."[10]

The boundaries established in the General Order offered technical guidance to the Allied and Japanese commanders. The relevant clauses read like an arid geography lesson. Colonel Bonesteel, who drafted the above provisions, was able to complete this complicated task in a short time primarily because he used the operational boundaries agreed upon at Potsdam as his guide. The one exception was Korea, on which he had received specific instructions from the State Department. Otherwise, he drafted the order as if all of the anticipated Allied operations had proceeded as planned. But such was not the case. Jiang's troops were not advancing into eastern and north China. Mountbatten's forces were not ashore in Malaya or the Netherlands East Indies. Nor had Chinese or British troops reached Indochina. Nevertheless, Japanese troops in those areas would be ordered to surrender to the designated Allied commanders, whenever they actually showed up. In the meantime, the Japanese were expected to retain control of the areas they occupied.

In this sense, General Order Number One was a great power agreement similar to great power agreements of the nineteenth century that partitioned Africa or China without regard to the desires of the inhabitants of those places. At least that is how it was bound to look to the insurgent or anticolonial forces in China, Korea, Indochina, and Indonesia that were excluded from participating in the surrender. This is not to say that the officers drafting the General Order could have acted differently. Decisions as to the future disposition of these areas needed to be made at the highest levels of the Allied governments. For the most part, all of the governments concerned had avoided addressing these issues. A month earlier, time had seemed to be on their side. The gradual re-conquest of the areas under Japanese control, it was thought, would solve most of these problems. Suddenly time had run out and with it, the patience of those groups that sought to change the prewar order in Asia.

On a geopolitical level the General Order favored the interests of great powers. At the same time it also glossed over potential points of conflict *between* the powers. To begin with, the order made no mention of the Kuriles, which were slated to become Russian as part of the Yalta Far Eastern agreement. But the existing operational agreements placed some of those islands in the American zone for naval and air operations. The order also omitted the crown colony of Hong Kong from the list of Mountbatten's responsibilities, thereby implying that the surrender would be taken by the Chinese. Finally, the order left Indochina north of sixteenth parallel north latitude in China's zone as well. Nevertheless, despite the protests that these provisions were likely to provoke from the Soviets, British, and French, they occasioned little discussion among the Joint Staff Planners and members of the State-War-Navy-Coordinating Committee.

After completing the draft of General Order Number One, the Joint Staff Planners also wrote a draft directive for outlining General MacArthur's responsibilities in order of importance. The occupation of Japan held the highest priority. Seoul was second. Landings on the China coast came last and were subject to the progress of the other two missions. Some time during August 11, the president revised the directive to include the occupation of Dairen and a port in Korea immediately after Japan surrendered. The Dairen operation, which had been stricken from the General Order the previous night, had come back to life. Only this time it was not included in the General Order. That meant that if MacArthur succeeded in getting troops into the Manchurian port they would arrive unannounced into what the Soviets were likely to think was their zone.

That same day, the Joint Chiefs received word from the British that they wanted to release elements of the Royal Navy from American control so that they could occupy Hong Kong. Continuing their balancing act, the Americans sought to avoid taking sides. Byrnes said only that the United States should not be asked to participate in or approve the operation without Chinese acquiescence. He recommended that the British take the matter up with the Chinese.

By this time, the General Order was beginning to look like a Christmas tree with various members hanging their own favorite ornament on its already sagging branches. On August 12, Assistant Secretary of War McCloy gained approval for landings at Tientsin on the north China coast just below the Great Wall. McCloy explained that landing at Tientsin might make the landing above the wall, at Dairen, "appear less pointed." McCloy seemed to think that landing troops elsewhere on the shore of the Yellow Sea would camouflage the Americans' true intentions in occupying Dairen. If challenged by the Russians, the Americans would say that the Dairen occupation was part of a larger plan to take control of the Yellow Sea from the Japanese. It is doubtful that the Soviets would be satisfied with such a flimsy pretext for the arrival of American forces into a key port in their zone. Nevertheless, MacArthur's directive was revised and one more port was added to his expanding responsibilities.

More was to come. After further discussions on August 12, Byrnes agreed to have Admiral Nimitz take the surrender of Japanese forces in the Kuriles below the operational line agreed upon at Potsdam. This would place Para-mushir and all of the islands to the south in the American zone. All concerned knew that the Yalta agreements stipulated that the islands would be turned over to the Soviets. Nevertheless, McCloy and some of the army's planners de-sired American landing rights on at least one of the islands to facilitate the oc-cupation of Japan. Rather than count on Soviet cooperation, they acted on the principle that possession is nine-tenths of the law. The Kuriles were now on the American itinerary although, like Dairen, they were not included in the General Order.

For the most part support for the enlargement of American responsibilities came from the president's civilian advisers. Ambassador Averill Harriman in Moscow, Byrnes, McCloy, and navy secretary Forrestal took the lead in calling for landings in Korea and Dairen and surrender operations in the Kuriles. In keeping with their responsibility for the broad outlines of American diplo-matic and military policy, these officials believed that the United States should capitalize on the unexpectedly sudden Japanese surrender to improve Amer-ica's ability to influence events in Northeast Asia. For the civilian policymak-ers, Allied unity, at least where the Russians were concerned, mattered less than the windfall opportunities presented by Japan's sudden collapse.

The army and navy staff officers charged with drafting directives to MacArthur saw the surrender planning from a different perspective. These of-ficers were aware of the political implications of the surrender, but they were most concerned with the technical challenges inherent in determining how to gather up America's far-flung naval and land forces on short notice and get them heading in new directions. With nearly three million Japanese troops outside of the home islands, the staff officers were especially concerned with making the surrender as orderly as possible. As the army's top planner, Brigadier General George A. Lincoln, later explained, they had to draft a Gen-eral Order that the Allies would accept or there would be chaos throughout Asia. Unannounced occupations in Dairen and the Kuriles increased the risk of undesirable confrontations. A breakdown in Allied cooperation risked more than could be gained by beating the Russians off the mark in Dairen or the Kuriles.

In keeping with that cautious view, the Joint Staff Planners drafted two memoranda addressed to Stalin from the president. The first would advise the Soviet leader that the occupation of Dairen was being undertaken to prevent the Japanese from destroying port facilities in the Yellow Sea and would not prejudice the final peace settlement. The second would inform Stalin at "the appropriate time" that the United States would be operating in the Kuriles.

The Joint Staff Planners' nervousness about confronting the Russians in Northeast Asia made them more circumspect than the president's civilian advisers. Their continued adherence to Roosevelt's minimalist approach to problems on the mainland also induced a general wariness about involving American troops in China. This view put them completely at odds with General Wedemeyer, the American chief of staff to Jiang Jeishi, and commanding general of American forces in China. When Wedemeyer learned that Japan might surrender well before the scheduled invasion he promptly beseeched the Joint Chiefs to make landings on the China coast MacArthur's first priority. Japan could wait, Wedemeyer insisted. China was the real powder keg in Asia. Wedemeyer explained that if Japan surrendered in the near future, Jiang's troops would be stranded in Southwestern China, far from the country's vital coastal areas. By the time Nationalist troops could move, Wedemeyer explained, the Communists would already be filling the void left by the surrender of Japanese troops throughout northern China. Once a race for control of Chinese territory began there would be no way to prevent the contest from escalating into a civil war. In light of this situation, Wedemeyer asserted that nothing short of making China the first priority for American forces would prevent war between the Communists and Nationalists.

The Joint Chiefs and MacArthur rejected Wedemeyer's pleas. The Chiefs dared not risk giving the Japanese time to change their minds. Japan remained the main destination of American forces in war or peace. Without enough shipping or troops to undertake all of his responsibilities simultaneously, MacArthur would have to make decisions based on the broad objectives of American policy. For the moment that meant China came in at a distant third behind Japan and Korea.

Lacking the resources to block Communist gains in north China, the Americans placed the onus on the Japanese to hold their ground until the Nationalists arrived. On August 14, the General Order was nearing completion when McCloy added one more provision. McCloy inserted new language in the order just below the paragraphs establishing the surrender zones that notified the Japanese that the Allied commanders listed in the preceding paragraphs were the only authorized recipients of the surrender. This clause effectively excluded the Chinese Communists and other Asian revolutionaries from participating in the surrender. It also temporarily drafted the Japanese army into the service of the Nationalists and, indirectly, the Americans.

The Americans would not have to wait long to see if this stopgap measure for China would work. At 7:00 p.m. on August 14, the same day that McCloy put the finishing touches on General Order Number One, President Truman called a press conference to announce that Japan had agreed to surrender. Truman referred to the capitulation as unconditional surrender. As we have seen, however, the Allies had committed themselves to several conditions in the Potsdam Declaration. Their eleventh hour stipulation that the emperor's right to govern would be subject to that of the Supreme Commander of the Allied Powers (SCAP) also carried with it the strong implication that the emperor would remain in place for the time being. These seemed like small matters in the nation's moment of triumph. The United States had achieved its main war aims without having to invade the home islands. Now the Americans would come as conquerors. Japan had yielded; its reign of terror in Asia had ended. The scramble for Asia was about to begin.

DA AND NYET: THE RUSSIAN RESPONSE TO GENERAL ORDER NUMBER ONE

Tokyo's announced intention to surrender did not produce an abrupt end to hostilities in Asia. Instead it signaled the beginning of a period of transition from war to peace. News of the decision to cease hostilities would have to be sent from Imperial Headquarters to the Japanese theater commanders and from those headquarters to the individual field commanders. Allied commanders would also have to be informed that their governments had accepted Japan's surrender. Once that information was in hand, the numerous Allied and Japanese commanders would have to communicate with each other and establish the terms for separate cease-fires throughout the region. Once a cease fire was in place and regular communications between the former belligerents were established, the Allied commanders could begin to disarm the Japanese troops in their area of responsibility. To begin this process, the Japanese commanders would need to know to whom they should surrender. For that, they needed instruction from Imperial Headquarters, which in turn, waited for instruction from the Allies, which meant that the Allies would have to agree on the territorial provisions of General Order Number One.

Truman started the ball rolling by sending the draft order to the Allies on the afternoon of August 15. As Dean Rusk later recalled, the army staff officers who had drafted most of the order were particularly nervous about how the Soviets would respond to the temporary division of Korea at the thirty-eighth parallel. They did not have to wait long. The next day, Stalin replied to Truman's message. Much to the relief of Rusk and his colleagues, the Soviet leader did not object to sharing surrender duties in Korea. Stalin reacted suspiciously, however, to the absence of any mention of Dairen and Port Arthur in the General Order. Not taking any chances, he reminded Truman that the Liaotung Peninsula, on which both ports were located, was part of Manchuria and therefore in the Soviet zone. Stalin also offered several "corrections" to the General Order. He requested the inclusion of all of the Kurile Islands in the Soviet zone and made a bid for a Soviet occupation zone on northern Hokkaido, the northernmost of Japan's home islands.

The Americans were relieved to learn that Stalin did not oppose the division of Korea. But the Soviet leader's cagey response regarding Dairen, the Kuriles, and Hokkaido necessitated an American reply. Responding to the Hokkaido "correction" would be easy. The Americans planned to use Allied forces in the occupation of Japan but they would serve under the Supreme Allied Commander, an American, and would not have control of a discrete zone. Responding to Stalin's request regarding the Kuriles and Dairen proved more difficult.

By the time the Americans received Stalin's message the Soviets had been at war with the Japanese for eight days. Already, AUGUST STORM was a stunning success. The Red Army offensive began in a driving rainstorm without an opening artillery barrage and caught the Japanese completely unprepared. Advancing on three fronts, one of which originated beyond the Grand Khingan Mountains in northwestern Manchuria, which the Japanese presumed to be impassable, Russian forces swiftly cracked through enemy lines and overwhelmed the paralyzed Kwantung army. To some extent, the achievement of AUGUST STORM has been overshadowed by the atomic bombs and Japan's decision to surrender. For our purposes, however, it is important to recognize the impact of the Manchurian campaign on American operations during the period of Japan's surrender. As David Glantz, the leading scholar of the campaign has noted, AUGUST STORM represented "the highest stage of military art the Red Army reached during its operations in the Second World War."[11] Certainly the Americans thought so. Recall that as late as July, the Americans were predicting that it would take the Russians thirty days before they began to gain ground. Instead, the Red Army was gobbling up territory in less than thirty hours. Even the Soviets were surprised by their overwhelming success. This extraordinary achievement looked even more spectacular since the offensive began at least a week before the Americans thought the Russians would be ready.

As the Americans sought to compose a response to Stalin's "corrections" the picture before them was of a crumbling Kwantung army and rapidly advancing Red Army columns stabbing deep into Manchuria. Having overcome the Japanese, the Soviets still had to conquer Manchuria's vast expanse. By August 17 Mukden and Harbin remained in Japanese hands. The Soviet advance into Korea stalled above the forty-first parallel, leaving much of the peninsula in Japanese hands. The Soviets did not reach Dairen in force until August 24. The assault on the Kuriles did not commence until August 18. Nevertheless, the awesome display of Soviet military power in the first week of the offensive convinced the already wary Joint Chiefs to abandon any thought of beating the Russians into Dairen or the Kuriles. When the Joint Chiefs predicted that the Soviets would take Dairen by August 19, Truman cancelled the Dairen operation.

Truman did not give up on the Kuriles so easily. In his reply to Stalin, the president agreed to place all of the Kuriles in the Soviet zone. On the advice of Secretary of State Byrnes and Admiral William D. Leahy, the president's representative to the Joint Chiefs, Truman added that the United States desired air base rights on one of the Kuriles. This reference to base rights was an awkwardly worded attempt to correct a prior failure on the part of the State Department to discuss with the Russians an American interest in acquiring emergency landing rights in the Kuriles for military and commercial aircraft during the occupation of Japan. Given the Soviets' record in these matters, Truman's request probably had little chance of success. Those odds were made slimmer by the message's reference to "base rights" which suggested a more substantial American presence on the islands than Truman intended. Nor did it help that this request was coupled with a rejection of Stalin's bid for an occupation zone on Hokkaido. After a sharp exchange in which Stalin claimed to be insulted by Truman's high-handedness, the Americans gave up on obtaining landing rights in the Kuriles.

The outcome did not surprise Rear Admiral Charles "Savvy" Cooke, the navy's top planner. Cooke complained that the Americans should have agreed to let Stalin occupy the Kuriles, but they should have also defined the Kuriles so as to exclude the southernmost two islands in the chain and the several much smaller adjacent islands. There was some basis for this distinction in that both of these, Etorofu and Kunashiri, and the smaller cluster were administered as part of Japan's home islands. Cooke thought Kunashiri could remain Japanese and Etorofu could be administered as an international trusteeship with landing rights provided to the United States.

We have no way of knowing if Stalin would have accepted Cooke's solution. After they dropped their bid for landing rights, the Americans acquiesced in the Soviet occupation of all of the Kuriles as well as the adjacent islands not previously considered to be part of the chain. As of this writing the Japanese government continues to insist that the islands mentioned by Cooke are Japanese territories illegally held by the Russians. The Americans support the Japanese. As a consequence, Japan and the Soviet Union have never signed a formal peace treaty. The dispute remained a bone of contention between Japan and the Soviet Union until the latter's collapse in 1991. The Russian government inherited the islands and with them the long running diplomatic wrangle over their ultimate disposition.

Of course no one could predict the long-term diplomatic consequences of the Soviets' opportunistic grab for all of the islands above Hokkaido. Most American staff officers thought the Kuriles had little value. Of more immediate concern was the haphazard way in which the exchange had been handled by the State Department. Despite repeated reminders that the issue of landing rights had to be taken up with the Soviets, the diplomats dropped the ball. At least that is how Deputy Chief of Staff General J. E. Hull saw the situation. "The State Department muffed this whole thing," he grumbled. Hull's epitaph for the Kuriles fiasco was symptomatic of a more general mood among the army and navy staff officers. It was also a harbinger of a widening fissure between the political and military sides of American policy making that would become more apparent when the war ended.

THE RESPONSE TO GENERAL ORDER NUMBER ONE IN THE CHINA THEATER

Unlike Stalin, Jiang Jieshi welcomed the provisions in the General Order. The General Order conferred some much needed international prestige on Jiang's Nationalist government by treating it as the only entity authorized to take the

Japanese surrender in the China Theater. General Wedemeyer recognized the symbolic importance of the surrender process and in the hour of his triumph urged Jiang to take full advantage of the occasion to impress upon Japanese and Chinese alike the superiority of the Nationalists' government. Nevertheless, the aura of irresistible power eluded Jiang. Neither his Communist adversaries nor his putative British allies regarded Jiang's edicts as sacrosanct. Jiang's precarious military position at the time of the surrender, his reliance on Japanese troops to maintain order, and his subordinates' staggeringly inept re-imposition of control over occupied areas further drained away much of the goodwill that accrued to Jiang in the moment of victory.

From the start, Chairman Mao had no intention of allowing the Nationalists to move unopposed into Communist held areas. The chairman understood that Japanese and American assistance would give Jiang the advantage in the race to reoccupy most of China's major cities, but he thought that the Communist People's Liberation Army (PLA) could improve its position in numerous lesser urban and rural communities. On August 10, Zhu De (Chu Teh), the PLA's commander-in-chief ordered his field officers to command the surrender of Japanese forces in their areas. Zhu's order also sought to take advantage of the precarious situation of Chinese collaborators, so-called puppet troops, to strengthen the Communists' ranks. Puppet soldiers were invited to turn in their arms before the Japanese formally surrendered and await further orders regarding their reorganization or disbandment. The alternative was harsh treatment. Faced with these stark choices, and aware that they could count on little sympathy from the victorious Nationalists, an approximate 75,000 collaborators went over to the Communists taking their equipment with them.[12]

Fortunately for Jiang, the Japanese proved to be more compliant. When they first learned of the emperor's intention to surrender, the commanders of the Japanese army in China insisted that they be allowed to fight on against the Chinese. Undefeated and unrepentant, the Japanese could not believe they were being told to surrender. Further resistance was scotched when the Imperial General Headquarters forcefully reminded its commanders in China of their obligations to serve the emperor. Fervently anti-communist, the Japanese officers also took some consolation in the belief that they might still serve Japan's interests by insuring an orderly transfer of power to the Nationalists. The Japanese commander in Nanjing curtly turned aside demands by a Communist representative that he surrender his forces to the PLA and awaited word from the Nationalists.

Contacts between the Japanese and Nationalists were opened, and a preliminary surrender ceremony establishing a cease-fire was held in Chikiang on August 21. During the ceremony, the Nationalists treated the Japanese representatives with a courtesy and politeness that eased the humiliation felt by the surrendering officers. The Americans found the ritualized politeness disconcerting and out of place. They had been surprised to learn that the Chinese even intended to use a roundtable for the exchange of surrender instruments as a gesture of equality between the two belligerents. The Chinese ultimately opted for two long tables symbolic of a more confrontational relationship between victor and vanquished. Nevertheless, the meeting ended with the Chinese officers, many of whom had studied in Japan, informally reminiscing with their former enemies about their youthful days in Japan. The Americans found such behavior mystifying to say the least. Personal experiences as well as traditional Chinese politeness help to explain the Chinese officers' conduct. But it seems equally likely that the Chinese officers' disinclination to gloat or deal coldly with the Japanese reflected their awareness of the military realities in China. In the days to come the Nationalists would be depending on the cooperation of what was in reality an undefeated Japanese army to facilitate the reassertion of Nationalist control over much of China below the Great Wall.

Unfortunately for Jiang, the British were not nearly as solicitous of his feelings as he was toward the Japanese. As soon as they learned of Japan's intention to surrender, the British requested the release of their naval forces under MacArthur's command for the purpose of reoccupying Hong Kong and otherwise showing the flag in China's treaty ports. On August 16, the British informed the Chinese government that they were readying a force to reoccupy the colony. The Chinese turned to the Americans for assistance, pointing out that General Order Number One placed Hong Kong in the China Theater. The British disagreed. According to their interpretation General Order Number One, which gave Jiang responsibility of Japanese forces "within China," did not apply to Hong Kong, since the colony was not, according to the British, within China. Prime Minister Clement Atlee sought confirmation for his views from President Truman. On August 18 Secretary of State Byrnes informed London that the United States had no objection to

British forces taking the surrender in Hong Kong providing they coordinated their operations with the Chinese.

The Americans still hoped to avoid taking sides but neither the British nor the Chinese seemed inclined to let that happen. After three more days of maneuvering by the British and Chinese, Truman directly advised Jiang that the United States wanted the British to take the surrender in Hong Kong. More negotiations between the British and Chinese followed. Some British officials recommended allowing Jiang's representative to cosign the surrender documents in recognition of Jiang's standing as the commander-in-chief of the China Theater. The British Foreign Office remained adamant that the surrender would be a British show. Jiang ultimately relented but the entire episode caused him considerable embarrassment. The Americans were also discomfited by publicly having to take a stand in support of the prewar colonial order in Asia.

THE RESPONSE TO GENERAL ORDER NUMBER ONE IN SEAC

In Korea and in China below the Great Wall, the Americans had taken care to draw the surrender boundaries to comport with their clearly defined interests. In Korea, the line reflected Truman's desire for an American presence on the peninsula when the future disposition of that luckless nation was decided. In China, where the United States had a stake in strengthening the Nationalists, Japanese troops were used to deny the Communists any part in the surrender. American interests in the territories claimed by the European colonial powers were less clearly defined. By the time the Allied leaders met at Potsdam, the State Department had taken the position that the United States would not stand in the way of a return of the Europeans to Southeast Asia. The Joint Chiefs had likewise agreed that the United States should not interfere in the restoration of colonial rule. All agreed that the best outcome would be for the Europeans to negotiate a gradual transition to independence, as the Americans were doing in the Philippines. But the State Department and the Chiefs also agreed that in view of the Soviet presence in Eastern and Central Europe, the United States should do nothing in Southeast Asia that would jeopardize Allied cooperation in Western Europe.

This clarification in American policy was imperfectly communicated to American representatives in Asia. The breakdown in communication impeded the execution of American policy in the final weeks of the war. Even more harmful to European interests, however, was the blithe indifference to colonial desires with which General Order Number One was drafted and implemented. This was particularly the case with Indochina. The French would long see American actions there as result of malign intent. In retrospect, however, it appears that the decisions that so adversely affected the future of French control over Vietnam were made in haste and without a clear understanding of what had been decided at the Potsdam Conference. Once the error made its way into the General Order, the Americans refused to correct it, more out of political convenience than anything else. In other words, the Americans did not set out to undermine French rule in Indochina, but that is what they did anyway.

The Americans antagonized the French by deciding to use the sixteenth parallel as the dividing line between the British and Chinese zones of responsibility. The Combined Chiefs of Staff, it will be recalled, had settled on the sixteenth parallel as the operational boundary for future operations. Mountbatten, in a classic British understatement had commented that "the French might find the proposition a little less agreeable."[13] But the British, who had been feuding with Wedemeyer over access to Indochina and Thailand, grudgingly accepted this compromise with the proviso that the line would be subject to revision as operations developed. Japan's surrender provided an opportune moment to adjust the boundary in favor of the British. In light of all of the additional territory being transferred to Mountbatten's theater the inclusion of northern Indochina would have been a minor inconvenience. That was how the French saw it. But as we have seen, in the absence of specific instructions Colonel Bonesteel and the Joint Staff Planners simply transformed the operational boundary into the surrender line. None of the officials in the administration who reviewed the General Order recommended any changes regarding Indochina. The General Order went out and was promptly met by protests from French officials in China.

The French thought that the best solution to the Indochina problem was to allow the 5,000 French troops presently in China to return to Indochina. The French representative in Chungking warned that if French troops were not able to return to Indochina it would "gravely prejudice" France's relations with China. He coupled that warning with an even stronger caution that there would be "serious trouble" if Chinese troops entered Indochina.[14] Secretary of State Byrnes brushed aside these alarms and informed the French government that the division at the sixteenth parallel was purely for military purposes and had no political significance. Byrnes added, somewhat unhelpfully, that if the Chinese and British agreed the French could be present at the surrender ceremonies in Indochina.

It is doubtful that Byrnes thought that his message would placate the French. But the secretary clearly felt little need to exert himself on behalf of French interests. French forces in Indochina had remained in Indochina during most of the war by cooperating with Japanese authorities, much as the French Vichy government had done with Germany. The Japanese eventually seized full control of the colony in March 1945. French forces resisted in a brief futile struggle before taking to the hills. Approximately 5,000 French soldiers fled into southern China. More than 10,000 languished as prisoners in Japanese camps. This belated resistance did little to improve France's standing in the estimation of American officials. Apart from the French prisoners or their compatriots in China, the only troops France had available for operations in Indochina had to be equipped and shipped into the Southeast Asian Theater. American shipping priorities made it clear that it would take months before those forces arrived.

The only alternative to a Chinese occupation of northern Indochina was to place the entire colony into Mountbatten's theater. Byrnes declined to seek that solution even after he learned that Jiang had spurned London's recommendation that China and Britain should make the immediate restoration of French authority and the return of French forces the primary objectives of their operations. Jiang countered that the General Order dealt only with the mechanics of taking the surrender of Japanese troops. It said nothing about the restoration of French rule. Clearly, trouble was brewing in Indochina. Nevertheless, Byrnes decided to leave matters where they stood. By this time, he was facing bigger problems in the looming Anglo-Chinese dispute over Hong Kong. The French were too weak to challenge the General Order, but the British were in a better position to cause serious trouble over Hong Kong. Bowing to these realities, Byrnes ultimately told Jiang that the Americans supported Britain's claim to Hong Kong. Byrnes avoided further offending Jiang by leaving northern Indochina in the Chinese zone.

For the French, to whom it was abundantly clear that a Chinese occupation of their colony could bring only trouble, this was a bitter pill. It is not clear what Byrnes thought the outcome of his decision might be. In light of the many problems arising from the surrender, it is not even clear that he gave the issue much thought. It needs to be emphasized, however, that Byrnes stuck with the sixteenth parallel despite strong opposition from the French. Most historians treat the division of Indochina as a decision reached at Potsdam. As we have seen, this was not the case. The line drawn at Potsdam was for operational purposes. That line was transformed into the surrender boundary by General Order Number One. But one did not automatically follow from the other. There was nothing about the operational lines agreed upon at Potsdam that dictated their being used as the surrender boundaries in the General Order. In Korea, the Potsdam operational line was revised for the General Order to accommodate American interests. In the case of the Kuriles and Hong Kong, the General Order was revised further to satisfy the Soviets and British. French pleas for similar treatment were rejected.

Even though they recognized French sovereignty over Indochina, the Americans would not rouse themselves on behalf of the French, especially if it meant further alienating the Chinese. The sixteenth parallel was the default choice but it was still a choice. Had they been able to anticipate the consequences of their decision the Americans would have acted differently. But at the time, few in Washington worried over how their decisions might affect the future of a relatively obscure French possession half a world away.

Had they not been preoccupied with regaining Hong Kong and with the preparations for taking the surrenders of Japanese commanders throughout their vastly enlarged theater, the British might have argued the French case more strenuously. As it was, Mountbatten's planners devoted most of their energy to making an impressive show of force when they returned to Singapore and Malaya. Having already completed preparations for Operation ZIPPER, the assault on Malaya, Mountbatten decided to mount his entry into the British colony as if it were an actual invasion. Mountbatten's armada was literally at sea when on August 19, MacArthur, who had been designated to take the main Japanese surrender in Tokyo, called a halt to the proceedings. Seeking to avoid any confusion in the field that might arise from numerous uncoordinated negotiations, MacArthur ordered Allied commanders to wait for the formal surrender in Tokyo before conducting surrender operations in their theaters. Mountbatten protested to his superiors, complaining that the delay would mean that British forces would not reach Singapore until nearly two weeks after the formal surrender in Tokyo. The movement of British forces into Saigon, the southern headquarters for the Japanese army, would take even longer.

Mountbatten worried that the interlude created by MacArthur's order would give nationalists throughout Southeast Asia a valuable opportunity to organize their resistance to the returning Europeans. Unlike the Americans, Mountbatten doubted he could count on the Japanese to maintain order during the long interval between the cease-fire and the actual arrival of British troops. Asia for Asians had been a dominant theme of Japanese propaganda for most of the war. In reality, of course, the Japanese had exploited the inhabitants and resources of Southeast Asia with a ferocity that might have made the Europeans blush. During the final stages of the conflict, however, the Japanese had actually taken steps to accord various Asian governments independent status, although in name only. Now that they had nothing to lose, no one could be certain how the Japanese would respond to the nationalist aspirations of their supposed brethren to the south. All that Mountbatten knew was that for the time being he would have to drop anchor and wait for the signal from the Big Chief before he could get under way again.

While Mountbatten fumed at MacArthur's theatrics, American and British officials found themselves enmeshed in another controversy that further underscored the lack of coordination between the two allies. When the Joint Chiefs learned that the British planned to show the flag in Chinese ports, they complained that those forces would be better employed in the main effort in Japan and Korea. The British surprised the Americans by replying that they had no plans to send troops to Korea. The Americans were baffled. They knew that as early as Yalta, discussions were underway among the Big Four to establish a trusteeship for Korea. The army had actually gone so far as to draw a preliminary map designating the main occupation zones on the peninsula. The British reply prompted a hurried search of the conference records by the army's planners. Much to their consternation they discovered that in postponing discussions about Korea with the Russians at Potsdam, the Americans had also neglected to raise the subject with the British. The Americans had intentionally delayed raising the issue with the Russians. But they had simply forgotten to discuss it with the British.

Searching their own records, the British quickly came to the conclusion that no one in their government had ever agreed to send troops onto the peninsula. Nevertheless, the British Chiefs of Staff recommended that in the

interest of Allied solidarity they would contribute a brigade group to the occupation of Korea if the Americans pressed the issue. By this time, the Americans, recognizing their error, decided to drop the whole subject. The
Americans would go it alone in Korea below the thirty-eighth parallel. The
British were not coming.[15]

THE SURRENDERS

As should be clear by now, arranging for the surrender of enemy forces was a
complicated and politically charged process. Boundaries and responsibilities
were negotiated and contested. Power, the ability to project force, remained
decisive. The outcome was tangible, easily measured in terms of territory
gained. Conversely, the culmination of this process, the surrender ceremony,
was a highly symbolic act. It was a drama suffused with ceremonial displays of
authority and power. Getting from the preliminary armistice to the final act
of surrender was in itself an important process that required staff officers to
address numerous technical matters. At the theater level, military staff officers
had to establish rules governing the implementation of cease-fires, the movement and activities of the surrendering forces, the treatment of prisoners of
war, and the care of enemy property. These were just a few of the issues that
demanded immediate attention.

At this stage in the surrender, the victors commanded the vanquished.
They ordered the surrendering commanders to present themselves at the
headquarters of the victors. The defeated were commanded to produce detailed information concerning troop dispositions, locations of prisoner
camps, inventories of stores and property. In the midst of defeat, however,
even a defeat as crushing as the one experienced by Japan, the Japanese
forces possessed a residual ability to influence the process and in small ways
shape it more to their own interests. Approximately three million Japanese
soldiers still held their ground across an immense empire. The army and the
Imperial General Headquarters remained intact within the home islands.
Japan's army in China controlled the cities most desired by Nationalists and
Communists alike. Japan's southern army, headquartered in Saigon, still
controlled much of the former Co-Prosperity Sphere. The opportunities for
mischief were enormous.

Allied commanders were alert to that potential. Their distance from the scene
made them all the more eager to make haste. At this point, the implementation

FIGURE 2.2
Japanese and American officers checking charts for the entrance of the U.S. Fleet into
Tokyo Bay, August 27, 1945.
Naval Historical Center, 80-G-490401

and enforcement of the technical terms of the capitulation collided with the
symbolic and ceremonial aspects of the surrender. As the newly appointed
SCAP, MacArthur deemed it necessary to take the formal surrender of the
Japanese government and Imperial General Headquarters in Tokyo before the
theater surrenders progressed. MacArthur justified this decision as necessary
to avoid confusion throughout Asia. As we have seen, Mountbatten complained strenuously about this restriction. Australian and Chinese officers also
criticized MacArthur's order as placing an unnecessary burden on their forces.
All suspected that SCAP's real intent was to focus world attention on the
drama he would enact in Tokyo Bay.

The general's entry into Japan provoked a wide range of responses. Some
observers commended him for his cautious preparations and attention to detail. The Japanese, with whom MacArthur arranged for the arrival of Ameri-

can forces, worried that they were not being given enough time to prepare for
the introduction of enemy forces into the homeland. Critics thought
MacArthur moved at a pace more suited for a royal procession. Mountbatten,
who was impatient to get on with his own ceremony, fell into the latter group,
as did at least a few American naval officers.

One of those was a pilot from a Third Fleet carrier who braved foul weather
to land at Atsugi airfield on August 27, one day ahead of an advanced party of
the 11th Airborne Division. When the paratroops arrived the next day they
were greeted by a large poster reading "Welcome to the U.S. Army from Third
Fleet." At dawn on August 30, the 11th began arriving in force. Also at day-
break the navy began landing elements of the 4th Marines at Yokosuka naval
base although according to one marine officer, "our first wave was made up
entirely of officers trying to get ashore before MacArthur." They succeeded.

FIGURE 2.3
General MacArthur speaking at the opening of the surrender ceremonies on the USS
Missouri. Behind him are representatives of the Allied powers, September 2, 1945.
Naval Historical Center, SC 213704

SCAP arrived at Atsugi in the afternoon and proceeded to take up temporary
residence at the Yokohama customhouse, one of the few buildings left reasonably intact by American bombings.

On Sunday, August 2, MacArthur boarded the USS *Missouri*, a 45,000-ton
battleship of the *Iowa* class. Anchored under cloudy skies in Tokyo Bay, the
"Mighty Mo" was laden with so much symbolism it was a wonder that it could
stay afloat. Flying above the decks was the flag that had waved over the Capitol on December 7, 1941. Commodore Matthew Perry's thirty-one star flag
was flown in from the United States in a special glass case and mounted on a
bulkhead overlooking the surrender deck. Admiral Nimitz's five star flag flew
from the main. When MacArthur came aboard his personal flag was run up
alongside Nimitz's. The choice of an American warship for the site of the sur-

FIGURE 2.4
General Hsu Yung-chang signs the Instrument of Surrender on behalf of the Republic
of China onboard the USS *Missouri*, September 2, 1945.
Naval Historical Center, SC 213698

render was a concession to the navy. The *Missouri*, which bore the name of Truman's home state and had been christened by his daughter, was selected at the president's behest.

The Japanese delegation performed their disagreeable task in an atmosphere of "frigid" formality. At MacArthur's side were Lieutenant General Jonathan Wainwright, who had surrendered American forces in the Philippines to the Japanese after MacArthur was evacuated, and British Lieutenant General Arthur E. Percival, the defeated commander of the Singapore garrison. VIPs, sailors, and cameramen hovered close by to glimpse the proceedings. A Russian photographer who slipped onto the surrender deck was ushered off by one of the *Missouri*'s officers. After a few minutes of silence, MacArthur stepped forward and read a brief address ending with an eloquent plea for a world where "freedom, tolerance, and justice" would flourish.[16]

There were two sets of documents on the table, one for the Allies and one for the Japanese. The instrument of surrender declared the unconditional surrender of the Imperial General Headquarters and all of the armed forces under Japanese control. It further commanded all civil and military officers to obey the orders of the Supreme Allied Commander and made the authority of the emperor and the Japanese government, subject to the Supreme Commander. A set of lines appeared below the text. Under each line ran the name of one of the countries participating in the surrender. Each delegate was to sign both documents on the line above his country's name. The Japanese foreign minister stepped forward and then paused, uncertain of where to sign. MacArthur tersely ordered his chief of staff to point out the line awaiting the foreign minister's signature. After the Japanese minister signed, MacArthur signed for the Allies, Nimitz for the United States, followed by military representatives of China, Britain, the Soviet Union, and the remaining allies, including France and Canada.

When the last representative had finished, MacArthur offered another brief prayer for peace and pronounced the proceedings closed. At that moment the sun broke through the clouds. Just then, a flight of nearly 2,000 American planes consisting of B-29s and carrier based fighters passed over head. MacArthur moved to a microphone and began a radio address to a world audience. "Today the guns are silent," began the now famous message. "A great tragedy has ended. A great victory has been won."

FIGURE 2.5
Navy planes over the USS *Missouri*, September 2, 1945.
Naval Historical Center, 80-G-472360

While MacArthur began his address, the Japanese delegates were looking at the signed instrument of surrender and talking among themselves. They were joined by several Americans, including MacArthur's chief of staff Lieutenant General Richard K. Sutherland. To some of the onlookers it appeared as though the Japanese were disputing something in the documents. One observer compared the huddle to a group of referees and team captains arguing over a penalty during a football game. It turned out that the problem was one of style rather than substance. The Canadian representative had somehow placed his signature below the designated line on the Japanese copy. Those who followed him compounded the error by signing out of place. General Sutherland saved the day by crossing out the names of the four countries above the misplaced signatures and rewriting them in below, where they belonged. Satisfied, the Japanese made their way down the gangway. The full ceremony had lasted no more than twenty-five minutes.

As one ceremony ended, another, this one staged in Washington, D.C., was about to begin. The Allies' copies of the surrender documents, which included the instrument of surrender, an imperial rescript, and the Japanese delegation's credentials, were placed in the care of a special courier, Colonel Bernard Thielen, who had delivered them to the *Missouri*. Now Thielen was supposed to bring the documents back to the Pentagon so that the secretaries of the war and navy departments, the secretary of state, and the Joint Chiefs could present them to the president in a ceremony at the White House. As an irreverent staff officer put it, the delegation would "assemble in a body and proceed in column of ducks over to the White House and present the Great White father with them. . . ."

Somehow, General Marshall's deputy received information indicating that MacArthur had circumvented the whole process by sending the instruments of surrender directly to the White House in the custody of his own courier. MacArthur's apparent effort to upstage the Joint Chiefs set off alarm bells in the Pentagon. During the next several days army staff officers worked the telephones to try to determine the identity and location of the mysterious major said to be escorting the documents. Orders went out to airfields near Washington, D.C., to hold the courier, by armed guard if necessary. This prompted one officer to ask "Aren't War Department orders usually sufficient to get someone here?" Under normal circumstances perhaps, but the army's staff officers clearly appreciated that given MacArthur's talent for self-promotion, these were not normal circumstances. "If General MacArthur has sent one of his men here with that document with instructions to go and deliver it to Mr. Truman," observed one officer, " I have no doubt but what all of your measures and ours will fail."

Happily for all involved, especially Colonel Thielen, MacArthur had not sent his own courier. Thielen arrived at the Pentagon with the documents and without incident. "A tempest in a teapot," sighed one of Thielen's trackers. The ceremony took place at the White House on September 7. A smiling Truman was shown pointing to what he presumed to be Hirohito's signature on the imperial rescript. Photographers recorded the event for posterity. The documents, explained an adjoining article, were headed for the National Archives where they would join the German surrender papers.[17]

Mountbatten finally got to conduct his own surrender ceremony at Singapore on September 12, four days after Truman received the instruments of surrender at the White House. Traversing a two-mile route lined at four-yard intervals by marines and soldiers, Mountbatten's party arrived at the downtown municipal building at 10:30 a.m. There he was met by four Guards of Honor representing the gathered might of the British Empire. Mountbatten inspected these units and additional troops drawn up on the parade ground and then entered the municipal building amid "thunderous applause" from the large crowd of spectators.

Major General Brian Kimmins, who Mountbatten described as the "'producer'" of the "marvelous show" had highlighted the international composition of the forces defeating Japan. Guards from India, Australia, the United States, and China assumed conspicuous positions inside the building. In the main chamber, long rectangular tables faced each other. Seated at the Allied table were representatives of China, the Netherlands, France, and the United States, as well as Britain, India and Australia. Mountbatten would take his place at a raised dais in the center. Before the Japanese delegation arrived, the assembled dignitaries and spectators were instructed not to rise. Once the Japanese were seated everyone in the room rose and stood for a minute of silence. At the end of that observance, Mountbatten entered through the double doors to take his place at the dais feeling "like some actor taking a cue at the climax of a great opera."

Speaking to the radio audience as much as the Japanese in the room, Mountbatten made a statement in which he called attention to the one-hundred-thousand-man Allied force that had begun coming ashore on September 9. Mountbatten explained that "the surrender today is no negotiated surrender. The Japanese are submitting to superior force now massed here."[18] As Mountbatten read the instrument of surrender, the Chinese delegate took out a camera and, much to the horror of the Japanese, began taking their pictures at the moment of their most extreme humiliation. As with much else that occurred during the ceremony, Mountbatten's assertion of the irresistibility of British power and the Chinese delegate's gloating over the vanquished enemy were intended to impress upon the Japanese the unconditional nature of their defeat. In the weeks that followed, however, the British, Chinese, and their American allies would find that the Japanese still had important duties to perform throughout Asia.

NOTES

1. JCS to MacArthur and Nimitz, 26 July 1945, ABC 387 Japan (15 Feb 45) sec. 3, RG 165.

2. Robert James Maddox, *The United States and World War II* (Boulder, CO: Westview Press, 1992), 267.

3. Samuel Eliot Morison, *The History of United States Naval Operations in World War II*, Volume 14, *Victory in the Pacific, 1945* (Boston: Houghton Mifflin, 1960), 354; D. Clayton James, *The Years of MacArthur*, II (Boston: Houghton Mifflin, 1976), 771. MacArthur's several communications on the subject are summarized in Memorandum for the Chief of Staff, 1 August 1945, OPD 014.1 TS, cases 50/2, RG 165.

4. Gallicchio, *Cold War Begins in Asia* (New York: Columbia University Press, 1988), 63.

5. James Forrestal to Harry Truman, 8 August 1945, Box 1, Forrestal Diaries, James V. Forrestal Papers, Seeley Mudd Library, Princeton University, Princeton, New Jersey.

6. Edward J. Drea, *MacArthur's Ultra: Codebreaking and the War against Japan, 1942–1945* (Lawrence: University Press of Kansas, 1992), 222–223.

7. Richard B. Frank, *Downfall: The End of the Imperial Japanese Empire* (New York: Random House, 1999), 276.

8. Waldo Heinrichs to his parents, 8 August 1945, unpublished letters collected and edited by Waldo Heinrichs as "Marking Time: Letters from Luzon, 1945–1946," copies in the author's possession. Copies of Heinrichs's letters are also in the manuscript collections of the Military History Institute, Carlisle, Pennsylvania.

9. Marc Gallicchio, "After Nagasaki: General Marshall's Plan for Tactical Nuclear Weapons in Japan," *Prologue* 23 (Winter 1991), 396–404.

10. Henry Stimson to James Byrnes, 11 August 1945, enclosing SWNCC 21/5 in SWNCC 21, State-War-Navy Coordinating Committee Papers (microfilm) Diplomatic Branch, National Archives, College Park, Maryland.

11. David Glantz, *August Storm: The Soviet Strategic Offensive in Manchuria* (Fort Leavenworth, Kansas, Combat Studies Institute, U.S. Army Command and General Staff College, 1983).

12. Louis Allen, *The End of the War in Asia* (London: Hart-Davis, MacGibbon, 1976), 244–246.

13. Minutes of the Combined Chiefs of Staff, 24 July 1945, Records of the Joint Chiefs of Staff, Part 1: Meetings of the Joint Chiefs of Staff and Combined Chiefs of Staff, microfilm, reel 4, University Publications of America, Frederick, Maryland.

14. Ambassador Patrick Hurley to the Secretary of State, 13 August 1945, *FRUS: 1945, The Far East: China*, 7: 498–499.

15. Chiefs of Staff minutes, 30 August 1945, 210th meeting, War Cabinet: Chiefs of Staff Committee, Public Record Office, CAB 79/37, microfilm; Gallicchio, *Cold War Begins in Asia*, 91.

16. This description of the surrender proceedings is taken from Morison, *Victory in the Pacific*, 360–370; James, *MacArthur*, 784–792; and the *New York Times'* coverage of the ceremony.

17. The saga of the search for Colonel Thielen appears in a sheaf of telephone transcripts in Executive File 17, Top Secret Files, Records of the Operations and Plans Division, Record Group 165, Records of the Army General and Special Staffs, National Archives, College Park, Maryland; "Truman Receives Surrender Papers," *New York Times*, 8 September 1945, 3.

18. The description of the Singapore ceremony and the related quotations are in Philip Ziegler, ed., *Personal Diary of Admiral the Lord Louis Mountbatten, Supreme Allied Commander, South-East Asia, 1943–1946* (London: Collins, 1988), 245–250. See also "Surrender Signed In Singapore," *The Times* (London), 13 September 1945, 4.

3

The High Water Mark

On the eve of Japan's surrender, Colonel J. Hart Caughey, one of General Wedemeyer's staff officers, stole a few moments from his hectic schedule to write his wife about what she could expect to see in the weeks to come. After eight years of war, he explained, everyone in China wanted to celebrate the coming of peace. Regrettably, everyone also knew that the elation would be short-lived. Bigger problems awaited them. "The communist business will flare up and wreak havoc—the question of control of Manchuria is between China and Russia [and] will give them concern, French Indo China is a problem and not the least of the worries is getting rid of the 2,000,000 Jap[anese] still in Asia. Our work has just begun," he wrote. "But even so it's a different kind of work—all mixed up in intrigue and political influence that will tend to make life most interesting." Caughey advised his wife to pay attention to General Wedemeyer's activities and American policy in the postwar period "because from a historical, if not immediate, point of view the period is critical and, as I said before, it will be interesting."[1]

Caughey's commanding officer saw the problems facing the United States in broader and more dire terms. "I view Asia as an enormous pot," wrote Wedemeyer, "seething and boiling the fumes of which may readily snuff out the advancement gained by the Allies in the last few years."[2] To keep the lid on, American forces were being sent to the Korean peninsula, north China, and the Japanese home islands. In the immediate aftermath of Japan's surrender,

American power reached its high water mark in Asia. More than 40,000 combat-ready marines landed in north China in September. During the second week of that month, two divisions went ashore on the Korean peninsula. MacArthur designated eighteen divisions for occupation duty in Japan and expected to need 500,000 soldiers for the first year. The remainder of MacArthur's planned invasion force lingered in the Philippines. All of these commands continued to rely on a vast network of naval installations, air bases, and supply depots stretching across the Pacific.

In the aggregate, this sudden assemblage of force represented a dramatic transformation in America's historic relationship with East Asia. But appearances deceived. Combat losses and implementation of the eighty-five-point threshold for discharging veterans had weakened some of the more seasoned divisions. Many of the units that took up occupation duties in Asia were refilling with raw recruits and inexperienced soldiers from Europe or the States. After V-J Day, the increased pressure to bring the boys home exacerbated an already difficult situation.

American troop strength became a wasting asset from the very moment that the United States assumed its enlarged responsibilities in Asia. The American public demanded quick solutions to complex political problems that seemed to lack solutions of any kind. In this tense atmosphere, differences of opinion within the American government occasionally escalated into public disputes further undermining attempts to forge coherent workable policies for the use of force to win the peace.

THE MEN ON THE SPOT

As American policy adapted to the new demands of peacemaking, American military commanders in Asia assumed new responsibilities as proconsuls and diplomats. Having come as conquerors and liberators, the American armed forces faced new challenges as occupiers and restorers of civil authority in Japan and its former empire.

The most prominent, visible and, not surprisingly, controversial, of America's military statesmen was General Douglas MacArthur. As Supreme Commander for the Allied Powers in Japan (SCAP) MacArthur wielded nearly unchallenged civil and military authority over the occupation. MacArthur welcomed his new responsibilities and jealously guarded what he viewed as his prerogatives from meddlers, foreign or American.

His father's experiences instilled in young Douglas a suspicion of politicians and a wariness of civil authority. A Civil War veteran and Congressional Medal of Honor winner, Arthur MacArthur commanded Americans sent to suppress Philippine resistance to the American occupation after the Spanish-American War of 1898. MacArthur had been called home after he lost a nasty political struggle with the colonial governor, William Howard Taft. Years later, Arthur MacArthur's bid to become Army Chief of Staff, the pinnacle of his profession, was blocked by the same Taft, who was now president. MacArthur ended his career in frustration and bitterness.

In the meantime, Douglas was launching his own career after having graduated first in his class at West Point. Douglas MacArthur's military genius, battlefield heroics in World War I, and carefully cultivated political and professional connections propelled him to a position of national prominence by the 1930s. In the midst of the Depression, as chief of staff during the administration of Herbert Hoover, MacArthur's fortunes tumbled suddenly when he was accused of using excessive military force to disperse down and out World War I veterans and their families who gathered in Washington to plead for early payment of their war bonuses.

MacArthur served his last two years as chief of staff under President Franklin D. Roosevelt. MacArthur loathed the new president and hotly protested when New Deal economies cut into the army's budget. MacArthur's sparring with Roosevelt endeared him to Republicans. For his part, Roosevelt privately regarded MacArthur as one of the two most dangerous men in Depression-wracked America. (The other was Louisiana Senator Huey Long.) When MacArthur's term ended in 1935, Roosevelt allowed the general to take a position as military advisor to the Philippine Commonwealth government in Manila.

MacArthur lived regally in the Philippines, which were a second home to him. When Japan began its southward march into Indochina Roosevelt called the recently retired MacArthur back into American service and charged him with building up the Philippines' military defenses. Defense of the Philippines was an impossible task, beyond even MacArthur's powers. Less excusable was an outcome in which his forces were caught unprepared by a Japanese surprise attack on the islands. Nevertheless, MacArthur was never made to face an inquiry as were the commanders at Pearl Harbor. MacArthur's reputation and political connections also led Roosevelt to order the general to leave the islands before they were completely overrun.

Vowing to return, MacArthur took command of American forces in the southwest Pacific and began the slow march back to the Philippines. As American forces battled for control of New Guinea and the Philippines, MacArthur fended off the navy and the White House. The General's eleventh-hour truculence over maintaining control of the invasion of Japan was only the latest in a long line of quarrels he waged with service chiefs and civilian authorities. The general was convinced that his adversaries in Washington were scheming to undermine his successes. Nevertheless, MacArthur had prevailed, almost by force of will. Now he stood ready to crown his military accomplishments by ushering in a new era of peace in Asia.

It was as if MacArthur's entire career had prepared him for the role of a benign overlord and lawgiver. The same could not be said for the other officers who had to deal with the complex politico-military problems arising out of the surrender of Japan. Across the Tsushima and Korea Straits on the Korean peninsula, MacArthur's subordinate, Lieutenant General John R. Hodge waded into a political storm for which he was professionally unprepared and personally ill suited. An Illinois native, Hodge saw combat in World War I, attended the army's staff schools in the interwar period and served on the general staff for five years before the outbreak of war. During the war he served mainly in field commands. Wounded on Bougainville, he led the Americal Division in the Solomons and took command of the XXIV Corps for the campaigns on Leyte and Okinawa.

Hodge was tapped to command the occupation forces in South Korea when Jiang Jieshi vetoed the appointment of his old nemesis, General Joseph Stilwell, for the job. The sudden rejection of Stilwell invites speculation as to how the ensuing occupation might have differed if "Vinegar Joe," an old China Hand, had been in command. Neither Stilwell nor Hodge could claim much skill as diplomats. But Stilwell possessed a deeper knowledge of Asian affairs and an instinctive sympathy for the region's oppressed peasantry. Stilwell's long-standing friendship with George Marshall also might have ensured that the army's problems in Korea received a fair hearing in Washington.[3]

Such speculation aside, it is generally agreed that Hodge was a poor candidate for the job of military proconsul in Korea. Sporting close-cropped hair, soft cap, and "Doug Junior" sunglasses, Hodge was by inclination a soldier's soldier.[4] The "Patton of the Pacific," he was a front line commander who endured the same hardships as his men. Instinctively conservative, Hodge took

his main job to be the imposition of law and order amid the social upheaval created by Japan's collapse. He would spend much of his time fretting about the Soviet threat just over the border which, compared to his daily aggravations in the South, at least had the virtue of being more recognizable and comprehended.

Moving across the Yellow Sea to north China, the Americans encountered many of the same problems that plagued Korea, only on a grander scale. The Japanese surrender created a potential power vacuum across the northern and coastal regions of the country. The Russians were already pouring into the three northeastern provinces of Manchuria but the north, below the Great Wall, was up for grabs. After fifteen years of Japanese occupation, both the Chinese Communists and the Nationalists (Guomindang), hungrily eyed these areas for the advantages they would provide in the looming civil war that most observers expected now that Japan was defeated. According to General Order Number One, Japanese troops below the Great Wall were supposed to surrender only to Jiang's Guomindang (GMD) troops. The Communists ignored that provision and ordered their troops forward to disarm the Japanese. Instead of ushering in an era of peace it seemed that Japan's defeat would become only a momentary respite from conflict, a transition from one catastrophe to another.

This was the situation that awaited the United States Marines as they prepared to go ashore in north China. Once they disembarked, the men of the III Amphibious Corps would come under the command of Lieutenant General Albert C. Wedemeyer, the Commanding General of United States Forces, China Theater. A native of Omaha, Nebraska, the forty-eight-year-old Wedemeyer served a brief tour with the 15th Infantry in China in the early 1930s and subsequently distinguished himself at the army's Command and General Staff School. A two-year stint at the German War College followed. Accustomed to American thinking about military strategy in narrow terms, he found the broader views propounded by the Germans to be more exacting and intellectually exciting. Wedemeyer's German and Irish upbringing, and his Jesuit education at a Catholic school in Omaha, also inclined him toward ready acceptance of his German hosts' hostility to the British Empire, strenuous anti-communism, and anti-Semitism.

The gregarious Wedemeyer befriended Charles Lindbergh when the aviator visited Germany and later sympathized with Lindbergh's isolationist pronouncements on the eve of World War II. Given Wedemeyer's ideological cal views and prejudices, it is not surprising that he would gravitate toward the isolationist wing of the Republican Party. That he did so and still managed to rise to prominence under the scrupulously apolitical George Marshall was a testament to Wedemeyer's abilities as a staff officer.

In 1941, while assigned in the War Plans Division, Major Wedemeyer served as the principal author of the Victory Program, the basic war plan that guided American strategic thinking and military production for most of the war. During the next two years he usually accompanied General Marshall to wartime conferences with America's allies and emerged as a vigorous proponent of opening a second front in France. In 1943, Marshall sent Wedemeyer to serve as second in command to Lord Louis Mountbatten in the newly

FIGURE 3.1
Major General Albert C. Wedemeyer, Ambassador Patrick Hurley, and Generalissimo Jiang Jieshi.
U.S. Army Photograph, Hoover Institution

formed Southeast Asian Command. Although he had clashed frequently with his British counterparts over the second front, Wedemeyer got on well with Mountbatten. In 1944, Marshall chose Wedemeyer to replace Stilwell as Jiang's chief of staff.

The meticulous Wedemeyer—Stilwell called him a "pompous prick"—was appalled by what he regarded as Stilwell's amateur staff work. In late 1944 it seemed as though Japanese forces were bent on the complete destruction of Jiang's regime. Tokyo halted its offensive, however, and began to prepare for Allied landings along the coast. Wedemeyer used that reprieve to continue the training of Nationalist troops begun by Stilwell and improve the cooperation between American advisers and Chinese officers. Having stared into the abyss, Jiang became somewhat more cooperative. It also helped matters that the Americans asked so little of Jiang that it was easy for him to comply.

By the summer of 1945, the newly confident American trained Chinese troops were moving on the offensive. Wedemeyer planned for a gradual extension of GMD control over Japanese held areas. Liberation of coastal areas promised to shorten supply lines and further strengthen Jiang's forces. Japan's abrupt surrender upset those plans and forced Wedemeyer to hastily improvise plans for replacing the Japanese, fending off the Communists, and generally preventing the spread of chaos throughout China. Sizing up the situation, Wedemeyer informed Washington that the Chinese had "no plan for rehabilitation, prevention of epidemics, restoration of utilities, establishment of a balanced economy, and redistribution of millions of refugees." Not surprisingly, Wedemeyer expected widespread "confusion and disorder," in the weeks ahead.

The residual problems of taking Japan's surrender and the resulting establishment of American military proconsuls in the region gave military professionals a central role in the development of American policy. The seething revolutionary conditions throughout Asia drew American military officers even more closely into the realm of policy making. In addition to these external circumstances, domestic bureaucratic factors also predisposed military officers toward a more active role in policy making. One problem was an exasperating level of administrative disarray within the State Department that seemed almost to beg for strong direction from outside. A second and related problem, from the military point of view, was the adoption of seemingly wrongheaded ideas by State Department members charged with implementing

American policy in East Asia. A collision was in the offing. After four years of planning for global warfare, military officers would not be content to acquiesce in decisions emanating from diplomats whose acumen they disparaged and loyalty they sometimes doubted.

THE STATE DEPARTMENT IN TRANSITION

Historians generally agree that American coordination of political policy and military strategy was inadequate to the point of being almost nonexistent before World War II. In particular, the JCS and their staffs had complained bitterly about the Roosevelt administration's assertive diplomacy in Asia during 1941. Many viewed the war with Japan as "Mr. Hull's war" or "Mrs." Hull as the navy preferred it. Military planners believed that coordination of policy and military strategy improved during the war but it would be more accurate to say that the military planning staffs achieved such coordination by effectively dominating the making of both policy and strategy. According to Brigadier General George A. Lincoln, the army's top planner, the armed forces had "carried" the State Department through the war.[5]

The pressure packed days bracketing Japan's surrender had necessitated intensive interaction between the State Department's Far Eastern specialists and the army's and navy's staff officers. The Joint Chiefs needed political guidance on a host of problems. Answers were slow in coming and often seemed couched in flabby generalities that offended the action oriented army and navy staffers. Important statements on pressing matters remained delayed or incomplete. As late as August 9, 1945, the Army General Staff was waiting for State Department guidance on twenty-five key policy questions pertaining to Japan's surrender. Among those were such matters as the nature of American policy toward the Chinese Communists and the goals of American policy in Korea.[6]

On matters where the State Department did provide guidance, the JCS were critical as well. According to the Joint Chiefs, the diplomats placed far too much importance on the United Nations as a guarantor of security in the postwar world. Similarly, the JCS hotly opposed the State Department's insistence that Japan's former League of Nations mandates be converted into U.N. trusteeships. Having fought for every inch of those Pacific islands, the Chiefs were loath to surrender control to an international body. Modification of unconditional surrender had been another point of contention between the military and the State Department.[7]

Much of the military officers' criticism of the State Department was merited. State's papers and staff work did not have the crisp concision of the army's. But State also labored under difficult circumstances. Hull's replacement, Edward Stettinius, served for only a year. He was replaced by James Byrnes, a former senator, Supreme Court justice, and head of war mobilization. Byrnes was a talented political deal-maker, but he was largely unconcerned with the administration of his department. His frequent trips abroad—he would spend nearly half his tenure overseas attending various postwar conferences—prompted one journalist to quip that "the State Department fiddles while Byrnes roams."

Byrnes's second in command as undersecretary was Dean Acheson who was newly promoted from his wartime position of assistant secretary for congressional affairs. Byrnes did not pick Acheson and had actually accepted his resignation as assistant secretary before changing his mind. It is probably more accurate to say that Byrnes's mind was changed for him. Acheson owed his appointment to Senator Fred Vinson on whom he made a favorable impression while acting as the State Department's liaison to congress. Vinson recommended Acheson to his former senate colleague Harry Truman. The president in turn appears to have urged Byrnes to keep Acheson.

It would be difficult to find two more different personalities than Acheson and Byrnes. "Jimmy" Byrnes was a self-made politician, a one-time court stenographer, and self-educated country lawyer who had risen to prominence by means of electoral politics in the one-party south. The son of an Episcopalian clergyman, Acheson entered government service by way of a partnership in a distinguished Washington law firm after having followed the path of many establishment figures by attending a New England preparatory school (Groton) and an Ivy League university (Yale).

The decision to make Acheson undersecretary had important ramifications for the department's East Asian policy. Although Acheson devoted most of his attention to European affairs and the daily operations of the department, he was committed to a thorough reform program for Japan. That view put him at odds with the Japan specialists in the department. Generally speaking, the Japan hands were unenthusiastic about undertaking a major reconstruction of Japanese society. They recognized the need to eradicate militarism and strengthen democratic institutions, but they scoffed at the idea of turning hordes of inexperienced New Dealers loose on Japan. During the summer of

1945 the Japan specialists, led by former ambassador Joseph Grew, had argued for offering the Japanese a chance to keep the emperor. Acheson had vigorously opposed Grew and the other "emperor worshippers" in the department who favored modifying unconditional surrender. When he became undersecretary, Acheson passed over the Japan specialists and selected liberal China specialist John Carter Vincent to head the Office of Far Eastern Affairs (FE). The older Japan hands saw the handwriting on the wall and resigned from service rather than endure the inevitable loss of influence that would follow from Vincent's appointment.

The new head of FE was a soft-spoken southerner and highly rated foreign service officer. As a young man he was attracted to Woodrow Wilson's internationalism and what he described as the "economic democracy" of FDR's New Deal. That liberalism was evident in his approach to American East Asian policy. Like Acheson, Vincent favored an extensive reform program for Japan. Unlike the more conservative Japan specialists, Vincent was also sympathetic to the nationalist aspirations of colonial peoples in the region. A proponent of gradual change, he was hardly a revolutionary. Nevertheless, his worldview differed significantly from the retreating Japan specialists. His views also put him at odds with men responsible for forming and implementing military policy in the region. This was nowhere more evident than in China.

China was Vincent's area of expertise. During his several tours in China Vincent came to view Jiang as the antithesis of the leaders he admired. Vincent thought it was in America's interest to have a democratic China emerge from the war, but he doubted that would happen with Jiang at the helm. Vincent warned that Jiang was impervious to constructive criticism and too beholden to corrupt interests in China to willingly change policies. The only way to get Jiang to reform would be to pressure him into doing so. Even then, it might be too late to keep the Communists out of power. Despite the sudden surge of American forces onto the mainland of Asia at the end of the war, Vincent believed that the United States would not have the ability to shape events to its liking. Vincent's wariness about challenging Soviet power on the mainland, his support for extensive reforms in Japan, extending even to the possible trial of Hirohito as a war criminal, and his strong criticism of Jiang, put him at odds with most military officers concerned with East Asia. During the first several months following Japan's surrender, as success eluded the Americans in China and Korea, some of his opponents in the Pentagon would begin to wonder if Vincent was actually trying to undermine American policy in the region

THE PHILIPPINES: LIBERATION AND RESTORATION

American officials' earliest encounter with the difficulties attendant in making the transition from war to peace came in the Philippines, MacArthur's home for much of the 1930s. The United States' return to the commonwealth began on October 20, 1944 when MacArthur's men came ashore on the island of Leyte. Amidst them, MacArthur and Philippine president in exile, Sergio Osmeña, slogged through the surf accompanied by the obligatory corps of photographers. MacArthur followed his triumphal return with a radio address broadcast to pro-American guerillas in the islands. "People of the Philippines," he declared, "I have returned! . . . Rally to me!" MacArthur's summons to battle implied that all Filipinos were united in their opposition to Japan, but the situation was more complicated than that. Many members of the elite, including officials in the commonwealth government and armed forces, had collaborated with the Japanese. These defections owed more to the elite's well-honed sense of self-preservation than to the allure of Japanese propaganda. Indeed, as the tide turned in the Pacific and the Americans return drew near, many of the collaborators initiated contacts with the anti-Japanese guerillas as a way of hedging their bets.

Divisions among the guerillas further complicated matters. Many guerilla units were comprised of members of the Philippine Constabulary. MacArthur's command assisted the guerilla forces and Americans sometimes led them. These forces were loosely organized under the United States Army Forces Far East (USAFFE). In the prewar era the Constabulary had been employed by the landowning and business interests to suppress peasant opposition to elite rule. They continued that practice during the war by occasionally attacking the independently organized peasant forces serving with the Hukbalahap (Huk) movement. The Huks, an indigenous Communist-led movement of revolutionaries and reformers located in the central provinces of the main island of Luzon, pursued their own agenda by attacking collaborationist landlords. Negotiations to bring the Huks under the overall direction of the American-led USAFFE guerilla units failed. Deprived of U.S. support, the Huks nevertheless acquired enough weapons to build a 15,000-man force during the war.[8]

Following the American landings on Luzon in January 1945, American forces and the USAFFE guerrillas began disarming the Huks when the opportunity arose. In one instance, a Huk group that helped American forces round up the Japanese on Bataan was summarily disarmed, its leader taken into custody. By the summer, USAFFE guerrilla forces were wreaking havoc on anyone suspected of having connections to the Huks. In short, despite his calls to Filipinos to rally to him, MacArthur did not plan on making room for the Huks in any postwar government.

The Americans were, however, much more willing to accommodate collaborators among the elite, including Manuel Roxas, MacArthur's close friend and business associate from the prewar days. In fact, the nimble Roxas received a special dispensation from MacArthur, which allowed him to resume his place at MacArthur's headquarters as if the previous three years of cooperation with the Japanese had never happened. Roxas, who soon began campaigning for the presidency against Osmeña, made it abundantly clear that his administration would not be overly concerned with prosecuting collaborators. Similarly, few if any of the officers in the commonwealth army were punished for collaborating with the Japanese, although one American report estimated that as many as 80 percent of the officers had done so.

By the time Japan surrendered, more than 100,000 Japanese soldiers and civilians remained at large throughout the islands. MacArthur's own forces had become worn down and widely dispersed in trying to subdue the remnants of General Yamashita Tomoyuki's forces. Yamashita had 50,000 men under his command on northern Luzon at the time of Japan's surrender.[9] The situation had become so troubling by July, that army planners began worrying that MacArthur would not be able to regroup and prepare his men in time for the invasion of Japan's home islands. The sudden end of the war relieved those anxieties, but other problems would soon develop. Principal among them would be the task of coping with thousands of American soldiers in the Philippines who were no longer needed for the invasion or occupation of Japan.

In the meantime, the United States was well on its way to reinstating most of the prewar elite in its accustomed position of power in the Philippines. Soon, the United States would begin equipping and training new military units to take the place of the discredited Philippine Constabulary. As the Filipinos prepared for independence, scheduled for July 1946, negotiations for

American base rights on the islands were also getting under way. Those who hoped for substantive reforms or for peasant representation in the new government were dismayed to see that the men who governed the islands before the war had resumed their familiar places of leadership in the islands.

IN THE HOME OF THE ENEMY

It was an irony of the immediate postwar period in Asia that Japan, the realm of the former enemy, was the least volatile area in the region. In part, this was because Japan's crushing total defeat inclined Japanese officials to end all overt resistance to the United States. But the relative calm the Americans experienced in Japan also owed something to MacArthur's astute leadership. Decked out in his trademark corncob pipe, sunglasses, and field marshal's cap, MacArthur was a master of performance. Subordinates often joked about MacArthur's penchant for stage-managed displays; Dwight Eisenhower once remarked that he studied drama under MacArthur in the Philippines. But in Japan MacArthur's theatrical talent was an asset.

MacArthur's tenure as SCAP began with typical flourish. As he winged his way toward Tokyo, the general casually told his staff how he planned to democratize Japan. He would begin by destroying Japan's ability to make war, and then he would enfranchise women, strengthen labor unions and agricultural organizations, destroy monopolies, establish a free press, end police repression, liberalize education, and decentralize political power.[10] Not surprisingly, the general's grasp of the task ahead impressed his admiring staff. During his soliloquy, however, MacArthur neglected to mention that the agenda he recited had been sent to him from Washington as the United States Initial Post-Surrender Policy.

The second act of MacArthur's drama commenced with the arrival of his plane at Atsugi airfield outside Yokohama. After the plane touched down the general appeared at the open door sporting his gold braided soft cap and corncob pipe. After pausing to gaze out on the crowd he descended the steps and greeted Eighth Army Commander Lieutenant General Robert Eichelberger with a nonchalant "How are you Bob?" The two men then climbed into a waiting car and began the slow drive to Yokohama past thousands of Japanese soldiers lining the roads. Winston Churchill later called MacArthur's arrival the "single bravest act of the war." The members of the advance team that prepared for the general's arrival might have questioned that assessment.

FIGURE 3.2
General Douglas MacArthur with his guest, Emperor Hirohito, at MacArthur's residence.
U.S. Army Signal Corps, Library of Congress

There is no doubting MacArthur's bravery but as one of the approximately 200 journalists present noted, the affair took place in the atmosphere of a "lawn party." Eichleberger also thought there were a lot of sightseers present. Nevertheless, MacArthur's self-confidence and composure had made its first favorable impression upon the Japanese.

As we have seen, the formal surrender ceremony aboard the *Missouri* was the main event in the unfolding drama of the conquerors' arrival in Japan. In terms of actual impact on the Japanese, however, the surrender ceremony may have run a distant second to MacArthur's meeting with the emperor in late September. To begin with, the emperor broke with tradition by going to meet MacArthur at his residence in the American embassy, rather than the other way around. MacArthur surprised the Japanese by arranging for a military photographer to be present. During the course of their meeting the two men posed side by side for a picture. The photograph showed MacArthur, hands on hips, tie-less in his pressed suntanned khakis. The emperor, a full head shorter, hands dangling at his side, appeared in formal attire, including a wing collar and striped tie. The photograph's message could not be any clearer: MacArthur was in charge. Shocked Japanese officials reached the same conclusion and tried to suppress the photograph. The Americans dismissed their objections and the photo appeared in the Tokyo newspapers on September 29. Seeing the emperor standing beside MacArthur as if he were some junior clerk convinced all Japanese who saw it of the finality of their defeat.[11] Policy makers in Washington had yet to decide on the emperor's fate. By this time, however, MacArthur was already finding that he would need the emperor in order to successfully conduct the occupation. In what would become common practice, MacArthur chose not to inform Washington of his meeting with Hirohito. That established a pattern. Using the Initial Post-Surrender Policy for guidance, MacArthur would be free to steer his own course in Japan for the next two years. It was not unusual for the JCS to give their commanders in the field wide latitude to complete their mission. But apart from a brief skirmish to be described later, the State Department also refrained from trying to direct the Supreme Commander. That was true also of Truman. In October, the president invited MacArthur to return to the United States to receive a well-deserved hero's welcome. Citing the "extraordinarily dangerous" conditions in Japan, MacArthur declined. It is not clear what conditions MacArthur was referring to since on September 17 he had announced that things were going so well that the United States would be able to reduce the occupation force to 200,000 men within six months. Truman might have recalled MacArthur for an explanation or he might have at least requested clarification of the situation. Given the president's many other concerns at the moment, and MacArthur's strong ties to the Republican Party, he did neither.

As MacArthur established his authority over the occupation, American forces proceeded with the main military mission of disarming and demobilizing Japan's war machine. This was a logistical challenge of monumental proportions. At the time of the surrender there were nearly seven million Japanese in uniform. About half of these as well as approximately three million civilians were overseas awaiting repatriation. The early occupation forces consisted of Eichelberger's Eighth Army, its headquarters in Yokohama, General Walter Krueger's Sixth Army, based in Kyoto but with troops also on

Kyushu, and the 4th Marine Regiment and Task Force 31 of the United States Navy's Third Fleet at Yokosuka Naval base. At their peak, the Americans numbered about 450,000 troops, but that number was reduced to about 200,000 with the departure of the Sixth Army in early 1946. The British Commonwealth provided an additional 40,000 troops, deployed on Western Honshu with its headquarters at Kure, but that number was also steadily reduced over the next two years.

In the last months of the war, the Americans had rejected allowing the Japanese to disarm themselves as a condition of a negotiated surrender. Once the war was over, however, they tacitly recognized that the only way to complete the job in a timely manner was to rely on the Japanese. American officers gave the orders, but the burden of locating and disposing of ammunition,

FIGURE 3.3
"Destruction Incorporated" crews dispose of more than 200 Japanese planes after the surrender.
Cpl. H. J. Grimm, USMC, National Archives, 127-N-139991

explosives, as well as other war material was placed on the Japanese military. Individual Japanese soldiers turned over their weapons to their officers. They, in turn, handed them over to the Allies. American "Destruction Incorporated" crews disposed of military aircraft, at first by burning them, but later by scrapping the planes and salvaging the parts for nonmilitary use. The Allied forces collected more than two and a half million rifles and carbines, and destroyed close to 13,000 planes and 3,000 tanks.

In the meantime, the navy made quick work of Japan's "fanatical arsenal" of midget submarines, human torpedoes, and suicide surface craft, numbering more than 2,500 vessels in all. Two hundred sixty-nine Japanese ships were pressed into mine sweeping service and one hundred thirty-eight repatriated Japanese from overseas. The Allies also divided Japan's remaining naval vessels, destroyer class and smaller, among themselves.

For the most part the destruction of Japan's arsenal went smoothly. Disposing of ordnance, always hazardous work, was made more so by the demobilization of trained experts in the Japanese and American armies. Spot inspections revealed an attitude of general compliance among the Japanese, but the almost monthly discovery of caches of weapons and explosives, some stored in school yards, indicated, as the occupation's official report delicately phrased it, that "the command structure had broken down," in some places. More serious was the Japanese government's emptying of its military warehouses and handing over of war materials to favored contractors immediately before the Americans arrived. This wholesale looting and disposal of government property contributed greatly to the rampant inflation that added to the misery of most Japanese in the early postwar years.

The demobilization of Japanese troops also became a lingering problem in the immediate postwar period. Japanese troops on the home islands were easily disarmed and sent home. But many of the roughly 3.5 million Japanese troops overseas remained there long after the surrender. In part this was a matter of logistics. As noted, there were approximately 6.5 million Japanese civilians and soldiers outside Japan when the war ended. Returning them to Japan was a huge task. But the repatriation of soldiers was deliberately impeded by the Allies, who found the Imperial Army troops to be a valuable source of manpower.

The fate of Japanese troops in Manchuria was a particularly notorious case. When the Red Army swept into the northeastern provinces of China during AUGUST STORM they bagged an estimated 1.6 million men. Most of these were put to work in Soviets camps in atrocious conditions. Hundreds of thousands were indoctrinated and sent back in a feckless attempt to subvert the Japanese government. Most of the returnees had little difficulty discarding their newly acquired ideology once they were home. By the time the Soviets announced the completion of their repatriation efforts in 1949 there were, according to the Americans and Japanese, more than 300,000 men missing and unaccounted for.

For more than a year after the surrender, the Americans held nearly 70,000 Japanese troops to use as laborers on bases in the Philippines and the Pacific. The British withheld more than 100,000 to assist in reconstruction in Southeast Asia. These construction crews were better fed and attended to than their unfortunate comrades in Manchuria. More controversial was the Allies' use of armed Japanese troops for military purposes.

In the chaotic aftermath of Japan's surrender the mostly undefeated Imperial troops held sway over vast areas of Asia. These troops became an indispensable auxiliary force for holding valuable territory until distant Allied troops could rush to the scene. In this way the military task of taking the surrender of Japanese troops became bound up with the unfolding political turmoil throughout Asia. This practice caused the most immediate controversy in Korea below the thirty-eighth parallel.

KOREA: LIBERATION OR OCCUPATION?

Hodge's XXIV Corps arrived in Korea on September 8 with only the barest instructions from Washington. As the army's official history notes, "If Washington or GHQ had given much constructive thought to Korean problems, it had not been reflected in orders issued to the Corps Commander."[12] Nominally under the authority of MacArthur, Hodge would soon discover that he was very much on his own. As Hodge prepared to embark for Korea he received word from MacArthur warning him that Russian troops might already have crossed the thirty-eighth parallel and entered Seoul. If such were the case, Hodge was to take control of the capital, establish friendly contact with the Soviet commander, and avoid creating any incidents. While en route to Korea, Hodge received several messages from the Japanese commander warning that Korean Communists planned to exploit the situation to cause unrest in the countryside. Primed to expect trouble, Hodge instructed the Japanese to maintain order until the Americans ar-

FIGURE 3.4
Vice Admiral Daniel Barbey and Lt. General John Hodge, with pipe, watch the landings
at Inchon, Korea. September 1945.
Naval Historical Center, 80-G-394169

rived. Hodge's preoccupation with maintaining order set the tone for the
first few days of the occupation.

On the morning of September 8 American troop ships carrying the first
wave of soldiers headed for Korea snaked along the narrow channel leading to
Inchon. Koreans who came down to the docks to greet the liberators were dispersed by Japanese police who fired into the crowd killing two. More shocks
awaited the newly liberated Koreans.

On September 9, the Americans took the surrender of the Japanese authorities in the government palace. The Americans took the victors' seats.
More than twenty officers in khaki sat with their backs to the large open win-
dows. In front of them was a long rectangular table draped in purple velvet.
On the opposite side of the table the small Japanese delegation sweated under
the hot lights brought in by photographers. As he signed over control of

FIGURE 3.5
The Japanese surrender Keijo (Seoul) Korea, September 9, 1945.
Naval Historical Center, 80-G-347701

Japan's wealthiest colony, Governor General Abe Nobuyuki put his handkerchief to his mouth and became briefly but violently ill. The ceremony completed, Abe staggered out of the room and vomited again on the marble floor.

Out in the streets the celebrations began, but they were curtailed by an 8:00 p.m. curfew imposed by the Americans. The next day, Koreans paraded through the capital to thank the Americans. By that time, the announcement that the Americans planned temporarily to govern through the existing colonial machinery made some wonder if there would be anything to celebrate. Governor General Abe was back at his desk and Japanese government news agencies continued to broadcast in Seoul. To the consternation of many Koreans, Japanese police wearing arm bands marked USMG (United States Military Government) patrolled the streets pulling down Korean flags and otherwise maintaining order. On September 11 after the surrender ceremony,

Koreans were marching again, this time to protest the continuation of Japanese in government positions.

Hodge came in for immediate criticism when news reached Washington that the Japanese remained on the job in their former colony. An anonymous State Department source expressed amazement at Hodge's decision to rely on the colonial machinery. Newspaper editorials seconded that opinion. The *New York Times* complained that in Korea "a common Japanese soldier would never know he has been defeated."[13] Hodge was already aware that his initial orders did not fit the conditions he found in Korea. He asked for and received permission to replace Abe with an American head of military government, Major General Archibald Arch. Hodge also removed the Japanese police and put American military police on their beats. That quieted things for a while, but it did little to resolve the larger problem of Korea's future.

In responding to the complaints about Hodge's use of the Japanese, American officials explained that they expected Korea to be placed under a four-power trusteeship that would include China and Britain. That idea was already a dead letter, however. The Chinese government had its hands full in reestablishing control over areas formerly held by the Japanese. As we have seen, the British were not told about the trusteeship proposal until after Japan announced its surrender. They had no plans to send troops to the peninsula and little interest in what happened there. For the time being this left the Americans and Russians staring at each other across the thirty-eighth parallel. As originally conceived, the trusteeship was intended to avoid just such a situation. Four-power supervision of Korea was supposed to prevent great power competition for control of the peninsula. The Americans' failure to reach agreement on the trusteeship before Japan suddenly surrendered had led to the temporary partitioning of the country.

Of course, any trusteeship would have been hotly opposed by the Koreans. By its very nature, a trusteeship was a paternalistic and humiliating half-step toward independence. But now the Americans faced the doubly difficult challenge of gaining Soviet support for a system of international supervision that no Koreans wanted. It did not take Hodge long to conclude that such a plan was futile. As the man on the spot, Hodge was in a better position to influence events than policy makers in the State Department. Within months of his arrival he began to support the creation of a Korean government in the South even while Washington continued to promote the trusteeship plan.

When Hodge arrived in Korea he found that a revolutionary group calling itself the Korean Peoples Republic (KPR) had established its main branch in Seoul and local committees throughout the countryside. Hodge suspected that the left-wing organization was a stalking horse for Moscow-directed Communists. According to the Japanese, Soviet agents had been active throughout the South right up to the time of Russia's declaration of war on Japan. Citing his instructions not to recognize any Korean government until the trusteeship had been created Hodge brushed aside a delegation from the KPR and turned to the Japanese for assistance. When that failed, Hodge instinctively turned for help to the newly formed Korean Democratic Party (KDP), which was led by landlords and industrialists, many of whom had collaborated with the Japanese. These members of the colonial elite quickly offered their services to the understaffed military government as a way of protecting themselves against a radical redistribution of property in the postcolonial era. In early October, the military government created a Korean Advisory Council composed mainly of KDP members.

Hodge also created a Korean national police force, comprised mostly of officers who had served under the Japanese. Rather than reorganize the police along local lines, Hodge opted for the expedient measure of working with the existing colonial apparatus. In part, his actions were dictated by manpower needs of the occupation force. Hodge understood that he could not count on receiving any more men. Pressure was growing at home to bring the boys back as quickly as possible. By reestablishing a police force Hodge hoped he could have trained Koreans relieving the Americans of police duty by January 1946.

Ideally, the new police force would attract officers untainted by collaboration with the colonial regime. In reality, the Korean National Police relied heavily on officers from the colonial era, most of whom would have reason to fear reprisals if the Left ever came to power. As a consequence of his suspicion of the KPR and his preoccupation with order, Hodge had provided the Right with the muscle it needed to keep its hold on power.

Although he was later unapologetic about his actions, at the time, Hodge seemed to recognize the unsavory reputations of the people on whom he relied. By way of defense, he complained that everyone was accusing everyone else of being collaborators. How was he to know who was telling the truth? At the same time, with the encouragement of the KDP, he began to lobby Washington and MacArthur for permission to bring back to Korea the leaders of the Korean Provisional Government (KPG), an exile group that had spent the war in Chungking. The Korean Right hoped that the returning exiles would provide it with a veneer of respectable patriotism while allowing it to consolidate its hold on the administration of the South. Hodge and the Right also favored the return of Dr. Syngman Rhee, an elderly exile living in the United States.

Shortly after arriving on the peninsula, Hodge also began to argue for the creation of a nascent military establishment for Korea. Hodge viewed the projected defense establishment as a constructive way of drawing many of the members of the numerous paramilitary groups in the south into a single institution capable of creating a national identity. Moreover, as one of his subordinates explained, a defense force was necessary because "National Defense is one of the primary functions of government."[14] That, of course, was the problem. According to Hodge's instructions, he was not to support or recognize any Korean entity claiming governing authority. More generally, he was proscribed from taking action that would prejudice the reunification of the peninsula under international trusteeship. Building an army in the south ran counter to those instructions. The Soviets would view Hodge's fostering of a defense establishment in the south as a clear sign that the United States was acting unilaterally to determine the make-up of the future Korean government. Recognizing the potential problems involved in building a military force for the south, MacArthur put Hodge on hold and referred the matter to Washington. In the meantime, Hodge's staff developed an alternative plan that would provide for a police reserve of 25,000 men to further relieve American forces of police duty.

As expected, the State-War-Navy Coordinating Committee instructed Hodge to postpone creating a military force. Hodge approved the alternate plan to create a police reserve for internal security purposes. The Korean Constabulary, as the new organization was called, began recruiting in the countryside in early 1946. Training sites were established and Japanese weapons provided to the new recruits. The program started slowly and operated on a shoestring for its first two years. Rapid turnover in American military personnel disrupted continuity and slowed progress. But the nucleus of an army was taking shape. Clearly that remained Hodge's goal. In spring, 1946 Hodge separated the Constabulary from the National Police and placed it under a Department of National Defense. He then thought better of that idea and renamed the new department Internal Security so as not to arouse Soviet and, one suspects, Washington's suspicions.

While Hodge took these steps toward establishing order in the south, the Russians were doing likewise in the north. During the first months of their occupation, the Soviets worked through a coalition of Koreans, many of whom had been in the Soviet Union during the war. Although the Soviets governed through indirect means, the Red Army made its presence felt in less subtle ways. On their drive to the thirty-eighth parallel, Soviet soldiers raped thousands of Korean women and plundered much of the countryside. Almost from the start, the Russians sealed off their zone. Machine gun emplacements and tangles of barbed wire marked what was supposed to be the temporary dividing line along the thirty-eighth parallel.

Although the Soviets clamped down on movement into their zone, they permitted a steady stream of refugees, almost 6,000 a day, to cross into the American sector. Many of these came from Japanese work camps in Manchuria. Others were Christians, collaborators, or members of the land-holding class fleeing south. No explanation for this migration was forthcoming. It is safe to say, however, that the steady stream of refugees added to Hodge's problems in the South while emptying the North of potential troublemakers for the Soviets.

Hodge's efforts to establish communications and commerce across the thirty-eighth parallel went nowhere. Privately, the Soviets were astounded that the Americans sought to restore commerce between the two zones. Instead, the Russians planned to treat Japanese industry in the North as war trophies and reparations for Japanese aggression dating to the Russian civil war era. They also expected to use Korean resources for development of the Soviet Far East. The Soviets did exchange small liaison groups, the Russians in Seoul and the Americans in Pyongyang, but they abruptly closed their office in mid-October. From that point on, the chief contact between the two sectors was by a mail train that ran once every two weeks.

Hodge's reliance on the colonial apparatus and Japanese collaborators did not go unnoticed by the Russians. Internal documents indicate that Soviet officials worried that the favored treatment given to the Right by Hodge signaled hostile intentions toward the Russians. Nevertheless, for the time being, the Soviets refrained from using the Korean Communist Party to disrupt conditions in the South. Publicly, officials in Washington and Moscow remained committed to the trusteeship proposal. For his part, General Hodge had already begun to doubt the feasibility, or even the desirability, of an international agreement on the future of Korea.

THE RESIDUE OF A LARGER PLAN: AMERICAN FORCES ARRIVE IN CHINA

American policy toward China in the immediate postwar period was an amalgam of long-standing policies and ad hoc decisions made in the days surrounding Japan's surrender. Truman remained committed to Roosevelt's public policy of supporting the development of a democratic China friendly to the United States under the leadership of Jiang Jieshi. At the same time, the United States would refrain from interfering in China's internal affairs. This position was confirmed in a hastily written order instructing Wedemeyer to assist in the movement of GMD forces into north China for the purposes of taking the surrender of Japanese troops. The same order enjoined Wedemeyer against aiding the Nationalists in a fratricidal war against the Communists. Wedemeyer quickly pointed out that by moving GMD troops north he would be aiding the Nationalists against the Communists. Faced with an apparent conflict in his orders, Wedemeyer recommended going ahead with the transportation of GMD troops while seeking to avoid direct confrontations with the Communists. The Joint Chiefs and Truman quickly approved the general's recommendation.

In early September, the president made it clear that China could count on continued American assistance during the transitional period from war to peacetime conditions. Truman agreed to provide shipping for the movement of Nationalist forces into Manchuria. He also pledged that the United States would fulfill its wartime promise to equip thirty-nine GMD divisions, even though the war had ended. Finally, the president also consented to the establishment of a military advisory group for China.

As Wedemeyer prepared to air and sealift Nationalist troops to the northern and coastal areas of China the first elements of the American Pacific fleet returned to Chinese waters in an impressive display of naval might. Watching from the deck of a captured Japanese ship, Captain Elmo Zummwalt, Jr. saw "stretching down the river, as far as the eye could see, meandering like an apparition through the flat fields of the river basin, a grim grey dragon of masts and guns and superstructures. The fighting fleet was back."[15] Shortly afterward, when Wedemeyer moved his headquarters and most of his command to the city, Shanghai became the seat of American power in China.

In late September the United States Marines III Amphibious Corps comprised of two divisions and supporting elements totaling approximately 40,000 men began landing in north China. An advanced team led by Brigadier General William A. Worton, a veteran with prewar experience in China, arranged for the marines' arrival. In Beijing, Worton had a late night conference with the Communist representative, General Zhou Enlai (Chou En-lai). Zhou warned Worton that the CCP would resist the marines' entry into Beijing. Worton replied that the marines were battle-tested veterans of the Pacific and that they would deal harshly with anyone who tried to keep them from completing their mission. On September 30, shortly after the confrontation with Zhou, the marines came ashore at Taku and began fanning out to key points in the northern coastal region. The Communists did not make good on Zhou's threat. Instead, the marines' entrance into Beijing was greeted by cheering crowds lining the ancient city's streets. The parade-like atmosphere was marred only by the disturbing presence of hand painted signs that read "Welcome U.S. Army."

Over the next several months, the marines' presence in north China would become more controversial. The III Marine Amphibious Corps (III MAC) was in China to help disarm and repatriate Japanese troops. The marines, who came under the command of General Wedemeyer once they were ashore, were under orders to avoid interfering in China's domestic strife. That proved impossible. The marines protected bridges, railroads, and key communications centers while Chinese Nationalist troops moved inland in pursuit of the Communists. Marine guards made sure that the Communists did not obstruct the shipment of coal and other vital supplies to Shanghai and protected traffic between Tianjin (Tientsin) and Beijing. They were aided in their mission by the 118th Division of the Japanese Imperial Army. As one marine officer recalled, the 118th's surrender in Tianjin, complete with "full fledged guard-of-the-day and band ceremony," amounted to having the Japanese report for duty. Within days, the Japanese were put to work guarding rail lines and repairing track damaged by the Communists. The marines soon jokingly referred to the Japanese troops as "III Marine Amphibious Corps (118th Division, Imperial Japanese Army, attached)."

The essential contradiction between the marines' orders and their mission vexed everyone involved. Sniped at and harassed, the marines felt as though their hands were tied by the strict rules of engagement issued by Wedemeyer.

Junior officers trying to decipher the confusing orders sought straightforward answers to questions such as "Does this mean we shoot 'em or not?" More revealing was the query "Who are we neutral against?"[16]

In some respects, officials in Washington were just as confused about the marines' role as the marines themselves. The Joint Chiefs originally contemplated sending the marines in to help repatriate the Japanese from north China. That was before they knew that the Japanese would cooperate peacefully after the surrender. Wedemeyer had requested landings along the coast, specifically at Shanghai, in order to keep the Communists out of the area until Jiang's troops could be flown in. During the discussions leading to the completion of General Order Number One, Assistant Secretary of War McCloy had recommended to Secretary of State Byrnes that the United States should send troops to several north China ports in addition to Dairen. McCloy conceived of the idea as a ploy to disguise the true purpose of the Dairen operation, which was to get troops ashore in Manchuria to use as leverage against the Russians.

The Dairen operation was scrapped, but the movement of the marines was not cancelled. Wedemeyer, who thought the landings were ordered in response to his entreaties, was puzzled to learn that American troops were heading for north China, instead of Shanghai. He was further dismayed to learn that marines, rather than regular army units, were being deployed. Perhaps no one was more surprised by the impending landings than John Carter Vincent. In the confusion surrounding the surrender and the assignment of occupation responsibilities, no one had bothered to tell him about the decision to send two divisions of marines into north China. The newly appointed head of the FE learned about the operation by reading about it in the newspaper. His first reaction was to try to get the operation cancelled.

Vincent believed that marines would increase rather than lessen the explosiveness of the situation. He knew that the Communists would see the presence of the marines as an intervention in Chinese internal affairs. Moreover, he was certain that such a show of force on Jiang's behalf would convince the Nationalist leader that he could count on continued American assistance in a showdown with the Communists. Even more troubling was the response that Vincent received when he asked about the marines' mission. At first, McCloy said that he thought that the III MAC's landings were "the residue of a larger plan," meaning the gambit to put troops ashore in Manchuria. McCloy added that there seemed to be no reason for the mission now and that it should be cancelled. That same day, however, he changed his mind. After talking with Wedemeyer, who was in Washington, he reported that the general wanted the marines to help with the repatriation of the Japanese and because they would be arriving "in the neighborhood where trouble was likely to start" between the Nationalists and Communists.

That was hardly the answer Vincent wanted to hear. Over the next several months he would continue to recommend that the marines be withdrawn as soon as possible. In the meantime, in the absence of any clearly defined national policy, more than 40,000 marines had landed in north China and placed themselves between two competing armed forces. The most that could be said of the confusing circumstances that sent them there was that the presence of the marines in north China resulted from an impulse by military officers and Pentagon officials to support Jiang Jieshi and counter the Soviet presence in north China.

A similar impulse led military officers to recommend the creation of the Military Advisory Group (MAG) for China. Like the marines' mission, however, the recommendation for a MAG in China served several purposes. And like the marines' mission, the proposal for a MAG encountered opposition from Vincent and the State Department. The driving force behind the advisory group was Wedemeyer. As Commanding General of American Forces in the China Theater, Wedemeyer planned to play an active role in the development of China policy. In early September he returned to Washington to lobby for continued aid to China. As part of that package he supported a MAG comprised of 4,000 officers and enlisted men modeled on the liaison system he had devised during the war. The group would include officers from the navy as well as the soon-to-be-independent Air Force.

Vincent opposed the MAG, arguing that the 4,000-man group would create a "semi-colonial Chinese army." Moreover, enlargement of the American military presence would almost certainly spark an armaments race with the Soviets in Northeast Asia at a time when the United States was seeking Russian cooperation on a host of problems in the region. Vincent also questioned aspects of the Chiefs' rationale for creating a postwar mission. One justification given by the JCS was that if the United States did not provide military advisers another country would. This hardly seemed like a reason for plunging more deeply into China's internal affairs. Vincent was concerned that a large advisory group, especially if it followed the model of the wartime Chinese

Combat Command, would bring American advisers into the field against Communist forces. Moreover, the size of the group and the justifications for it, suggested that the MAG was designed with bureaucratic and career interests in mind.

Vincent's fears were well founded. Later reports indicated that American military officials believed that advisers would have to provide operational advice to be effective. Indeed, Wedemeyer's staff officers had made such a proposal at the end of the war. It was also the case that the individual services had a bureaucratic stake in the creation of the mission. Planning for the MAG became the occasion for much inter-service squabbling over roles and missions. Although bickering continued over lines of command, a large mission at least had the advantage of providing each service with a piece of the action. Individual career interests were also better served by a large mission to China. As the armed forces began their rapid contraction after the war, many professional officers viewed the postwar advisory group as a way of finding a secure berth, possibly at their present rank. One of Wedemeyer's staff officers privately acknowledged that career considerations played a role in shaping the MAG. "[T]he whole damn mission was a worse pyramidal setup than we had in China during the war," he observed. "Everybody wants to be a General apparently."[17]

Finally, China also held a special appeal for those who had prewar experience as China Marines or members of the army's 15th Infantry Regiment. Attended to by servants, and insulated from many of the hardships of Depression era America, officers on the China station had enjoyed a life of ease and comfort as privileged members of an international community. Service folklore about China was so widespread that even those who had not served there before the war found the prospect of a postwar tour in China alluring.

After considerable debate, Vincent succeeded in whittling the MAG down to 900 officers and enlisted men. He also managed to win approval for instructions that prohibited Americans from offering operational advice to the Nationalists. In battling the army and navy over the size and role of the advisory group, Vincent had earned the enmity of the men in the Pentagon. In the months to come, as the situation in China worsened, these officers would lead a growing chorus of complaints about State Department subversion of America's China policy. Vincent's opposition to the MAG would become Exhibit A as the military built its case against alleged subversives at State.

By late October the Truman administration had established the contours of its postwar assistance to its Chinese ally. The program consisted of the MAG, the use of marines in north China to repatriate Japanese troops and protect communications from the Communists, the continuation of military aid to Jiang's regime, and an agreement to ferry GMD troops into Manchuria. This assistance would go forward while the United States encouraged Jiang to reform his regime and negotiate with opposition groups, of which the Communists were the most important. This approach to China's problems was endorsed in a new policy statement produced by the State-War-Navy Coordinating Committee after considerable disagreement between the State Department representatives and the uniformed officers who usually represented the War and Navy Departments at the working level.

In its final form, the statement repeated America's commitment to the creation of a friendly, unified, and democratic China. To secure that goal, the United States would advise and assist China in creating a modern military establishment. These forces would be used to provide for China's internal security and to ready its troops for occupation duty in Korea and Japan. The policy statement also declared that American assistance would be terminated if Chinese forces became involved in a civil war. As is often the case with such compromises, the most difficult decisions were postponed for another day. And as is also usually the case, neither side in the debate was satisfied. Vincent's efforts to keep the marines out of China and use American assistance as a carrot to induce Jiang to undertake significant reforms had been rejected. By the same token officials in the Pentagon disliked the language that threatened to withhold American assistance in the event of civil war. Reviewing the policy statement, navy secretary James Forrestal put his finger on the issue that would plague policy makers for the next four years. Forrestal, who strongly favored support for the Nationalists, asked "How do you draw a line between internal security and internal war?" Admiral Ernest King, the navy's representative on the JCS answered in a manner that foreshadowed the contentiousness that lay ahead. "That," replied King, "is done arbitrarily."

INDOCHINA AS AFTERTHOUGHT

In mid-September, as U.S. occupation forces took up positions across Northeast Asia, a small cadre of American advisers accompanied Chinese Nationalist troops into French Indochina. Led by Brigadier General Philip Gallagher, the Americans' main purpose was to assist and advise the Chinese in the repatriation of Japanese troops currently in Indochina above the sixteenth parallel. In accordance with General Order Number One, British colonial troops commanded by Major General Douglas Gracey assumed responsibility for repatriating Japanese troops south of that line. As in Korea and China, however, the sudden collapse of Japanese authority turned the ostensibly military task of managing the surrender of Japanese soldiers into a complicated political one.

In the brief period between Japan's surrender and the arrival of Chinese troops, the Vietminh, a coalition of Vietnamese nationalists led by Ho Chi Minh's Communists, seized control of most of the north and parts of southern Indochina in what has become known as the "August Revolution." On August 24, Ho, quoting liberally from the American Declaration of Independence and the French Declaration of the Rights of Man, proclaimed the independence of the Democratic People's Republic of Vietnam. The Japanese chose not to interfere in these dramatic events. In the weeks that followed they stood aside as the Vietminh expanded their organization into the countryside. The Japanese also declined to free the nearly 4,500 French soldiers they had imprisoned following the overthrow of the Vichy government the previous March. In a belated demonstration of solidarity with their fellow Asians some Japanese officers covertly transferred captured French weapons to the Vietnamese. Approximately 5,000 Japanese soldiers went even further and joined the Vietminh, providing the nationalists with valuable technical advice and instruction. In mid-September, when anti-French violence broke out in the South, Japanese troops did nothing to quell the attacks.

Japanese apathy convinced General Gracey to arm approximately 1,400 newly freed French troops. The French quickly took control of the government buildings in Saigon but the situation disintegrated as both sides engaged in atrocities and reprisals. As the fighting escalated, the Japanese began to cooperate more closely with Gracey's occupation force. Gracey's Indian troops held the city center while the Japanese were employed to clear roadblocks and patrol outside of Saigon. Charged with the supposedly nonpolitical task of taking the surrender of Japanese troops, Gracey now found himself increasingly enmeshed in an anticolonial revolution. Gracey's emphasis on maintaining order, which led him to ignore the Vietminh, had produced the opposite result.

Unfortunately for the British, it looked as though Gracey would have to muddle through for the next several months since it appeared that French troops were not slated to arrive from Europe until late December. French colonial troops, black soldiers from Madagascar, were available, but colonial officials vetoed their use, insisting that only white troops could restore French prestige. Faced with mounting criticism of his actions at home, especially his use of Japanese troops, the beleaguered commander changed course and encouraged negotiations between the French and Vietminh. By late October, as a tenuous truce emerged, French troops wearing American uniforms, riding in American Jeeps, and armed with American weapons, began to arrive earlier than expected.

Above the sixteenth parallel, Chinese Nationalist troops under warlord General Lu Han, the "old Indian" as Gallagher referred to him, continued to hold sway. In contrast to Gracey in the South, General Lu kept the French at arm's length and did nothing to interfere with the newly proclaimed Vietminh government. Lu's ostensible mission was to disarm and repatriate the Japanese and transship his own troops to Manchuria and Formosa through several ports in Vietnam. But Lu, who took up residence in the Governor General's palace, was in no hurry to leave. It soon became clear that the Chinese intended to exploit the French colony's resources for their own purposes, the most effective method being through currency manipulation. Although the Chinese did not make it a priority to aid the Vietminh, they nevertheless provided the revolutionaries with valuable support as a consequence of their anti-French actions.

In the meantime, the Chinese heaped insult on injury by refusing to fly the French flag at the September 28 surrender ceremony. At first, Lu planned to exclude the Union Jack as well, but he changed his mind after intervention by Gallagher on behalf of the British. Gallagher also tried, unsuccessfully, to persuade Lu to fly the French tricolor. Lu refused to budge, justifying his position by saying that only the flags of the four countries that signed the Potsdam Proclamation would be represented. That explanation ran contrary to practice at other ceremonies throughout Asia but pointing out this discrepancy did the French no good. The brief ceremony took place in the Governor General's palace, a small group of Americans on hand to watch the Japanese approach the Chinese seated behind a long cloth draped rectangular table. Unwilling to attend the ceremony as a guest in what might reasonably be considered his

FIGURE 3.6
General Lu Han at the surrender ceremony in Hanoi, French Indochina, September 28, 1945.
Phillip E. Gallagher Papers, U.S. Army Center for Military History

own house, General Marcel Alessandri, the French representative declined Lu's invitation to observe the proceedings.

Throughout the Chinese occupation, the French complained bitterly to American officials in Washington, Chungking, and Hanoi. "The Americans in China," declared a French official, "have right along been playing the Chinese game, although unwittingly." For his part, Gallagher was more worried about the Japanese, who he suspected of aiding the Vietminh. Privately, he sympathized with the Vietnamese desire for independence and regarded the French as a "pain in the neck," but he held no illusions about Ho, who he described as an "old revolutionist . . . a product of Moscow, a communist." Stuck in a highly visible yet nearly impotent position as adviser to Lu, Gallagher tried his best to coax the Chinese into fulfilling their mission and cooperating with the French. Gallagher, however, worried that Lu was intimidated by the Japanese. The best solution, as Gallagher saw it, was to remove the Japanese, of whom there were approximately 20,000 in northern Indochina. Once the Japanese were repatriated that would officially end the Chinese mission and hasten the movement of the Nationalists to north China thereby "permitting the French a free hand in settling their score with the [Vietnamese]."[18]

Gallagher realized, however, that Japanese repatriation from Indochina ranked far down on MacArthur's list of shipping priorities. By late October, the Chinese remained in control of the north even though several Chinese armies were transiting through Indochina en route to other parts of China. The Japanese had been rounded up, disarmed, and organized for repatriation. The Vietminh continued to use this strange interlude to extend their influence into the countryside. The French, having begun to reclaim control of the south, awaited an opportunity to assert their authority above the sixteenth parallel.

NOTES

1. J. Hart Caughey to his wife, 10 August 1945, J. Hart Caughey Papers, George C. Marshall Library, Lexington, Virginia.

2. Marc S. Gallicchio, *The Cold War Begins in Asia: American East Asian Policy and the Fall of the Japanese Empire* (New York: Columbia University Press, 1988), 41.

3. William Stueck, *Rethinking the Korean War: A New Diplomatic and Strategic History* (Princeton, NJ: Princeton University Press, 2002), 35–36.

4. Michael C. Sandusky, *America's Parallel* (Alexandria, VA: Old Dominion Press, 1983), 272, 289–292.

5. Mark Stoler, *Allies and Adversaries: The Joint Chiefs of Staff, the Grand Alliance, and U.S. Strategy in World War II* (Chapel Hill: University of North Carolina Press, 2000), 332, n. 25.

6. Col. Charles Bonesteel to Lincoln, 9 August 1945, ABC 387 Japan (15 Feb 45), sec. 1-B, RG 165, (Army General and Special Staffs) Modern Military Records Branch (MMRB), National Archives.

7. Lester Foltos, "The New Pacific Barrier: America's Search for Security in the Pacific, 1945–1947," *Diplomatic History* 13 (1989), 317–342; Stoler, *Allies and Adversaries*, 266.

8. Lawrence Greenburg estimates Huk strength at the end of the war at 15,000. D. Clayton James estimates that it may have been as a high as 30,000 during the war. Major Lawrence M. Greenberg, *The Hukbalahap Insurrection: A Case Study of a*

Successful Anti-Insurgency Operation in the Philippines, 1946–1955 (Washington, DC: U.S. Army Center of Military History, 1987), 17; D. Clayton James, *The Years of MacArthur, II, 1941–1945* (Boston: Houghton Mifflin Company, 1975), 507.

9. Richard Frank, *MacArthur* (New York: Palgrave Macmillan, 2007), 115; James, *Years of MacArthur, II*, 690.

10. Michael Schaller, *The American Occupation of Japan: The Origins of the Cold War in Asia* (New York, 1985), 24.

11. Historian John Dower has suggested that the photo opportunity also managed to convey an additional message. MacArthur was showing the Japanese that he would stand by the emperor in the weeks ahead. John W. Dower, *Embracing Defeat: Japan in the Wake of World War II* (New York: W. W. Norton & Co., 1999), 293.

12. James F. Schnabel, The United States Army in the Korean War series, *Policy and Direction: The First Year* (Washington, DC: U.S. Army Center of Military History, 1972), 14.

13. *New York Times*, 11 September 1945, 9.

14. Robert K. Sawyer, *Military Advisers in Korea: KMAG in War and Peace* (Washington, DC: Office of the Chief of Military History, 1962), 9.

15. Edward J. Marolda, "The U.S. Navy and the 'Loss of China,' 1945–1950," in Larry I. Bland, ed. *George C. Marshall's Mediation Mission to China, 1945–1947* (Lexington, VA: George C. Marshall Foundation, 1998), 409.

16. Quotes in this section are from Henry Aplington, II, "Sunset in the East: A North China Memoir, 1945–1947" in the author's possession. Waldo Heinrichs edited a version for publication. See Henry Aplington II, Colonel USMC (ret.), "Sunset in the East: A Memoir of North China, 1945–1947," *Journal of American East Asian Relations* 3 (Summer 1994), 2: 155–175.

17. Gallicchio, *Cold War Begins in Asia*, 101.

18. Brig. General Philip Gallagher to Maj. General, Robert McClure, 20 September 1945, and 26 October 1945, Philip E. Gallagher Papers, U.S. Army Center for Military History, Washington, DC.

4

Domestic Politics and Foreign Policy

The abrupt termination of the war and the subsequent movement of U.S. forces into the vacuum created by Japan's defeat provided little time for taking stock and assessing America's position in Asia. In Japan, years of wartime planning had provided a solid foundation for policy. Thus, despite the last minute decision to govern through the existing regime, the occupation proceeded smoothly toward achievement of its main objectives of disarmament and political reform. In Korea, Indochina and, most important of all, China, the arrival of American forces owed more to reflex and spasm than long-term planning. American objectives in these places were clear enough: a friendly non-communist China under Jiang Jieshi; a united, friendly and non-Communist Korea; and a resumption of French control over Indochina as the first step in a gradual transition to independence. How American forces could be employed to achieve these ends remained less clear. Local conditions played havoc with any American effort to construct a coherent policy for the use of force to achieve political ends.

With the benefit of hindsight we can see in each of these problem areas the seeds of much larger crises that would plague the region in the years to come. At the time, however, the turmoil in Asia shared the spotlight with a host of other foreign and domestic problems confronting a harassed President Truman. Following V-E Day, the United States faced the enormous task of reconstructing a flattened Europe. Complicating this herculean task was the fraying relationship with the Soviet Union.

Soviet power had defeated the bulk of the German army. The Russians paid a terrible price in lives and treasure for that victory but their sacrifices had brought the Soviet Union to the center of Europe where they appeared prepared to stay. In the autumn of 1945 Stalin's plans for the newly occupied countries in Eastern and Central Europe remained unclear to outside observers. The future of Germany was even more important to the United States but Stalin's plans for the defeated enemy appeared equally uncertain. In September, early attempts to resolve differences at the London Conference of Foreign Ministers had ended in disappointing failure. Although no clear pattern of Soviet behavior emerged, the very nature of Stalin's secretive repressive government encouraged American officials to see malign purpose in every action. Deadlock only seemed to favor the Russians. Economic turmoil and continued uncertainty about the future of occupied territories fed a generalized despair which seemed to benefit the Communist parties in Italy and France, as well as in Eastern Europe.

The Truman administration's uneasiness about developments abroad was matched by an equal uncertainty about its ability to manage affairs at home. Heading the list of administration concerns was the daunting task of conversion to a peacetime economy. The officials charged with managing the wartime economy and the president's various economic advisers could not agree which posed the greater danger, inflation or unemployment. In the ten days following V-J Day, 1.8 million workers lost their jobs, raising fears of a return to Depression-like conditions. At the same time, the vastly enlarged national debt, increases in household savings, and pent-up consumer demand heightened fears that the lifting of price controls would trigger runaway inflation.

Disagreement was to be expected given the unprecedented scope of the transition. But policy recommendations often reflected political orientation which, in turn, reflected the growing tensions within Roosevelt's and Truman's coalition style governments. Conservatives sought to remove economic controls and cut taxes; liberals urged continued controls, especially on prices, and a gradual easing of limits on wages. Truman steered between both positions, which only managed to anger everyone. As an economic traditionalist, Truman worried about balanced budgets and excessive interference in the economy. In mid-August, he permitted the War Production Board to revoke more than 210 orders governing production of household appliances while maintaining restrictions on wages. Truman's actions led one prominent labor leader to complain that the president had turned the task of reconversion over to the industrialists "without so much as asking labor to kiss his royal ass." Despite these complaints, Truman remained committed to his predecessor's social welfare programs. In September, he antagonized Republicans by pledging his support for Roosevelt's Economic Bill of Rights and tacitly endorsing a full employment bill. "This begins the campaign of '46," declared one Republican leader in Congress.

By mid-autumn, Truman appeared to be losing control. A growing number of high-profile strikes, rising prices, commodity shortages, and public quarrels between administration officials left liberals and conservatives wondering if the president were up to the job. Even Truman's occasional holidays came in for criticism. The president's many critics regarded his favorite recreational pursuits, poker, horseshoes, and piano sing-a-longs, all lubricated by the occasional bourbon, as beneath the dignity of his office and an irresponsible flight from the pressing needs of the country. Truman, of course, saw such criticism as unfounded, but he got the message and toned down the frolicking. Confined to the White House, which he likened to a prison, the president continued to wrestle with a mounting list of domestic problems. "Sherman was *wrong*," he told an annual gathering of reporters and politicians, "I'm telling you I find peace is hell. . . ."[1]

THE POSTWAR MILITARY ESTABLISHMENT: DEMOBILIZATION AND UNIFICATION

Truman's task of overseeing the conversion to a peacetime economy was greatly complicated by the pressing demands of postwar military planning. As American soldiers and marines took up their positions in Korea, China, and Japan, officials in the War and Navy Departments began to grapple with a host of operational and policy problems brought on by the sudden end of the war. The earlier than expected surrender of Japan also meant that the postwar era had arrived bringing with it many of the postwar issues that policy makers had thought would not require attention for at least another six months.

Heading the president's to-do list was the need to establish a policy for atomic weapons. Truman also made Universal Military Training (UMT) a high priority. The dawning of the atomic age and the rise of American air power promised to further complicate the conversion to a peacetime military establishment. With the independence of the Air Force a foregone conclusion, there would be a new claimant demanding a slice of the shrinking defense pie. The search for missions, assignment of roles, and establishment of new theaters of command promised to make the perennial inter-service battle of the budget an especially fierce contest.

In a category by itself was the politically explosive issue of demobilization. The path from a wartime force of twelve million men and women in uniform to a much smaller peacetime establishment was seeded with political land mines. Assuring a fair and orderly system of demobilization was just part of the problem. Plans were needed for integrating the returning soldiers into the economy with as little disruption as possible. The president and his military advisers also had to weigh the public's desire for a swift demobilization, to say nothing of the GIs', against the ongoing needs of American foreign policy. In Europe, a sudden withdrawal of American forces would handicap the administration's diplomatic efforts to settle boundary questions and other postwar issues with the Soviet Union. In Asia, a pell-mell rush to disarm seemed likely to undermine the occupation of Japan and lessen the chances of achieving stable friendly governments in China and Korea.

As previously noted, during the summer, the mounting demands to lift wartime economic restrictions and start bringing the boys home led some public figures to float the possibility of a negotiated surrender for Japan. Those calls ended with Japan's abrupt collapse in early August. But Japan's sudden surrender also intensified the pressure on the Pentagon to hasten the return to peacetime conditions. Worried by the public's impatience, the Joint Chiefs urged the president not to use the words "end of war" or "end of hostilities" in his victory proclamation lest he inadvertently start the clock ticking on the government's legal authority to maintain in uniform men who had been drafted for the duration of the war. As we have seen, the logistical challenges involved in bringing the boys home, mounting occupation operations, and simply rolling up the vast array of bases and installations were enormous. Nevertheless, a skeptical public refused to be satisfied by the administration's explanations for the perceived delays. In late August Congressman John Vorys (R-Ohio) cast aspersions on the military by urging the Joint Chiefs to "allay suspicions that our armed forces are being held together so as to avoid a loss of rank by officers, through shrinkage of their commands, and the suspicions that there are undisclosed imperialistic or militarist plans in the making." Trying to calm the public, Truman declared, "There will be no padding in our armed forces. America is going to keep the full strength she needs for her national commitments. But the rest of the men are coming back home as fast as the Services can get them out."[2]

Robert Patterson, who replaced Stimson as Secretary of War, stood by the existing point system for discharges, explaining that it was fair and understood to be so by the soldiers. He also explained that the "red tape" soldiers complained about was necessary to guarantee that every soldier left the service with the proper documentation so as to be eligible for a wide array of benefits. But the War Department also sped up the discharge process, operating centers twenty-four hours a day and cutting the time needed to release a soldier from eighteen days to forty-four hours. Despite these improvements, public criticism mounted. By late autumn the quickened pace of demobilization only seemed to sharpen the frustrations of those still in uniform. Soon, the soldiers overseas would add their voices to the chorus of complaint rising at home.

As demobilization became disintegration, in Truman's apt description, the Joint Chiefs worried that the declining effectiveness of American forces would tempt the Soviets to probe beyond the ample territories already under their control. The public's clear desire to enjoy the fruits of peace at home and the sharp reductions in force size posed serious problems for policy makers intent on securing American objectives abroad. But the process of demobilization with its priority given to points accumulated by individual GIs exacerbated the problem. The departure of high point men often deprived units of their most experienced soldiers or those with vital technical expertise. By October, it was clear that volunteers and draft calls would not make up the shortfalls. Marshall hoped that adoption of a system of UMT would provide the necessary replacements, but given the mood at home UMT was a remote possibility.

As the JCS watched the dismantling of their once mighty force, they confronted the additional problem of reaching agreement on the size and shape of the postwar military establishment. Apart from UMT the main issue concerned the unification of the armed services. Beginning with the Pearl Harbor disaster, the war had highlighted the need for more efficient management of the armed forces. Many observers concluded that some form of unification was required in order to eliminate the costly duplication of missions and ensure better coordination between the services. Representatives of the army and navy concurred on the need for reform but they sharply disagreed on the means to achieve that end. Backers of the army were more in favor of actual administrative unification whereas the navy, which feared it would become an escort service for the larger army, supported a looser form of coordination and cooperation. The navy also worried that unification, which envisioned three separate services for air, land, and sea would eliminate or reduce the significance of the marines and the navy's air arm even though both branches had proved their worth in the Pacific campaigns.

Truman, who as a senator had written an article on the subject, tended more closely toward the army's position. His proposal called for a melding of the services into a Department of National Defense, presided over by a Secretary of Defense. The army air force would become a separate service with its own commander, who along with the army and navy commanders would meet with a single Chief of Staff to advise the secretary and president. According to this plan, the navy would keep its integrated structure, meaning its air arm and the marines. But there would be a single supply service to eliminate waste. The navy, however, had gotten the jump on the army by presenting its own plan, including its own postwar manpower estimate, to the sympathetic House Military Affairs Committee. Army staff officers were livid. They complained bitterly that the navy's special pleading before Congress proved that in the absence of true unification the admirals would always pursue their own narrow interests on matters that affected all of the services.

The unification controversy was finally resolved, at least temporarily, with the National Security Act of 1947. The final organization tilted more toward the navy's ideal than the army's. In the interim, however, the intramural feuding infected nearly every other aspect of defense policy. Army staff documents during this period are filled with critical commentary questioning the navy's motives on a range of policies. Forrestal's diary is likewise strewn with accusations against army and War Department officials who, he was convinced, constantly plotted to do in the navy. It is not too much to suggest that the mental illness that eventually drove Forrestal to suicide began to manifest itself during this period. It is perhaps more telling that the secretary's tenacious defense of service interests did not seem all that unusual in the harsh world of defense politics.

RIPPLES ACROSS THE AMERICAN LAKE

In many respects, the battle over unification continued into peacetime the fierce army-navy skirmishes that had colored the making of wartime strategy. In the final months of the war, each service had advanced its own plan for the defeat of Japan, the navy recommending blockade, the air corps strategic bombing, and the army invasion. The final plans had incorporated some aspects of all three but, as readers will recall, by early August the navy was challenging MacArthur's command of the invasion while the general fended off any attempts to compromise his overall control of operations. That particular intramural quarrel continued into the postwar period, threatening to mar the surrender ceremonies and casting a pall over the future command structure in the Pacific.

The struggle over service unification hindered policy making to such an extent that one respected military commentator concluded that the military feuding "delayed the nation for a year or two in grappling with the already dire state of world affairs."[3] The unification debate certainly influenced the formulation and implementation of policy in East Asia. But its effects were often subtle and not immediately perceivable to contemporary observers. In contrast, the troublesome consequences of the breakneck pace of demobilization were more obvious to contemporary observers. Together, however, the intramural quarrels and demands of demobilization shaped and limited the American response to developments in the region. In this way, Washington politics made its impression on Asian policy. But events in the field also had the potential to shape Washington politics and, consequently, Asian policy. The Pacific Ocean was fast becoming an American lake, but its vast size undermined control from any single source and encouraged initiatives from all directions.

In mid-September, Truman abruptly realized his own tenuous control of that initiative when MacArthur unexpectedly announced that things were going so well in Japan that he would soon be able to reduce the occupation force to 200,000 men. The new shogun's statement was widely seen for the political act it was by everyone but the general's friends in Congress. In fact, MacArthur made his announcement shortly after being warned by a prominent Republican backer that administration officials were conspiring to use the need for a large occupation army as a justification for continuing the draft. MacArthur was advised that the best way to avoid being blamed for the continuation of conscription would be to make it clear that he would need fewer troops, say 200,000 to 300,000 to govern Japan. MacArthur settled on the lower number and in the process embarrassed an administration already under pressure to speed the rate of demobilization.

Although MacArthur's announcement certainly surprised the administration, it is doubtful that it added to the public's already strong desire to bring the soldiers home. On the other hand, the episode did little to help Truman while simultaneously serving MacArthur's own political purposes by positioning him on the side of those who wished to reduce the size of the armed forces. The general's statement also alarmed those, including Acting Secretary of State Dean Acheson, who suspected MacArthur of wanting to administer a soft peace for his own political advantage. Acheson, who at the time sided with those favoring a thorough reconstruction of Japanese society, publicly rebuked the general for seeking to make policy. MacArthur's friends in Congress sought retribution by trying, unsuccessfully, to derail Acheson's nomination as undersecretary. The episode gave Truman more reason to mistrust the man he once privately called "Mr. Prima Donna, Five Star, Brass Hat MacArthur," but the general soothed matters by issuing an insincere apology to Marshall.

Not long after he made his unhelpful contribution to the demobilization process, MacArthur entered into a longer, less public quarrel with the Joint Chiefs over the boundaries of his command. MacArthur hoped to prevent disputes such as those that had arisen during the war by once and for all gaining authority over all army forces in the Pacific. The navy, led by Admiral Nimitz, countered that it made little strategic sense to have MacArthur in Tokyo in command of army forces in Hawaii. Instead, the navy argued for geographical theaters similar to those in place in Europe. To MacArthur's dismay, Army Chief of Staff Dwight Eisenhower was inclined to compromise with the navy. The dispute dragged on for more than a year, during which time an embittered MacArthur refused army requests to publicly endorse UMT, unification, and renewal of the draft. The final arrangement designated MacArthur as Commander in Chief, Far East, with control over Japan, Korea, the Ryukyu Islands, Philippines, Marianas, and Bonin Islands, but placed Hawaii and the remaining Pacific islands under a naval Commander in Chief Pacific. A special arrangement placed forces in China under the direction of the Joint Chiefs, but gave routine operational control of naval units to the Pacific commander.

MacArthur's collisions with military and political leaders over demobilization and command structure demonstrated how high level officers in the field could thwart or disrupt policy making in Washington. In the fall of 1945, however, administration officials encountered an unexpected challenge to their authority when normally powerless enlisted personnel and their loved ones at home attempted to have a say in how the American government projected its military power across the Pacific. American soldiers stationed throughout Europe and the Pacific protested what they perceived as the slow pace of demobilization but the sharpest complaints were directed at the marines' involvement in China's incipient civil war. By early winter, as violence spread throughout northern China, GI disapproval of War Department policy was placing serious limitations on the Truman administration's ability to deploy armed force in the service of its national policy.

THE SLOW BOAT TO CHINA

As the eventual command arrangements indicated, the Chiefs recognized China as a special case. The explosive political situation was one reason for the unusual setup. Inter-service rivalry was another. Once they landed, the marines came under the control of General Wedmeyer, a step he demanded as part of a larger program to bring order to the overlapping jurisdictions in the theater. Wedemeyer had already battled the navy when he tried to rein in Naval Group China a special intelligence gathering operation that had worked closely with Jiang's secret police during the war. Wedemeyer and his predecessor Joseph Stilwell regarded the group's leader, Commander Milton "Mary" Miles, as the self-aggrandizing head of a rogue organization that operated outside any recognizable chain of command. For his part Miles claimed that his sailors had performed inestimable service collecting meteorological information, coast watching, and training Chinese guerilla fighters. The army, however, suspected that Miles's main task was to maintain the navy's bureaucratic stake in China until the fleet could return. Shortly after V-J Day Miles left China after suffering a nervous breakdown brought on by side effects of medication taken to combat malaria. By that time, however, the fleet was back and the Navy Department had obtained a place in the postwar advisory group being organized for China.

While Wedmeyer sparred with the navy, he established his headquarters in Shanghai and plunged into the task of coordinating the sea and airlift of

Nationalist troops into the Japanese occupied areas of coastal and northeastern China. Eventually, about 500,000 Nationalist troops were transported from China's interior. The first of those troops arrived at airfields and ports guarded by Americans. Once they landed, Jiang's men moved inland in pursuit of the Communists, leaving the marines to protect the ports and communications centers in the rear of the advancing GMD armies.

In early October, Wedemeyer briefly returned to Washington to push for continued aid to Jiang. The general assured fellow officers that the strength of Mao Zedong's Communist forces had been overrated in the United States and that Jiang could handle the Chinese Communists provided they did not receive aid from the Soviets. The main problem Wedemeyer faced was getting GMD forces into position to take over from the Japanese while simultaneously ensuring that the marines did not get drawn into any clashes between the Nationalists and Communists. By early November this was proving increasingly difficult. During their first month of occupation, the marines had been unmolested by the Communists. In late October, once GMD troops began arriving, the Communists became more confrontational. In one incident, they attacked a convoy and injured several marines. The increasingly tense situation convinced Wedemeyer that his orders to avoid involvement in a fratricidal war were rapidly being overtaken by events.

Soviet actions added to the list of challenges Wedemeyer was facing. In October, Russian officials had turned American ships carrying Nationalist troops away from Manchurian ports, forcing Jiang's forces to march overland from below the Great Wall. In the meantime, Soviet officers brushed aside Nationalist representatives sent into Manchurian cities to prepare for the establishment of Chinese sovereignty, transferred captured Japanese weapons to the Chinese Communists, and began systematically hauling off Japanese machinery to Russia as war booty. The latter action was especially troubling since the Chinese expected to use Japan's industrial empire to help rebuild their war-ravaged country.

American officials now worried that Stalin was going back on his agreements at Yalta. Jiang was even more disturbed by the Soviets' duplicity. Soviet actions in Manchuria certainly appeared to fit into a larger pattern of Russian misbehavior already evident in Central Europe, Iran, and Korea. Before long, however, the Chinese Communists also had cause to worry about Stalin's intentions. In early November, Russian authorities ordered the Chinese Communists out of Manchurian cities. Their stunned Chinese comrades protested: "The army of one Communist Party using tanks to drive out the army of another Communist Party. . . . Can this kind of action be acceptable?"[4] Evidently it was. Mao's forces withdrew to the countryside and waited for further developments.

Communist brotherhood was all well and good, but Stalin's main goal was to secure the fruits of operation AUGUST STORM and ensure the safety of the Soviet Union's Far Eastern provinces. Toward that end, he was willing to aid the Chinese Communists' return to Manchuria. But Stalin doubted that Mao's forces could prevail in a contest with the Nationalists, especially if the Americans came to Jiang's aid. Nor did Stalin view a Chinese Communist victory as an unalloyed blessing for the Soviet Union. Perpetuation of the struggle between the Nationalists and Communists would render both Mao and Jiang dependent on Moscow's favor. Stalin was playing warlord politics, turning the clock back to the 1920s and keeping China's contending parties seeking assistance from outside.

To American officials it appeared their fears had been realized, Stalin was not living up to his agreements. After all, the Yalta agreements were supposed to restrain Soviet expansion in Manchuria. Now it looked as though the Soviets were settling down in Manchuria and stepping up their interference in Chinese internal politics. Stalin could counter that the Americans were also skirting the agreements. The increased American military presence in China after Japan's surrender, the invaluable assistance being given to Jiang by the marines, the previously unplanned occupation of South Korea, and the exclusion of Soviet influence from the occupation of Japan indicated that the American ambitions in northeast Asia were expanding beyond the minimalist goals of the Yalta agreements. The Americans of course did not believe they were threatening Russia, nor did they think that their postwar assistance to Jiang exceeded limits imposed by wartime agreements. Quite the contrary, American officials argued that American and Soviet recognition of Jiang's government as the only legitimate authority in China had been the central fact of the Yalta agreements. That recognition entitled the Nationalists to American assistance in the reoccupation of all of China, including Manchuria.

Nevertheless, some Americans, notably Secretary of State Byrnes, began to question the wisdom of unconditional support to Jiang. Byrnes believed that the marines were needed to repatriate disarmed Japanese troops. He was beginning to agree with John Carter Vincent, however, that American aid to Nationalists only fed Jiang's desire for military victory and risked further Soviet interference in China. As Byrnes reconsidered China policy, his counterparts in the War and Navy Departments grew increasingly convinced that the United States needed to stand firm in its commitment to the Nationalists. A series of fractious meetings between State Department members and military staff officers on the interdepartmental State-War-Navy Coordinating Committee only sharpened the lines of disagreement and increased the uniformed officers' frustrations with what they saw as State's muddled response to the worsening situation in China.

In early November, shortly after returning to China, Wedemeyer notified the Joint Chiefs that he had refused Jiang's request for help in transporting more Nationalist soldiers into north China. Wedemeyer said that Jiang already had enough troops in the area to disarm the Japanese. Inasmuch as the Communists posed the more serious threat to Nationalist control, any additional aid would violate his instructions against involvement in China's fratricidal war. Wedemeyer advised withdrawing the marines as early as November 15 so as to avoid being drawn into a firefight with the Communists. Wedemeyer may have wanted to pull the marines out of China, but it is more likely that what he really sought was a change in his directive. His request to begin extracting the marines on less than two weeks notice was unlikely to be accepted. Wedemeyer's warning did, however, force policy makers in Washington to confront the China problem and end what many in the Pentagon saw as the aimless drift in national policy.

If that was Wedemeyer's intention, he succeeded. During the remainder of November, officials in Washington sought to hammer out a new policy for China. They did so in an atmosphere of increasing criticism and complaint from GIs, their family members, and their representatives in Congress. Restless servicemen waiting to be shipped home from U.S. bases in Europe, the Pacific Islands, and Asia launched letter-writing campaigns to hasten their return home for discharge from the military. Feelings of neglect were widespread but they were especially acute for the marines who patrolled rail lines and roads in the damp cold of north China's approaching winter. As one marine recalled, "We were fugitives from the law of averages. . . . We had survived fierce combat in the Pacific and now none of us wanted to stretch his luck any further and get killed in a Chinese civil war. We felt a terribly lonely sensation of being abandoned and expendable."[5]

A TEMPORARY SOLUTION

As clashes erupted between the Americans and Communists some marines and their family members began to condemn American intervention in China's civil war. Liberals at home also questioned why Japanese soldiers were being used to protect communication lines if the marines were in China to repatriate enemy troops. Although administration officials acknowledged the legitimacy of these complaints they nevertheless attributed much of the criticism of American policy to the work of Communist sympathizers. Many officials also took it for granted that Communist sympathizers in the State Department were responsible for the government's muddled China policy. Forrestal complained about "left wing boys" in the press and listened sympathetically when Ambassador Patrick Hurley warned him about Communist supporters in the State Department. Staff officers in the army and navy, referred to "pinkies" in the State Department, and withheld classified material from Vincent, who according to the head of the Office of Strategic Services, was under investigation by the FBI as a possible Soviet agent.[6]

Seeking to quiet public opposition, Secretary of War Patterson issued a statement explaining that the marines were in China to help the Nationalists take the surrender of the one million Japanese soldiers scattered throughout the countryside. In referring to one million Japanese troops, however, Patterson knowingly inflated the size of the enemy force under arms. War Department statistics shown to Patterson put the number in north China at 203,000. Several hundred thousand soldiers remained under arms elsewhere in China, including the island of Formosa, but they were not near the area occupied by the marines. In any case, Patterson's men put the total at about 600,000, well below the more impressive-sounding one million used by the Secretary. Patterson's press release, and a similar announcement from the Navy Department, failed to satisfy those calling for the marines' return.

In the meantime, the Chinese Communists applied added pressure on American policy makers by attacking marine convoys and patrols. Wedemeyer warned that the fighting was likely to escalate and urged that marines be withdrawn. At the same time, however, he offered a bleak forecast of what would follow the marines' evacuation. The Communists, Wedemeyer predicted, would view the evacuation of the marines as a success for their policy of intimidation. Moreover, once the marines withdrew, the Communists would disrupt the flow of vital supplies, especially coal, to Shanghai, a key city for the Generalissimo. The ensuing chaos would weaken Jiang's hold on the north and move the country closer to civil war.

Once again, the uniformed officers and civilian officials in the War and Navy Departments took Wedemeyer's warnings as proof that the administration had to modify China policy to allow for the possibility that the marines might become involved in the developing conflict. To that end, Forrestal and Patterson sent a joint memorandum to Byrnes urging the secretary of state to amend American policy to permit Wedemeyer to continue supporting the Nationalists. The two secretaries impressed upon Byrnes the importance of adjusting policy lest the region pass under Soviet control. When Forrestal and Patterson met with Byrnes the pugnacious navy secretary bluntly declared that the United States "could not yank the Marines out of China now." Forrestal recommended equally blunt conversations with the Russians but Byrnes countered that the Soviets had already publicly stated their support for the Nationalists. Byrnes then surprised his colleagues by suggesting that the United States try to force the Nationalists and Communists into a compromise by warning Jiang that the United States would withhold aid to his government unless he cooperated.

Following their meeting the three cabinet members proceeded to a formal session of the full cabinet at the White House. The president opened the proceedings by entering the room with a White House teletype sheet in his hand and exclaiming "See what a son-of-bitch did to me!" Truman explained to the surprised group that Ambassador Patrick Hurley had just announced his resignation on the grounds that Communist sympathizers in the State Department were subverting his attempts to bring about the unification of the Chinese government under Jiang's auspices. Only a day before the erratic ambassador had told Truman he was returning to China. Instead, Hurley had suddenly complicated an already difficult situation by providing Congress with a justification for investigating the operations of the State Department.

The president already had enough headaches in China. Apart from the looming civil war, he worried about Soviet intentions in the region. The American reparations commissioner had recently told the president that the Soviets were stripping Manchuria and northern Korea of Japanese factories and machines. In explaining the situation to his cabinet, Truman predicted that unless they were stopped the Russians would take Japan's place in Northeast Asia. The president needed time to formulate a more effective policy for China. That necessitated finding some means to reassure the public that American interests were in safe hands. Thinking that a dramatic appointment would "steal thunder" away from Hurley's announcement, Secretary of Agriculture Clinton Anderson recommended sending General Marshall to China on a fact-finding mission. Truman jumped at the idea and phoned Marshall at his home in Leesburg, Virginia, the same day.

Although he had begun his retirement only eight days earlier, the general dutifully accepted his new job. Marshall hoped to keep the news from his wife until after that evening's dinner but a radio news bulletin broke the story while everyone was seated at the table. Katherine Marshall took the announcement stoically, but she later expressed her true feelings to one of the general's former aides. "This sounds bitter," she wrote, "Well I am bitter. The president should never have asked him in a way that he could not refuse." Mrs. Marshall's indignation was well founded. The general had maintained a grueling pace during the war. Exhausted and weary of Washington's incessant battles, he allowed himself to begin thinking about retirement after Germany's surrender. Now after only the briefest of vacations his sense of duty was taking him back to Washington to prepare for his new mission. Once his preparations were completed, the general would fly halfway around the world to enter a world of political intrigue that made Washington's infighting seem tame.

Nevertheless, Marshall approached his new job with the can-do spirit typical of the military professional. As a professional officer, Marshall was also used to making sure officers in the field possessed clear instructions and enough autonomy to carry out their mission. He would require the same. Therefore his first order of business was to insure that his instructions did not tie his hands or inhibit the execution of policy. That task brought the staff officers in the Pentagon into conflict with the State Department. Believing that Jiang would not cooperate unless the United States threatened to withhold aid, John Carter Vincent recommended that any new movement of Nationalist troops north should be made dependent on a truce and a calling of a national political convention open to all parties. Marshall and the officers in the

General Staff's Operations and Plans Division (OPD) rejected Vincent's proposal as too vague to serve as the basis for a new directive for Wedemeyer. Moreover, Marshall believed that withholding support from Jiang would give the Communists a reason to stall while allowing the Soviets to take advantage of the growing chaos in north China. Accordingly, Marshall had the officers in OPD revise Vincent's proposal so that it permitted continued support for the Nationalists. Vincent made a tactical retreat to what he thought was a more defensible position. He added a statement to the revised instructions that called for a moratorium on troop movements if they endangered the negotiations. The War Department rejected that restriction as well.

What the officers in OPD wanted, and what Vincent was not providing, was a "firm and unequivocal" policy statement that put the United States squarely behind Jiang. Without such a statement, they told Marshall, "You, the JCS and the War and Navy departments may continue to be hamstrung by the vague, indecisive, delaying tactics which have characterized U.S. policy toward China since the Japanese surrender."[7] The dispute was finally resolved in the army's favor during a series of three high-level meetings, the latter two attended by the president. Marshall's final instructions provided that Jiang's troops could be transported into Manchuria to take the place of Soviet forces when they withdrew. Wedemeyer would be instructed to secretly prepare for additional troop movements into the contested region of north China. Jiang would not be told of these preparations so as to give him some incentive to negotiate in good faith with the Communists. Marshall would give Wedemeyer approval to resume transporting Guomindang troops into the north if the negotiations progressed to the point where they would not be hindered by additional troop movements. But the Americans would also move the troops north if negotiations between the Nationalists and Communists broke down, even if the talks collapsed due to Jiang's intransigence.

This last point was consistent with Marshall's view that it was in American interests to have Nationalist troops control north China. But it also made the withholding of U.S. aid a hollow threat. Byrnes, in accordance with Vincent's recommendation, thought that if Jiang obstructed the talks, the United States should repatriate the Japanese as quickly as possible and then withdraw the marines, even if it left north China up for grabs. Marshall was unwilling to accept that solution. During the second of the three meetings, this one attended by the president, he raised the matter again. Truman agreed with Marshall that even if Jiang torpedoed the talks, the United States would have to resume shipping GMD troops north.

Marshall now had the instructions he and the JCS desired. The United States would maintain its support for the Nationalists while Marshall tried to broker a settlement between the Nationalists and Communists. Wedemeyer would have the information he needed to plan for the next transfer of GMD troops north and the marines would stay in China for the time being. As the historian Gary May has noted, Marshall's final instructions were a triumph for him and the military. Marshall would soon discover, however, that the movement of Nationalist forces north would not produce the stability that he thought essential to American interests. Instead, Jiang, as he had done before, would call the Americans' bluff, believing that he could count on U.S. support in a showdown with the Communists.

For the moment, however, Truman could take some consolation from having muffled the shock waves from Hurley's resignation. Marshall's appointment had taken the China problem off Truman's desk and left the president time for the myriad domestic issues bearing down on him. Within days of Marshall's departure for China, however, a new crisis overtook the administration when tens of thousands of GIs began demonstrating in mass rallies to demand their immediate repatriation.

NO BOATS. NO VOTES

The magnitude of the logistical difficulties entailed in returning the millions of servicemen and women from overseas are difficult to overstate. The duration of ocean voyages, two and a half months round trip from Manila to San Francisco, twenty-three days from Le Havre, France to the East Coast, meant that thousands of GIs would be stranded for months until their ship came in. To meet the demands of demobilization, the navy scrounged for bottoms and converted cargo vessels to transports. These efforts were vitiated, however, when the United States agreed to return to Britain the liners *Queen Elizabeth*, *Queen Mary*, and *Aquitania*. All three ships had been on loan to the United States for use as troop ships but were now much needed by Britain. Despite the enormous challenges involved in demobilization, the army soon discovered that it was discharging men at a rate that jeopardized the government's ability to meet its postwar commitments. Before demobilization had moved into high gear the army had planned to maintain 2.5 million men in service

by July 1946. That number would allow the United States to meet its occupation obligations and keep a small force stateside. By December 1945, however,
Army planners found to their dismay that the actual pace of demobilization
was racing ahead of their scheduled rate of discharge. The army expected to
release a little over 2.5 million men by the end of 1945. Instead, they were on
track to discharge twice that number.

The furor that erupted in early January was in some respects the result of
the military's own efficiency. Instead of reassuring soldiers that the army was
doing all it could to get them home, the rapid pace of demobilization worked
on the GIs' insecurities. As troop ships left ports laden with homeward bound
GIs, those left behind wondered when their turn would come. For most of the
soldiers scattered throughout the Pacific, especially those in the Philippines or
on Okinawa, "the island of despair" as one dejected marine put it, the dull
routine of the peacetime military added to the frustrations of those itching to
resume civilian life back home. As conscripts, most soldiers had tolerated the
rigors of military life, but few felt any fondness for the hierarchical structure
and stiff discipline of the armed forces. Soldiers found the military "caste system" that separated officers from enlisted men in most social settings offensive to their democratic sensibilities and they took umbrage at the preferential
treatment accorded officers. For their part, professional officers believed that
a formal code of behavior and sharp distinctions in social settings were essential to good order.

One senses the skeptical attitude that the defenders of tradition had toward
any social leveling from the FBI file compiled on the activities of Lieutenant
Colonel Evans Carlson, a maverick marine who gained fame as the leader of
the group Hollywood dubbed "Carlson's Raiders." Before Pearl Harbor, Carlson had spent time in China with the Communist Eighth Route Army and had
written and lectured about his experience. After the war he came under
scrutiny for participating in protests against American involvement in Chinese internal affairs. In mid-September, shortly after V-J Day, political gossip
columnist Drew Pearson reported that Carlson had suggested to "White
House friends" that there were "thousands of well trained troops in China and
that the use of these Chinese troops would permit thousands of American
troops to return home." Appearing in the press within days of MacArthur's
surprise announcement that he would need fewer troops than anticipated for
occupation duty, Carlson's comments aroused the concern of the White

House as well as the Navy and State Departments, all of which asked the FBI for information on the outspoken marine.

In building its case on Carlson's allegedly subversive activities, the FBI reported that Carlson drew on his experience with Mao's army to abolish officers' privileges and the officers' mess. "It was said," the report continued, "that all the raiders wore the same clothes, carried the same equipment and lived alike." Quoting a news story the report added that "'discipline is firm but informal, based on knowledge, reason and individual volition.' It was likewise said that Colonel Carlson has adopted the Eighth Route's method of group meetings where problems were threshed out and the men heard talks on Democracy, freedom of speech, press, and religion."[8]

Carlson's practices were rare, perhaps nonexistent elsewhere in the marines and army. Those GIs who served in less socially innovative units, dealt with the petty annoyances and more serious inequities in a variety of time-honored ways. Grousing, at least privately, was a soldier's privilege. Writing to his parents aboard a ship headed, ultimately, for the Philippines, the historian Waldo Heinrichs, who was then a noncommissioned officer, complained about "the advantages offered officers on board ship in comparison with enlisted men. We sleep six deep in small compartments." A typical day topside fed that resentment. "We bask in the sun and play bridge, sweat out interminable chow lines, see the officers, secure behind the omnipotent dark glasses gaze at us from the lofty heights of the quarter deck as one would gaze on a mass of slaves on the way to our South or, as I actually heard one officer remark, like the cattle pens of Chicago." The caste system that galled GIs functioned in even the most rugged conditions. Following the battle of Okinawa, marine private Eugene Sledge and his companions fumed over having to spend an exhausting day clearing brush and killing snakes so that officers could pitch their tents in the shade of some pines growing on a hill. As they worked, the marines "voiced many profane, and profound, complaints regarding having to clear a place for officers' tents that was so snake-infested."[9]

When private complaints failed as a vent for their anger, GIs had other means of seeking redress. Following their arduous day clearing brush, Sledge and his comrades were ordered out in a rainstorm to fasten the flaps of a tent sheltering several second lieutenants newly arrived from the states. The marines took out their frustrations on the young officers by releasing the ropes on the canvas flaps so that the tent blew off, instantly soaking everyone and everything inside. Once he arrived in the Philippines, Heinrichs and a crusading group of colleagues turned the regimental newspaper into an outlet for soldiers' grievances. The main targets of these complaints were officers, especially newly minted West Point lieutenants. In a particularly mischievous moment the writers on the paper created a fictitious officer, one Lieutenant T. S. Truscott, as a caricature of the new crop of officers arriving in the Philippines to torment the homesick GIs. The regiment's commanding officer, who was a reservist as opposed to regular army, tolerated the publication of soldiers' complaints, or "bitch letters" as they were called, and even let the paper have its fun with the imaginary Truscott because he believed friendly criticism of officers would be a harmless way for his men to let off steam.

Lieutenant Truscott soon took on a life of his own. Many readers, including some officers, were convinced he was real. It turned out that he was. Several weeks after the paper began reporting on the fictitious Truscott, a young Lieutenant Lucian K. Truscott III, whose father was the Commanding General of the Third Army in Europe, joined the division. Faced with a troublesome case of life imitating art, and realizing that the islands were not big enough for two Truscotts, the regimental commander put an end to the imaginary Lieutenant.[10]

To its credit, the Pentagon recognized that GI animosity toward officers was widespread. Responding to these complaints, and the stark fact that the army was not meeting its postwar enlistment goals, Secretary of War Patterson commissioned war hero Lieutenant General Jimmy Doolittle to investigate and recommend reforms for the peacetime army. Patterson acknowledged the legitimacy of some of the GIs' grievances and approved changes in rules regulating interactions between soldiers and officers off base. But he vetoed the panel's recommendation that the terms "officers" and "enlisted men" be dropped in favor of the blanket term "soldiers."

Over the long term, the Doolittle commission, which did not convene until March 1946, would help ameliorate some of the GIs' grievances. It could do little, however, to quell the calls to bring the boys home. Nor could it address the soldiers' growing sense that they had become unwilling pawns in a regional power struggle. The marines in North China resented being placed in the middle of China's internal strife, but their proximity to the front lines and their professionalism prevented them from publicly voicing their complaints. That task was taken up by family members back home who protested to their

congressmen. GIs elsewhere in China could also be more outspoken. "If any-
body had meddled in our civil war," complained a soldier to a Shanghai newspaper, "we'd shot the hell out of him."[11] In the Philippines, American soldiers
were convinced that shipping was available to take them home. Some concluded that the army was being kept in the islands to demonstrate the American commitment for conservative candidates who were being challenged by
the Hukbalahap movement, the left-wing resistance group that controlled
much of central and southern Luzon.

The demobilization crisis finally boiled over into mass demonstrations in
the first week of January 1946. The outbreaks flared up at army bases in Europe, the Pacific, and China, the latter occurring just as Marshall was beginning the arduous process of bringing the rival Chinese parties together for
negotiations. The GIs took to the streets after they learned that the army was
revising its timetable for the return of low point men. That earlier schedule
had been announced by Marshall, who in a rare political misstep, had inti-
mated that soldiers with two years service would be discharged by March 20.
By late October, however, administration officials decided that they would
have to slow the pace of demobilization in order to maintain the commitments they deemed necessary for the achievement of postwar objectives. That
announcement, followed by press conference comments by Patterson that revealed his feeble grasp of the details of demobilization, infuriated soldiers and
sparked the protests. Patterson, who was touring Pacific installations at the
time, became the target of especially harsh criticism from the GIs who could
not fathom how the secretary could be so uninformed of their plight. "[I]f the
secretary of war doesn't know what's going on," read one complaint to the
president, "who the hell does?"[12]

On January 7, approximately 20,000 soldiers rallied in downtown Manila
to protest the announced slowdown. The orderly crowd booed lustily at the
mention of Patterson's name and listened approvingly as numerous speakers
questioned the continued presence of troops in the Philippines. Many of the
speeches were laced with complaints that officers were "getting almost all the
comforts and luxuries while 'sweating it out' overseas." But the GIs also
weighed in on matters of national policy. Most of the demonstration's orga-
nizers saw ulterior motives behind the slowdown. They began by noting that
the islands were not enemy territory in need of occupation. They also voiced
concern about a report in the regimental newspaper in which the division's

chief of staff was cited as saying that the 86th division would resume combat training to prepare for guerilla raids during the spring election campaign. The protestors objected to any American intervention in the Philippines and extended their complaints to include U.S. involvement in China and the Netherlands East Indies as well. In doing so, the homesick GIs leveled a broadside at the Truman administration's emerging postwar policy in Asia.[13]

As Patterson traveled across the Pacific, he encountered rallies and demonstrations at nearly every stop. President Truman issued a statement on January 8, in an effort to calm the situation. But more action was needed. Unaccustomed to such displays, commanding officers at some U.S. installations too freely characterized the protests as mutinies. For the most part, however, high-ranking army officers, including MacArthur, inclined toward more charitable interpretations. Meanwhile, reports of the protests triggered new inquiries on Capitol Hill into the demobilization program. In mid-January the newly appointed Chief of Staff Dwight D. Eisenhower addressed Congress on the problem. Eisenhower sought to calm the furor by stressing the already speedy rate of demobilization and reminding Congressmen of America's overseas obligations. Three days later, the general followed his testimony with a nationwide radio address. Ike's sterling reputation and reasonable demeanor were valuable assets in winning over the public and the soldiers. Even more helpful was his announcement that men with thirty months service would be home by April 30 and soldiers with two years service would return by June 30. The latter date amounted to a delay of three months from the one Marshall declared in October. But the soldiers were gratified to hear the army recommit itself to a firm timetable.

By the end of January, demobilization and protesting soldiers ceased to be front-page news. Administration officials welcomed the restoration of order, but they still had to deal with the inescapable reality of vanishing military power. Comparatively speaking, the new schedule slowed the pace of demobilization from a mad dash to a stately gallop. Assessments of this situation differed according to one's perspective. Occupation duties and plans for the maintenance of overseas bases meant that the United States would retain the largest peacetime force in its history. But the changing international circumstances and a new definition of national security that stressed the importance of forward basing and control of resources fed a growing sense of insecurity. In short, expanding American responsibilities

and dwindling forces left military officials feeling there were not enough resources to go around.

In this atmosphere, the political criticism voiced by the soldiers' spokesmen
was easily construed as Communist inspired. According to the army's official
history, the protesting GIs and their stateside kin had unwittingly found
themselves dancing "to the tune played by the Communists."[14] Some professional officers regarded the soldiers' complaints about serving Wall Street's interests or Yankee imperialism as telltale signs of Communist propaganda.

It would be reasonable to conclude that some of the demonstrators had
been involved in left-wing politics during the Depression and New Deal years.
But it is equally plausible that men in the ranks had absorbed the rhetoric of
Franklin Roosevelt's Four Freedoms and former vice-president Henry Wal-
lace's "Century of the Common Man" and applied it to the conditions they
found in Asia. Most Americans did not need to be indoctrinated to sympa-
thize with the underdog or colonial subject.

Of course, most of the protestors probably wanted nothing more than to
get home to their families, find a job, a house, and restart their lives. Many of
the demonstrators probably never publicly protested government policy again
in their lives. Indeed, they probably forgot that they ever had. But even at their
most apolitical, the GIs forcefully displayed an unwillingness to cooperate
with the Truman administration's developing policy in Asia.

Given the difficulty the United States faced in sustaining its military presence in the region, it is easy to understand why John Carter Vincent and James
Byrnes opposed unqualified support for Jiang's government. Both men had
sound reasons for doubting that American assistance would produce the stable friendly regime the United States desired. The Nationalists' inherent de-
fects and the Communists' latent strengths worked against a favorable
outcome. It also seemed clear that any escalation of American involvement in
China would be readily matched by the Soviets. American power on the mainland had reached its high-water mark in the first two months after Japan's surrender. Now, just as swiftly, the tide was running out. The draining away of the
American presence on the mainland persisted, each drop in the combat effectiveness of American troops readily apparent to anyone who could read the
newspapers.

In light of this situation, Vincent urged the administration to pressure
Jiang into negotiations and reforms, even if it meant withholding aid from the

Nationalists. But neither Truman nor his military advisers were prepared to take such drastic steps. None of these officials expected progress in China to be easy. But they believed too much would be lost if the United States quit China now. A top-secret portion of a new statement on United States–China policy starkly explained what was at stake. The success of American policy would require the continuation of American naval and ground forces in China for the foreseeable future. Those expenditures would be "minute" in comparison to those already made to restore the peace shattered by Japanese and German aggression. "They will be infinitesimal," according to the statement, "by comparison to a recurrence of global warfare in which new and terrible weapons that now exist would certainly be employed. The purpose of which the United States made a tremendous sacrifice of treasure and life must not be jeopardized."[15]

This was strong stuff. The Truman administration had quietly concluded that the failure to support a China friendly to the United States could lead to a new global war. American ground and naval forces in China were being called on to save the peace so recently won at enormous cost. The transformation in the assessment of China's importance was remarkable. During the summer of 1945 army strategists had floated the possibility that the United States might have to learn to accept the reality of a truncated China heavily influenced by a Soviet presence in the northeast. This controversial proposal never received much consideration. Less than a month after it was written, Japan's sudden collapse saved China and opened the country to large scale American support for the first time since 1942. The war had ended on a note of optimism for the American Army officers advising and training Chinese forces. The navy had steamed back to the China station for the first time since 1941. Surely this dramatic change in China's fortunes argued against any hasty abandonment of America's wartime objectives. Service interests provided an additional reason for continuing the American military presence in China. Bureaucratic politics were not sufficient cause for intervention. The Army-Navy rivalry did, however, push the two services forward while making any independent reassessment of China's strategic importance increasingly unattractive.

Much hinged on the Soviet Union's intentions. For this reason, one unstated purpose of Marshall's mission was to ascertain the extent of Russian support for the Communists. Without a doubt the Soviets were making Jiang's recovery of Manchuria difficult, but thus far they had refrained from giving Mao their full support. It appears that the arrival of the marines in China surprised and worried Stalin. When Marshall's mission was announced, Stalin urged Mao to join the negotiations lest the outbreak of civil war lead to even greater American involvement in China. In this respect, Patterson and Forrestal were correct in believing that an American show of force would deter the Soviets from meddling in China's internal problems. But Byrnes and Vincent were also correct when they predicted that the continuation of American military support would stiffen Jiang's resolve to destroy the Communists once and for all. If that happened and civil war erupted, the Truman administration would face a new round of decisions regarding the application of force on the Asian mainland.

NOTES

1. Quotations in this section are from Robert J. Donovan, *Conflict and Crisis: The Presidency of Harry S. Truman, 1945–1948* (New York: W. W. Norton, 1977), 111, 115, 125.

2. James Schnabel, *The Joint Chiefs of Staff and National Policy. Volume I: 1945–1947* (Wilmington, DE: Michael Glazier, Inc., 1979), 206; Jack Stokes Ballard, *The Shock of Peace: Military and Economic Demobilization in World War II* (Washington, DC: University Press of America, 1983), 89–90.

3. Walter Millis, ed., *The Forrestal Diaries* (New York: Viking Press, 1951), 143.

4. Odd Arne Westad, ed., *Brothers in Arms: The Rise and Fall of the Sino-Soviet Alliance, 1945–1963* (Stanford, CA: Woodrow Wilson Center Press, 1998), 7.

5. E. B. Sledge, *China Marine* (Tuscaloosa: University of Alabama Press, 2002), 40.

6. Gallicchio, *Cold War Begins in Asia*, 121, 133; Marc Gallicchio, "About Face: General Marshall's Plans for the Amalgamation of Communist and Nationalist Armies in China," in Larry Bland, ed., *George C. Marshall's Mediation Mission to China* (Lexington, VA: George C. Marshall Foundation, 1998), 392.

7. Lt. General John E. Hull to George C. Marshall, 8 December 1945, *FRUS 1945*, 7: 758–759.

8. Evans Fordyce Carlson, FBI File in the author's possession, obtained through the Freedom of Information Act.

9. Waldo Heinrichs to his parents, 28 August 1945, "Marking Time: Letters from Luzon, 1945–1946;" in Sledge, *China Marine*, 4.

10. Waldo Heinrichs to his parents, 12 November 1945, "Marking Time"; *Tandem Times* (341st Infantry regimental newspaper, Luzon), 8 November 1945, in possession of Waldo Heinrichs.

11. Mark Wilkinson, "A Shanghai Perspective on the Marshall Mission," Larry I. Bland, ed., *Marshall's Mediation Mission to China*, 333.

12. Jack Stokes Ballard, *The Shock of Peace: Military and Economic Demobilization in World War II* (Washington, DC: University Press of America, 1983), 98.

13. *New York Times*, 13 January 1946, 8, Waldo Heinrichs to his parents, 5 January 1946, "Marking Time"; *Tandem Times*, 3 January 1946.

14. John C. Sparrow, *History of Personnel Demobilization in the United States Army* (Washington, DC: Center of Military History, United States Army, 1951, facsimile edition 1994), 292–293.

15. "Top Secret Portions of U.S. Policy Toward China," copy in folder C-2 (4), Box 158, OP 30 (Operations) Naval Historical Center, Washington Naval Yard, Washington, DC.

5

Occupational Hazards

As Marshall began his mission to China, Secretary of State James Byrnes was heading for Moscow for a meeting with the foreign ministers of the Soviet Union and Great Britain. By excluding France and China, Byrnes hoped to turn the Moscow meeting, as much as possible, into direct negotiations with the Russians. Byrnes, it seems, also hoped that the more exclusive gathering would make it easier to conclude agreements based on principles of *realpolitik*. One of his main goals was to win Soviet agreement for an American-sponsored plan for the international control of atomic energy. Here Byrnes was persuaded by Soviet specialists in Washington who argued that little progress could be made with the Russians on other issues until he addressed their security concerns stemming from the American monopoly over atomic weapons. Byrnes hoped that the American plan would satisfy those concerns. But he was also prepared to accept only cosmetic changes in the Russian sponsored Bulgarian and Rumanian governments as a condition for signing peace treaties with those former Axis allies. East Asian issues also figured prominently on the agenda. In particular, the foreign ministers agreed to discuss Allied control of Japan, the Korean trusteeship, repatriation of Japanese in China, and the restoration of Manchuria to Nationalist control. The continuing Allied occupation of Iran rounded out the agenda. On this issue, Byrnes hoped to obtain Soviet guarantees that Russian troops would leave northern Iran by the previously agreed date of March 2, 1946.

As Byrnes embarked for Moscow he was largely unaware of the tenuous-
ness of his own position within the administration. Only recently, Truman
had voiced concerns about what he viewed as Byrnes's failure to clear public
statements with him. In fact, it appears that Truman had already asked Marshall to consider taking Byrnes's place after the general completed his mission
to China. Byrnes had also irritated Admiral Leahy, the president's representative to the JCS, by his willingness to cease aid to the Nationalists if they obstructed Marshall's mission. Key senators similarly raised concerns that the
plan for international control of atomic energy Byrnes was bringing to
Moscow amounted to a giveaway of America's hard won monopoly. Truman
remained uncertain about the best course of action toward the Russians.
Many around the president had already concluded that the Russians needed
to adhere to their wartime agreements, as interpreted by the Americans. They
wanted to see Byrnes make a stand on principle rather than compromise.

Of course Byrnes did not plan to relinquish anything he thought the Americans could hold. But he saw little advantage in insisting on conditions over
which the Americans had little power. In the end, the conference yielded a traditional great power accord that addressed most of the issues on Byrnes's list.
The Russians complained about the marines in China, but did not insist on
their immediate removal. Stalin also settled for the creation of a toothless Allied Control Council to advise MacArthur in Tokyo. Regarding Korea, the Soviets and Americans agreed to create a joint commission for the purpose of
forming a provisional government comprised of different groups in Korea.
The entire process would be supervised by a four-power trusteeship which
would last for no more than five years. Concerning Europe, the Russians were
less flexible. They brushed aside British and American complaints about the
Bulgarian and Rumanian regimes and refused to discuss the Iranian situation.
Byrnes settled for minor adjustments in the governments of the two former
German satellites and agreed to omit Iran from the final communiqué. Most
significantly, as far as Byrnes was concerned, the foreign ministers agreed to
the American proposal on atomic energy with only minor changes. As one
historian has summed up the final communiqué, "Byrnes traded the Russians
token concessions in Japan for token concessions in the Balkans, and American troops stayed in China while Soviet troops remained in Iran."[1]

Unfortunately for Byrnes, his detractors in Washington viewed the outcome of the conference as a setback for the United States. Byrnes, who re-

turned home convinced he had saved the alliance, was accused of "loitering around Munich" as Republican Senator Arthur Vandenberg put it. Admiral Leahy likewise branded the communiqué an "appeasement document." Truman at first seemed satisfied by Byrnes's explanation of the agreements but his opposition grew over the next several days. The drumbeat of criticism coming from Byrnes's opponents fed the president's uneasiness about his secretary. But the final break came in early January when Truman learned that Byrnes had withheld from him a highly critical report on the Soviet backed governments in Rumania and Bulgaria. Truman disavowed Byrnes's handiwork in a sharply worded "Dear Jim" letter to his former senate colleague. Soviet misconduct put the president in an uncompromising mood. Truman insisted that the United States should demand free elections in Rumania and Bulgaria and that the Red Army should leave Iran in accordance with its promises. Regarding Asia, Truman wrote that "[W]e should maintain complete control in Japan. . . . We should rehabilitate China and create a strong central government there. We should do the same in Korea."[2]

Although Byrnes's handling of Asian matters seemed beyond reproach, Truman's strongly worded reaffirmation of American policy implied a criticism of the secretary. More important, it also indicated that Truman held the Soviets accountable for much of the turmoil in the region. In the aftermath of the war, Truman had come to regard Soviet activities in Asia as part of a larger pattern of aggression, subversion, and opportunism originating in Eastern Europe and extending through the Middle East to the Korean peninsula. Five months after Japan's surrender, the United States maintained control over Japan, but Korea remained divided and China lurched toward civil war. Frustration over these conditions had given way to a growing feeling within the administration that the Soviet Union and its fellow travelers in the United States were responsible for thwarting American policy. Truman reflected this trend in mid-January when he intemperately denounced critics of his China policy as "those people in this country who are more loyal to the Russian government than they are to their own."[3]

Historians have tended to view Truman's "Dear Jim" letter as the president's declaration of Cold War against the Soviet Union. But his reckless accusations about those who criticized American intervention in China were an equally significant milestone in the transformation of Truman's thinking. By impugning the loyalty of his critics, Truman had sunk to the level of those around him who saw "pinkies" sabotaging American policy in Asia. Such allegations would become a common feature of Cold War rhetoric in the years to come. Indeed, Truman's reaction to events in Asia exhibited many of the features that characterized American foreign policy in the Cold War. The president and his advisers minimized local causes for the upheaval in Asia and all too readily attributed those convulsions to the machinations of the Soviet Union and its agents. In this atmosphere, negotiation was taken as a sign of weakness, or worse. It was one thing, however, to fume about critics of American policy and insist on tougher action. It was altogether more difficult, insofar as Asia was concerned, to formulate a coherent strategy to translate those impulses into action.

"YOU CAN DO ANYTHING WITH A BAYONET EXCEPT SIT ON IT"

By early 1946, American officials had reason to agree with Napoleon regarding the shortcomings of the bayonet. After nearly four years of arduous campaigning, American military forces had come to rest in garrisons spread across the western shores of the Pacific. Having achieved a welcome peace soldiers and sailors let down their guard and eased into the less strenuous routines of occupation duty. As we have seen, many of the veterans sought nothing so much as a speedy exit from military service. New enlistees and conscripts derisively referred to as "high school commandos," trickled into the overseas posts in numbers too small to maintain the occupation forces at full strength. The result was a steady erosion of the combat effectiveness of American forces in East Asia at a time when the presence of those forces was intended to demonstrate the Truman administration's resolve.

In Korea, the army's XXIV Corps slipped from three to two divisions, both of them under their wartime complement of troops. Over the next two years the numbers fluctuated as veterans returned home and eighteen-month enlistees took their places. Despite occasional increases in manpower, the trend was steadily downward. Hodge entered Korea in September with 77,500 officers and enlisted men. By October 1946, the strength of the XXIV Corps, redesignated United States Army Forces in Korea (USAFIK), fell to less than 36,500. The numbers rose again briefly but by 1947 they were headed down once more. Occupation forces in Japan likewise dwindled from a high of 250,000 in early 1946 to 83,000 by the outbreak of the Korean War in June

1950. Well before then, however, the Eighth Army's commander was warning that his force had become nothing more than a "supply organization with no combat soldiers, just a cadre."[4]

The restless GIs in the Philippines, equally ill prepared for combat, were barely able to carry out the minimal duties assigned to them. As noted earlier, soldiers in the 86th Division complained that they were being kept in the islands to help ensure the victory of America's chosen candidate in the upcoming presidential elections. Those suspicions seemed borne out when in February, a poorly equipped battalion of the 86th, lacking ammunition, antitank weapons, and machine guns, motored through northern Luzon for what was supposed to be a training exercise. Most of the men inferred, however, that their real mission was to demonstrate the ability of the army to move freely about Luzon for the purpose of maintaining order on the eve of election. Toward the end of the journey the unit camped for several days in the vicinity of a tribe of Negritos. The soldiers watched with admiration as the tribesman displayed their prowess with bow and arrow all the while wondering "who was intimidating whom."[5]

By mid-1946, the marines of the Third Amphibious Corps, despite their proximity to the skirmishing between Communists and Nationalists, were also losing their fighting trim. Attrition through the departure of high point men posed a constant challenge for the small detachments "strung out along the railroad like beads on a string." But the boredom of guard duty and the anomalous experience of being a spectator at someone else's fight brought the marines' guard down and dulled their instincts and discipline. In July, troopers guarding a bridge at Liu-Shou-Ying were captured by Communists after the marines defied orders and left their compound in search of ice to restock their beer cooler. The attempted rescue of the negligent marines was hampered by the need to whip the pursuit force into shape. Their commander would have preferred weeks for that task but given the emergency he settled for two days of conditioning hikes. With only a minimal tune up, the grossly understrength battalion of 250 men confirmed their commander's doubts about their stamina. Early into the pursuit the "battalion" was further reduced when a staff officer was ordered to take the "worst cases" back to their temporary base. Several days into the pursuit, the Communists spared the marines further aggravation by returning the captured troopers with a warning that they should keep out of "liberated areas."[6]

When they were not pressed into action, the remaining low point men and recent draftees and volunteers who comprised the occupation forces tried to make the best of the often less than desirable living conditions. Housing and recreational facilities were a glaring problem in Korea and Okinawa, both places where the future and duration of the American presence remained in doubt. In Korea, the declining morale of the occupation forces was directly attributable to what one USAFIK unit history candidly described as "rugged" living conditions. Existing Japanese army housing was inadequate, often lacking reliable plumbing, heating, and water. Facilities for dependents were almost nonexistent. Recreational facilities of the type American soldiers were used to—athletic fields, tennis courts, gyms, golf courses, and pools—were also scarce. Eventually, these and other amenities, including nearly one hundred movie theaters, seventy-two Post Exchanges (PX), and even several ice cream plants were constructed for use by the soldiers.[7]

For nearly two years after the war, Okinawa remained in administrative limbo. Military government marked time in an atmosphere of administrative uncertainty and neglect. As the armed services directed their scarce resources and talent elsewhere, the island's inhabitants endured an occupation that seemed unconcerned by the enormous destruction and dislocation caused by the war's last battle. That indifference extended to the American enlisted military personnel whose misfortune it was to be assigned to occupation duty there. Officers in the military government were convinced that they received the army's cast-offs. MacArthur reinforced that impression when he sought to punish two writers for *Stars and Stripes* by banishing them to Okinawa. As late as 1949, an army inspector categorized living conditions, recreational facilities, and training as well below army standards. The chairman of the JCS more bluntly referred to dependent housing on Okinawa as "slums."[8]

Fraternization, especially in the form of sexual encounters between GIs and females in the local population produced its own set of difficulties. Occupation forces throughout the region suffered from alarmingly high rates of venereal disease. Korea, with an infection rate of 93 men per thousand boasted the lowest rate in the Far East Command. Following liberation, the venereal disease rate in the Philippines shot up an astounding 2,000 percent. In Japan, the Eighth Army reached an infection rate of 27 percent in February 1946 before strenuous efforts by military authorities brought the rate down to a more tolerable 50 per thousand in combat units. As one historian has noted, "apparently American troops had brought more than goodwill and freedom with them to Japan." [9]

American officials sought to combat the rise in infection through various means, including educational campaigns and improving recreational opportunities for GIs away from local red light districts. Regulating or licensing brothels was another, less publicized, means of dealing with the problem. Although, the *New York Times* reported that on Okinawa the rule against fraternization was strictly enforced, unit commanders surreptitiously arranged trips for their men to local red light districts. On Japan proper, the Supreme Commander Allied Powers (SCAP) initially cooperated with the Japanese-run Recreation and Amusement Association (RAA), a government subsidized agency that recruited women quite literally to sacrifice their honor in order to keep the occupation forces from preying on the larger female population. The occupation authorities and the Japanese government agreed to this exercise in sexual accommodation for different reasons. Japanese officials' fear that the occupation soldiers would engage in an orgy of rape and plunder owed much to their knowledge of how Japanese soldiers had behaved overseas in conquered areas. American officials were willing to endorse the use of RAA facilities, even though they knew that at least some of the women had been coerced into service, primarily because they thought the licensed houses would reduce the risk of venereal disease. When venereal disease rates continued to climb, MacArthur ended the social experiment by outlawing prostitution in Japan. [10]

Fraternization continued, however, with implications for Japanese and American societies that few of the authorities would have anticipated in August 1945. The presence of several hundred thousand astonishingly wealthy GIs contributed to a relatively new phenomenon in Japanese society, the freelance streetwalker, universally known as the *panpan*. Before the war, young women entered brothels under contractual obligation to support their families. Only a small number of the most desperate prostitutes worked the streets. During the occupation the number of *panpan* rose dramatically. Depending on one's perspective the emergence of the independent *panpan* could be seen as a disturbing sign of social breakdown or an exhilarating harbinger of personal liberation. The *panpan* no longer fit the stereotype of destitute women driven to the streets. Rather, surveys indicated that many cited reasons other than family hardship for their choice of profession. Some shapers of Japanese popular culture glamorized the image of the alluring westernized prostitutes as women who had broken free of the shackles of traditional Japanese society. But others viewed the *panpan* and her uncouth public displays as a further humiliation to be endured during the occupation. Sadly, but not surprisingly, the offspring of these sexual encounters between American and Japanese were usually abandoned by their transient fathers and treated as pariahs in Japan.

MacArthur also found fault with the promiscuous behavior of what he termed "Japanese women of immoral character." Nevertheless, SCAP refused to outlaw fraternization for the simple reason that MacArthur thought it could not be enforced. Somewhat ingenuously, given the continued prevalence of the *panpan*, the General insisted that most of the men under his command were seeking more innocent contacts with Japanese women. SCAP took a more progressive step in 1947 when the occupation authorities legalized marriages between Americans and Japanese. That decision led to a sharp increase in interracial marriages at a time when most states in the United States refused to recognize such unions.[11]

"AMBASSADORS OF ILL WILL"

In their efforts to maintain their troops in a state of readiness, American commanders throughout Asia battled boredom, substandard living conditions, and venereal disease at rates reaching epidemic proportions. Crime in all forms, including rape, robbery, assault, and generally reckless behavior, provided an additional challenge for officers seeking to maintain good order among their men. When GIs engaged in criminal or antisocial activity, however, it also undermined American efforts to win the support of local populations and in some instances complicated or seriously hindered the achievement of policy objectives.

One of the most common forms of outrages perpetrated by GIs involved what historian John Fairbank described as the problems arising from the convergence of "wine, women, and jeeps." In Manila, Americans were involved in 50 percent of the accidents resulting in fatalities despite owning only 20 percent of the automobiles. Complaints about GIs' contempt for speed limits and other traffic laws were common. The problem became so acute that President Manuel Roxas lodged a formal complaint with the U.S. embassy. Longtime American residents commonly referred to the obstreperous GIs as "ambassadors of ill will." Civilian observers, as well as some of the army's officers blamed the poor training given to the "juvenile rabble" that was being sent out to replace the returning veterans. Remarking on the unkempt appearance and slovenly behavior of the "smart aleck kids" who filled the ranks, one journalist claimed he spent twenty days in Manila without seeing an enlisted man salute an officer. In defending their young recruits against these criticisms, their commanding officers acknowledged that the soldiers lacked adequate training, but they insisted that the prevalence of malefactors among the troops was no greater than one would find anywhere groups of Americans gathered. Given the rather large number of men gathered in the islands, however, Filipinos might not have found that a reassuring thought.[12]

In Japan, Eighth Army commander Lieutenant General Robert Eichelberger also blamed "troops in their teens" for widespread misconduct including rape, assault, housebreaking, and thievery. Even American civilians felt threatened. Eichelberger warned that GI lawlessness had gotten so bad that it was threatening the mission of the occupation. Although statistics were difficult to come by because of SCAP censorship, reporters cited one instance in which an unspecified combat unit brought more than one hundred of its new recruits before courts martial in a single month for having committed crimes against Japanese. Indulging in some instant psychological analysis, journalists speculated that the draftee-delinquents were roughing up Japanese as a way to compensate for their own lack of combat experience. Whatever the cause, most observers agreed that the occupation troops were a poor substitute for the splendid soldiers who were leaving the army in droves.[13]

By 1946 it seemed that American troops all over Asia were behaving deplorably. A crime spree in March left General Hodge in a state of disbelief that Americans would prey on helpless Koreans who looked to the United States for assistance. Hodge attributed the crimes to "a few outlaws and thugs" among the troops, but like Eichelberger, he worried that the miscreants were "blocking our ability to accomplish our mission as well as destroying the prestige of America in the Orient."[14]

China, particularly Shanghai, may have been the area where American rowdiness had the potential to do the greatest harm to American policy. As General Marshall began his sensitive mission as mediator, the inhabitants of Shanghai were losing their patience with the raucous GIs who streamed into the city after V-J Day. Some of those soldiers relocated to Shanghai from Chungking after General Wedemeyer moved his headquarters to the once bustling port city. Many others came to sample the pleasures Shanghai had to offer anyone with money. According to one unit history, "Examples of the laxness that was Shanghai can be quoted almost endlessly. So many men AWOL from other commands were living in Shanghai that it became necessary to issue identification cards to those military persons authorized to be there."[15] To the inhabitants of Shanghai it must have seemed that every American owned a jeep. By April there were 1,600 registered U.S. vehicles in the city burning 7,500 gallons of gasoline a day. The Americans and their ever-present jeeps quickly got into trouble with the city's residents. Between September 1945 and the start of the new year American drivers were involved in over 400 traffic accidents. Even when out of their vehicles, Americans were capable of producing considerable mayhem. As historian Mark Wilkinson noted, "Servicemen brawled in cafes, beat up Chinese laborers, crashed into rickshaws, assaulted Chinese women, and fought with local police."

Like their counterparts elsewhere in Asia, China theater commanders recognized the seriousness of the problem and sought ways to bring their men under control. They assigned military police to patrol in tandem with Chinese police, canceled shore leave for American sailors, and, as mentioned above, tried to keep unauthorized personnel from loitering in the city. Military intelligence reports underscored the potential harm being done by noting a rise in anti-American feeling among Chinese regardless of political affiliation. In March, as if to underscore that point, a newspaper run by the Ministry of Information called for someone to rein in the disorderly GIs. Staff officers in Shanghai also detected a troubling change in the attitude of the city's residents. According to the unit history cited above, Chinese women dating Americans were abused by other Chinese and crowds picked fights with GIs while Chinese police looked on. "We are in charge now," screamed Chinese onlookers, "We can run our own country—you get out!"[16]

The misbehavior of American troops, which was not confined to Shanghai, remained a sore point in Chinese-American relations for most of Marshall's stay in China. In October, Dr. Chang Tang-sun of Peiping's Yengching University and a chairman of the liberal Democratic League, issued a lengthy complaint against the U.S. presence in China, much of which centered on what he termed "the practice of wanton deeds," by American servicemen. Chang's ultimate goal was to get the Americans to cease their support for Jiang Jieshi's undemocratic government. Reducing the American presence would be an important step toward achieving that objective. In making the case for the American withdrawal Chang highlighted the misdeeds of the servicemen roaming Beijing's streets. "As we know perfectly well," Chang declared, "they have given themselves over to drunkenness, gambling, seeking women, smuggling, illegal sale of government properties, robbery, manhandling, killing through reckless driving, insulting and violating Chinese women and what not."

Lieutenant General Alvan Gillem, the ranking American officer in Peiping, defended his men against Chang's sweeping accusations. In doing so, however, he acknowledged that GI discipline had been bad, although the demobilization of most of the servicemen in China had resolved that problem. Gillem also seemed to concede Chang's point when he noted that he expected complaints to diminish as army, marine, and Chinese police began patrolling the city's streets together. According to the press account of this episode, the new policing system served a dual purpose: it would minimize problems stemming from the language barrier while also heading off the potential for bad feeling between the two branches of the American armed forces.[17]

Gillem had his hands full. In addition to providing support for Marshall's mediation effort, he had to clamp down on unruly GIs while making sure that the ever-present rivalry between the army and the navy (marines) did not spill out onto the city's streets and provide ammunition for opponents of the continuing American presence in China.

Apart from the unusual accusation that American GIs were guilty of committing "what not," Chang's complaints against the Americans were similar to charges being made against American troops across Asia. The situation in China was particularly sensitive, but American commanders in Japan, Korea, and the Philippines were similarly vexed by the indiscipline of their men. As the American commanders indicated, their goal was to win the confidence of the peoples under their control, not intimidate them into sullen submission. This desire to win the hearts and minds of the people of Asia, to borrow an expression from a later era, was a long-standing ambition rooted in America's image of itself. But short-term policy imperatives reinforced such an approach. Given the ongoing reduction in American forces, the success of American policy depended on local support throughout the region.

By early 1946, American commanders in the region had reason to fear that they might lose that support. When asked to explain the reasons for these developments, they pointed to the replacement of experienced enlisted men and noncommissioned officers with poorly trained and motivated teenagers as the main source of the problem. Given enough time, better training, and more resources, those problems were treatable. In the spring of 1946, however, it was not clear if enough time remained to rectify the situation.

HOLDING THE LINE: CONSIDERATIONS OF RACE IN MILITARY POLICY

When American officers addressed the problem of GI misconduct in private communications, they often singled out African American soldiers as the leading culprits. Black soldiers were more likely to be arrested and face courts martial than whites. Given the wide discretion wielded by local commanders, however, it also appears that black offenders were more likely to be held to the letter of the law than white soldiers. White officers pointed to the disproportionately high crime rate among black soldiers as evidence of their unfitness for military life. They ignored the corrosive effects of segregation and daily discrimination on the morale and discipline of black troops and tended to see black misconduct as a sign of racial inferiority, which, they argued, justified the system of segregation.

For the most part, the men in charge of the armed forces at the end of World War II remained at ease with their prejudices. During the war, notably during the desperate moments in the Battle of the Bulge, the army yielded slightly, and then only grudgingly, to necessity. Small units of black soldiers were absorbed whole (as opposed to integrated) into larger white combat commands. When the war ended those experiments did also. Jim Crow segregation had survived World War II intact despite increasing criticism regarding the inefficiencies inherent in the system.

Toward the end of the war, Assistant Secretary of War John McCloy initiated a comprehensive study to address what he saw as the glaring inadequacies in the army's use of manpower. Completed under the supervision of Lieutenant General Gillem in November 1945, shortly before he assumed his position in China, the report recommended an approach described by one historian as "modified segregation." The Gillem Board called for an enlistment quota of 10 percent to reflect the percentage of African Americans in the national population, increased opportunities for black enlisted men, noncommissioned officers, and officers, and a continuation of the experiments in limited integration conducted toward the end of the war. If the army accepted this last recommendation it would eliminate large division-size organizations of all black troops in favor of smaller, but still all black, units attached to larger white commands. Taken in its entirety the Gillem report was viewed by most observers at the time as a step forward in creating an integrated army. But the Gillem Board also made it clear that full integration remained a long way off.

For his part, McCloy criticized the report for accommodating segregation instead of challenging it. He also complained that the 10 percent quota would exclude qualified men from service at a time when the army was badly in need of recruits. Nevertheless, McCloy accepted the report's conclusions as the best he could hope for under the circumstances. Gillem's recommendations became army policy in April 1946, but they promptly encountered opposition from American commanders. The new policy came at a time when the percentage of black troops in the army was increasing owing to the demobilization of white troops and a disproportionately high rate of black enlistment and re-enlistment. As a consequence of this demographic reality, the general staff had already mandated that black soldiers would comprise 15 percent, as opposed to the previous 10 percent, of overseas commands.

These changes were not welcomed in the field. For the next several years, American officers continued to treat black units as a burden to be endured if it could not be avoided altogether. Officers frequently sought to remove black units from their jurisdiction by denigrating their fitness for service or accusing them of committing a disproportionate share of the crimes against local inhabitants. They were also quick to protest whenever it appeared that the percentage of black troops under their command threatened to climb above the prescribed 15 percent. Moreover, officers resisted even the Gillem Board's modest recommendation for assigning small black units to larger white ones. Instead, officers preferred to designate black units as "attached" rather than "assigned" units, an administrative arrangement that confirmed their status as separate and inferior units.

After the war, the continued discrimination against black troops in the Pacific and Japan seemed especially pernicious in light of the prominent role race had played in the war. Japan had presented itself to colonial East Asia as the champion of the darker races and the foe of white imperialism. Early in the war that message had seemed so potent that Military Intelligence, the Office of Naval Intelligence, and the Federal Bureau of Investigation had conducted surveillance of African American groups to make sure they did not succumb to Japan's propaganda. At the same time, civil rights leaders had argued that America would have to jettison its racial prejudices if the United States hoped to blunt Japan's message and win the support of Asia's nonwhite peoples. American military planners appeared to accept at least part of that argument. As the war came to an end, the Joint Chiefs and SWNCC agreed that "Orientals" should be included in the occupation forces to demonstrate that a multiracial alliance had opposed Japan's bid for leadership of Asia's nonwhite peoples.[18]

The JCS saw little reason, however, to alter how they treated nonwhite servicemen under their command. Black leaders had insisted that the war made the American dilemma an international problem. The achievement of racial equality, they argued, had become vital to the defense of the nation. American officers not only rejected that argument, they stood it on its head. As American forces took up their stations in East Asia and the Pacific, their commanders insisted that the presence of African American servicemen in the occupation forces endangered the success of American postwar policies. American theater commanders brushed aside Washington's attempts to improve the status of black GIs and argued instead that one way to foster harmonious relations with the region's peoples would be by minimizing the presence of black troops in the occupations.

Major General James Christiansen, Acting Commanding General of U.S. Army Forces Western Pacific, claimed that Filipinos blamed African American troops for most of the crimes committed by Americans. Citing concern for future American base rights on the islands, Christiansen urged a reduction in the number of black GIs so as to ensure good relations with the Philippine Republic. Similarly, Major General Whitney Griswold resisted the assignment of black units to the Marianas by arguing that the residents objected to the introduction of black GIs into the islands. Officers on Okinawa likewise blamed African Americans for the majority of crimes committed against islanders. According to these officers, reductions in the number of black soldiers on the island would solve the problem of crime on the island.[19]

Black soldiers were not considered a problem in China for the simple reason that they were all but excluded from the theater by agreements made during the war. Jiang initiated the ban in anticipation of the arrival of black engineer battalions who were building a road through northern Burma to connect Ledo, India with Kunming in western China. Albert Wedemeyer, the Commanding General of U.S. Forces China Theater and chief of staff to the

Generalissimo, thought the ban would be unworkable given that the African Americans comprised 60 percent of the of the troops building the road. Nevertheless, he accepted the restriction while cautioning Jiang to keep the delicate matter out of the press. That proved difficult. Reporters soon peppered American and Chinese officials with questions about a rumored ban on black troops. The Americans headed off any immediate controversy by quickly adding some black drivers to the first convoy entering Kunming.

It also became evident that the token inclusion of black drivers would not suffice. Black troops would be needed to continue working on the road and its adjoining pipeline inside China. As Wedemeyer later explained, there were "so many service elements in the India-Burma Theater, I am compelled to accept them." Jiang responded by agreeing to allow black soldiers into China as far west as Kunming. If necessity dictated, they could be used farther east. In relaying those instructions to his subordinates, Wedemeyer added a stipulation that the soldiers not be permitted to enter Kunming. This proscription was added because Wedemeyer worried that the black GIs would get into trouble in the city. Resorting to stereotypes, Major General Gilbert X. Cheves, the head of the Service of Supply in the theater, put the matter more bluntly. "Kunming is nothing; a rotten town," Cheves confided to reporters in an off-the-record meeting. "In these dark streets if fights were to start a colored man would start to cut; records show that he is a good cutting man," Cheves explained.[20]

The restrictions remained in place after Japan's surrender. In late August, Wedemeyer's headquarters advised General MacArthur against deploying a port company comprised of black troops in China. Wedemeyer's representative acknowledged that the request placed an additional burden on MacArthur's overworked staff, but he insisted that the prohibition imposed by Jiang was part of a "very firm policy." Six months later, Wedemeyer continued to block the use of black soldiers in China on the grounds that Jiang opposed their presence in China. According to Wedemeyer, Jiang worried that the Communists would denounce the Americans for replacing white troops with black soldiers in order to achieve their imperial ambitions. It is not clear, however, why Jiang or Wedemeyer thought that the introduction of black troops into the theater would be any more provocative than the well-documented use of Japanese troops. In light of what we know about Wedemeyer's previous disposition regarding African American soldiers, it seems that the postwar proscription of black troops from the theater was as much his decision as Jiang's. As we have seen, during the war the Generalissimo had been willing to ease restrictions on the use of black troops in China as conditions determined. It appears, however, that Wedemeyer preferred to interpret the ban as unequivocal in order to limit the use of African American GIs in China. Like his colleagues elsewhere in the Asia Pacific region, Wedemeyer found it convenient to argue that the presence of black soldiers in his theater ran counter to the wishes of his hosts.[21]

In contrast to China, black soldiers entered Japan with their white counterparts. GIs entering Japan were treated to an instructional film advising them that "We can prove that most Americans do believe in a fair break for everybody regardless of race, or creed, or color."[22] In reality, black units in Japan encountered discrimination similar to that which they faced at home in the areas of housing, recreation, assignments, and promotions. Historians have also concluded that black GIs in Japan, as elsewhere, were unfairly blamed for a disproportionate number of crimes and punished more harshly than their white comrades. Although SCAP paid lip service to the ideal of equality, the statements and actions of its officers made it clear that they considered the presence of black troops a nuisance to be endured. General Eichelberger reflexively blamed black soldiers for the low morale of the Eighth Army and attributed interracial skirmishes between GIs to black soldiers who "liked to get out at night in the Mohammedan heaven furnished by some millions of Japanese girls." MacArthur's staff officers also seemed to have had difficulty thinking of black soldiers as contributing members of the same army. In official documents dealing with the allocation of black GIs in the theater MacArthur's men repeatedly referred to the "problem" under the subject heading "shipments of Negroes." For his part, MacArthur never voiced any concern about the treatment of black soldiers under his command until the Korean War, at which time civil rights advocates and inquiring journalists prompted him belatedly to profess his devotion to a color-blind army.[23]

The persistence of discrimination in the armed forces in the aftermath of Japan's surrender is, of course, well known. It is surprising, however, that despite the importance that American officers placed on high morale and unit cohesion, few of them were willing to concede that segregation and routine discrimination would erode the effectiveness of the black troops under their command. Occasionally some officers recognized the deeper sources of the problems and sought creative remedies. In Europe, General Clarence Huebner instituted training and educational programs that raised the morale and standardized test scores of black soldiers under his command. As the army's official history notes, however, "The tragedy was that the education program was never applied throughout the army, not even in the Far East or United States where far more black soldiers were stationed than in Europe."[24]

The adherence to Jim Crow practices by U.S. commanders in East Asia is important for our purposes for what it tells us about the use of American forces to implement national policy. The resistance of theater commanders to the Gillem Board's recommendations and the quotas mandated by the War Department showed that policies emanating from Washington were subject to revision and outright rejection in the field. Domestic pressure and overseas protests had accelerated the pace of demobilization beyond what the Pentagon thought conducive to the tasks assigned to the armed forces. Resistance to racial quotas and the Gillem reforms had further thwarted Washington's plans for the efficient use of personnel.

The persistence of discrimination within the armed forces owed much to the reflexive desire of American commanders to maintain the status quo. The dire circumstances that had led to experimental integration in the war against Germany had passed. Now that the threat to national security had been overcome there did not appear to be any need to experiment further with race reform in the military. Much to the consternation of American military officers, that same sense of receding danger fueled the broader public's insistence on the rapid demobilization of the armed forces. Throughout the region the transition from war to something approximating peace played havoc with the discipline and morale of the remaining occupation forces. The sudden collapse of Japanese resistance had left thousands of soldiers on the Philippines who were no longer needed for invasion or occupation. As they waited impatiently for their ship to come in, they protested and wrote their congressmen. Their young replacements got into jeeps and then into trouble. The young draftees who replaced veterans in Japan and Korea exhibited a similar penchant for misconduct. The ad hoc nature of the decisions that had placed Americans ashore in Korea and China added to the confusion. Jurisdictional quarrels and unanswered questions about the future disposition of territory, most notably the battered island of Okinawa, prolonged the misery of occupiers and occupied alike.

The mood was one of drift and uncertainty. Across the region the entire military enterprise seemed improvised and lacking definition. Within the Truman administration, wariness and a hardening of attitudes toward the Soviet Union and their suspected Communist allies was more of an inclination than a policy. The boundaries of American interest and the purposes to which armed forces could be put became the subject of debate. Over the next several months limits were explored and considered as policy makers looked to see how regional concerns meshed with global imperatives. Gradually inclination gave way to policy.

NOTES

1. Quoted in Patricia Dawson Ward, *The Threat of Peace: James F. Byrnes and the Council of Foreign Ministers, 1945–1946* (Kent: Kent State University Press, 1979), 76–77. This discussion of the Moscow conference also relies on Marc S. Gallicchio, *The Cold War Begins in Asia: American East Asian Policy and the Fall of the Japanese Empire* (New York: Columbia University Press, 1988), 128–135; Arnold Offner, *Another Such Victory: President Truman and the Cold War, 1945–1953* (Stanford, CA: Standford University Press, 2002), 116–124; and Melvyn Leffler, *A Preponderance of Power: National Security, the Truman Administration, and the Cold War* (Stanford, CA: Stanford University Press, 1992), 4–49.

2. Robert Ferrell, ed. *Off the Record: The Private Papers of Harry S. Truman* (New York: Penguin, 1980), 78–80.

3. Truman to Congressman Hugh DeLacy, 12 January 1946 and DeLacy to Truman, 13 February 1946, China-1946, President's Subject File, Harry S. Truman Papers, Harry S. Truman Library, Independence, Missouri.

4. D. Clayton James, *The Years of MacArthur: Volume III, 1945–1964* (Boston: Houghton Mifflin, 1985), 84.

5. Waldo Heinrichs, 28 August 1945, "Marking Time: Letters from Luzon, 1945–1946"; Sledge, *China Marine*, 28.

6. Henry Aplington, II, *Sunset in the East: A North China Memoir, 1945–1947*, unpublished manuscript, 64–67.

7. United States Army Forces in Korea, XXIV Corps, G-2 Historical Section, "Record Regarding the Okinawa Campaign, U.S. Military Government in Korea . . . ," RG 544 Records of the GHQ, Far East Command, Supreme Commander Allied Powers, and the United Nations Command, MMRB, NA, College Park, MD; James I. Matray, *The Reluctant Crusade: American Foreign Policy in Korea, 1941–1950* (Honolulu: University of Hawaii Press, 1985), 53.

8. The writers were suspected of Communist affiliations. Their reassignment to Okinawa drew protests from the newspaper's staff since the island was widely recognized as a "less desirable" assignment. The two men eventually were sent to

Yokohama. "MacArthur Backs Ouster of GI Writers," 2 March 1946, *New York Times*; Nicholas Evans Sarantakes, *Keystone: The American Occupation of Okinawa and U.S.–Japanese Relations* (College Station: Texas A&M University, 2000), 39.

9. United States Army Forces in Korea, "Record Regarding the Okinawa Campaign, U.S. Military Government in Korea . . ."; Holly Sanders, "Prostitution and Indentured Servitude in Modern Japan," Ph.D. dissertation, Princeton University, 2005.

10. "Uncomfortable truth: U.S. troops ignored sex slave atrocity, used Japanese-run brothels," 26 April 2007, *Mainichi Daily News*; John W. Dower, *Embracing Defeat: Japan in the Wake of World War II* (New York: W. W. Norton & Co., 1999), 122–132; John Hunter Boyle, *Modern Japan: The American Nexus* (Fort Worth, TX: Harcourt Brace Jovanovich, 1993), 308–309; Sanders, "Prostitution and Indentured Servitude in Modern Japan."

11. James, *Years of MacArthur*, III, 285–287.

12. "U.S. Manila Forces Held Slur on Army," 20 October 1946, *New York Times*; "Aged Filipino Beaten," and "Manila Generals Reply to Criticism, 30 October 1946, *New York Times*; John King Fairbank, *The United States and China*, 3rd edition (Cambridge, MA: Harvard University Press, 1971), 306; Nick Cullather, *Illusions of Influence: The Political Economy of United States-Philippines Relations, 1942–1960* (Stanford, CA: Stanford University Press, 1994), 49; Violet Elizabeth Wurfel, "American Implementation of Philippine Independence." Ph.D. dissertation, University of Virginia, 1951, 445–448.

13. "Curb on GI Crimes Ordered in Japan," 14 July 1946, *New York Times*; James, *Years of MacArthur*, III, 286.

14. "Soldiers Upbraided for Crimes in Korea," 5 March 1946, *New York Times*.

15. McNeil Folder, Box 8, Alvan Gillem Papers, Military History Institute, Carlisle, Pennsylvania.

16. This discussion of Shanghai is taken from Mark Wilkinson, "A Shanghai Perspective on the Marshall Mission," in Larry I. Bland, ed., *George C. Marshall's Mediation Mission to China, December 1945–January 1947* (Lexington, VA: George C. Marshall Foundation, 1998), 332–335.

17. Although he was a member of the Third Way Group, the so-called middle of the roaders, Chang was moving toward support for the Chinese Communist Party at this time. Edmund S. K. Fung, "Socialism, Capitalism, and Democracy in

Republican China: The Political Thought of Zhang Dongsun," *Modern China* (Fall 2002), 399–431; "Much China Crime Laid to Our Troops," 13 October 1946, *New York Times.*

18. Yukiko Koshiro, *Trans-Pacific Racisms and the U.S. Occupation of Japan* (New York, 1999), 20–21.

19. Hal M. Friedman, *Creating an American Lake: United States Imperialism and Strategic Security in the Pacific Basin, 1945–1947* (Westport, CT: Greenwood Press, 2001), 127–134; Sarantakes, *Keystone: The American Occupation of Okinawa and U.S.-Japanese Relations,* 37–38.

20. Conference, Newspaper Correspondents—Brooks and Bolden, 10 February 1945, Afro-American Soldiers file, 3-G, Commanding General U.S. Forces China Theater, Wedemeyer Papers; John D. Stevens "Black Correspondents of World War II Cover the Supply Routes," *Journal of Negro History* (1972), 398–404; Marc Gallicchio, *The African American Encounter with Japan and China: Black Internationalism in Asia, 1895–1945* (Chapel Hill: University of North Carolina Press, 2000), 193–198.

21. It is unclear why Chiang initiated the ban. His stated reason was that the Chinese living in the remote western areas would not know how to interact with the strange foreigners. Black reporters believed that Madame Chiang, who attended school in the American south, was behind the ban. In any case, once they entered China, black troops encountered few problems.

22. Yukiko Koshiro, *Trans-Pacific Racisms and the U.S. Occupation of Japan* (New York: Columbia University Press, 1999), 55. John Curtis Perry, *Beneath the Eagle's Wings: Americans in Occupied Japan* (New York: Dodd Mead, 1980), 170–172.

23. Friedman, *Creating an American Lake,* 132; John Curtis Perry, *Beneath the Eagle's Wings: Americans in Occupied Japan* (New York: Dodd Mead, 1980), 170–172; Eiji Takemae, *Inside GHQ: The Allied Occupation of Japan and Its Legacy* (New York: Continuum, 2002), 129–131; James, *MacArthur,* III, 568–569.

24. Morris J. MacGregor, Jr., *Integration of the Armed Forces, 1940–1965* (Washington, DC: Center of Military History, United States Army, 1981), 216–219.

6

A Lingering Presence

By spring 1946 it was clear that American forces in Asia would be reduced to a barely tolerable minimum required for occupation duties. It was less clear, however, how Washington would determine which stations required even a token American military presence. Japan, of course, would remain under American control for the foreseeable future. But the duration of the marines' mission in China and the army's occupation of Korea remained undecided. Ideally, American policy makers would be able to choose how to deploy military force based on calculations of national interest and an assessment of local and regional conditions. The growing consensus on the need to counter Soviet influence would figure prominently in any such deliberations. Advocates for a continued military presence on the mainland could also point to the Truman administration's publicly declared support for a unified China friendly to the United States and an independent Korea as justifications for their positions. Nevertheless, domestic factors, most notably retrenchment of the armed forces and concomitant budgetary reductions, tipped the scales toward withdrawal.

Faced with these competing impulses, American military commanders sought alternative means to exert their influence over developments in the region. One method was the military advisory group (MAG). As we have seen, the establishment of a MAG for China had been approved by late 1945. Others would follow in the Philippines and Korea. A second approach entailed the transfer of military supplies at minimal cost, either under lend lease or heavily discounted as military surplus. A third approach, closely related to the first two, was to support local forces willing to cooperate with the United States.

On the face of it, these programs seemed a common sense, even natural, solution to the problem of diminishing American resources. After all, one of the stated objectives of American policy was to aid America's friends so that they could defend themselves. On the other hand, all three forms of military support required the United States to take sides in countries where the legitimacy of the recognized authorities was being contested. In China, for example, General Marshall faced the daunting task of convincing the Chinese Communists to accept him as a disinterested mediator at the same time the United States showered their Nationalist adversaries with numerous forms of military assistance. More problems arose when it turned out that the forces most able to help the United States in the region were those of the defeated Japanese enemy or indigenous groups that had collaborated with the Japanese during the war. Reliance on Japanese troops in China or on Japanese collaborators in the Philippines and Korea seemed to negate the very purposes of the war. In order to deflect criticism from this practice, American officials stressed the temporary nature of such partnerships, reorganized the controversial military units to obscure their past service, and in extreme cases hid the suspect partnerships from the American public. These evasive maneuvers bought the Truman administration additional time to sort out its priorities in the region. But the close connections forged between the United States and corrupt and reactionary forces during this period would remain a lingering influence on American policy in Asia.

RESTORATION AND INDEPENDENCE IN THE PHILIPPINES

As American officials prepared for Philippine independence, slated for July 1946, they looked for ways to relinquish control over the islands without sacrificing American economic and security interests. At the same time, civilian and military officials in Washington sought to make the transition to independence as smooth as possible. That proved difficult where economic matters were concerned, in part because the United States Congress and the executive branch disagreed over which economic interests needed protecting. On security matters, however, Congress deferred to the administration. A consensus quickly developed within the Pentagon which, in turn, provided American negotiators and officials in the islands the clear directions needed to implement policy.

American security objectives in the Philippines followed the usual formula; a stable friendly government that would welcome U.S. military bases in the postwar era. In theory, the Americans preferred a democratically created reform-minded popular government in Manila. In reality, however, they were willing to accept a return of the traditional elites to power, especially since many of the popular movements in the islands, most notably the Huks, challenged the economic arrangements propping up elite rule. This desire for stability led Truman administration officials to soft-pedal calls for a purge of Japanese collaborators from the Philippine government. Any serious inquest was likely to foment divisions within Philippine ruling circles. American-sponsored purges also ran the risk of awakening anti-American feeling and jeopardizing base rights in the islands. In the end, the United States left the matter in Philippine hands, which, as historian Stephen Shalom has noted, had the effect of leaving the prosecution of collaborators in the hands of the Filipino elite, many of whom had collaborated.[1]

As preparations for the spring 1946 presidential elections got underway, American officials set about reforming the Philippine armed forces. In addition to proposing the establishment of a new Philippine army, MacArthur recommended the creation of a Military Police Command to assume responsibility for internal security. This new organization replaced the Philippine Constabulary, which had done the bidding of landlords and the Japanese during the occupation. In many cases this reorganization amounted to little more than a change of costume. For the most part, the new Military Police consisted of USAFFE guerillas who had fought the Huks during the occupation as well as Constabulary officers who had belatedly joined the guerillas on the eve of the American invasion.

The new Military Police Command wasted little time in settling scores with the Huks. By January 1946 the MP units and civilian guards organized by landlords were waging a campaign of intimidation and terror in the parts of central Luzon sympathetic to the Huks. The MPs also targeted meetings of the Democratic Alliance, a peasant-based political coalition formed by the Huks and left-wing urban groups. The struggle intensified following the April election. Manuel Roxas, who owed his political rebirth to MacArthur's sponsorship, won a narrow victory over Osmeña. The Democratic Alliance, a reform party supported by the Huks, also made a strong showing, however, winning seven of eight legislative seats in central Luzon. Shortly after the election, Roxas moved to disqualify the Alliance legislators so he could win approval for a controversial provision in the United States–Philippine trade bill.

With the electoral path to power closed off, the Huks resumed the insurgency, resorting to guerilla tactics against the better-equipped and supplied MP. The MPs, armed with American weapons, including sub-machine guns, could also call on the newly reorganized Philippine army for heavier weapons, including artillery and armor. Nevertheless, Roxas was taking no chances. After a visit to Washington in May, the new president obtained an additional $100 million in arms and equipment for the Philippine army. The transfer occurred shortly before the islands gained their independence on July 4. By October, although the rebellion persisted, Roxas was downplaying the danger calling the insurgency more of a "newspaper problem" than a political one.[2]

In the meantime, Washington and Manila pressed ahead with negotiations for American base rights on the islands. Philippine officials were more than willing to conclude a bases agreement, in part because they viewed it as a means of guaranteeing continued American interest in the well-being of the newly independent nation. Roxas insisted, however, that the Americans locate their installations away from heavily populated areas. That meant abandoning the Fort McKinley–Nichols Field complex adjacent to Manila. At first the army balked at this concession. MacArthur was particularly adamant. By late 1946, however, the Army General Staff concluded that the drastic cuts in the size of the peacetime army as well as continuing obligations elsewhere reduced the usefulness of the Philippines bases. New plans called for naval and air bases with only a token army force. Agreement followed quickly. In March 1947, the United States and Philippines agreed to a treaty that granted the United States ninety-nine year leases on twenty-three base areas. Chief among these were what became Clark Air Force base, a 130,000-square-acre complex that occupied a tract in Central Luzon, larger than the District of Columbia. The navy established its main installation at Subic Bay, but held options on other ports as well.

Concurrently with the base negotiations, the two parties collaborated on a Military Assistance Agreement. Although aid was distributed to the Philippine army, American and Philippine officials agreed that the islands were already safe from external threat. The real goal was to provide for internal security. In one sense, the agreement only formalized the disbursal of military aid that had been underway since the previous summer. But the pact also established a Joint U.S. Military Advisory Group (JUSMAG). Limited at first to a skeleton staff of twenty officers, the JUSMAG nevertheless worked closely with Philippine officials on matters of internal security, including drawing up plans for the creation of a national police force and the coordination of Philippine intelligence services.[3]

Most officials in Manila welcomed the additional military assistance and few objected to the strings the Pentagon attached to Philippine independence. Those strings restricted Philippine sovereignty, but they also bound the United States to look after the islands' security. Despite American military and economic assistance, however, the Huk insurgency continued unabated during the next several years. Changes in leadership (Roxas died unexpectedly in 1948) failed to stem the tide. The Philippine government proved politically unwilling to address the rebellious peasants' concerns and militarily incapable of stamping out the armed revolutionaries who moved among the villages and forests of central Luzon. By the late 1940s, American officials were becoming concerned that what Roxas had once termed a "newspaper problem" had the potential to threaten the U.S. military presence in the islands.

INDOCHINA: A PROBLEM FOR ANOTHER DAY

American officials hoped that the granting of independence to the Philippines would serve as a model to other colonialists, especially the French in Indochina. Despite surrendering sovereignty over the islands, the Americans maintained favorable economic relations and strategically valuable bases in the former colony. The French were willing to go through the motions of granting the Vietnamese nominal "independence within the French Union," but they were not prepared to surrender their colony without a fight. Full-scale warfare did not erupt, however, until after the Americans and Chinese departed the north.

While the Chinese settled down to plunder northern Indochina, the tense political conditions drew Gallagher grudgingly into the role of mediator. Like most of the approximately sixty Americans in Hanoi, Gallagher was impressed by Ho Chi Minh and sympathetic to the idea of eventual independence for the Vietnamese. Unlike several officers from the Office of Strategic

FIGURE 6.1
General Phillip E. Gallagher and General Lu Han.
Phillip E. Gallagher Papers, U.S. Army Center for Military History

Services (OSS), Gallagher tried to avoid interfering in the interactions of the French, Chinese, Vietminh and its nationalist rivals. In particular, Gallagher accused OSS operative Major Archimedes Patti of meddling in ways that were potentially harmful to American objectives. Gallagher, a career officer, believed that Patti had obtained much useful information on the Japanese, but he denigrated Patti's melodramatic style and mysterious behavior. "When I enter a room, I expect to see him come out from under a rug," Gallagher complained. "Would just as soon he be relieved by someone a little less spectacular," he added.[4]

For the most part, Gallagher concentrated on his primary tasks of advising Lu Han on the repatriation of Japanese soldiers, the evacuation of Allied prisoners, and the transshipment of Chinese troops to north China and Formosa. Gallagher spent much of October 1945 in the port city of Haiphong attending to the latter mission. The biggest problem he encountered there involved the presence of American mines sown across the harbor during the war. It appeared that before the Chinese could board the waiting American Liberty ships the mines would have to be swept from the harbor. But clearing the harbor would allow the French to enter before they had reached an agreement with the Vietnamese. That in turn would almost certainly lead to violence, something Gallagher sought to avoid. Gallagher's team solved the problem by removing only enough mines to permit the Liberty ships access to the outer part of the harbor so that Chinese troops could be ferried out to the vessels in small lighters.

Gallagher returned to Hanoi in late October to an economic crisis brought on by the Chinese manipulation of the local currency. By enacting an arbitrary and highly favorable exchange rate for Chinese dollars, the Chinese were able to scoop up real estate and goods at cut-rate prices. At the same time, they also extracted a series of forced loans from the French Bank of Indochina. Gallagher's warnings about the harmful consequences of these unsound practices failed to move Lu Han. The French took matters into their own hands by trying to restore some control over the colonial currency. They announced that all 500-piaster notes would have to be turned into the bank and held in blocked accounts and that all notes of the same denomination printed by the Japanese after the March coup would be invalidated. As the 500-piaster note was the most commonly exchanged note, this measure hit the Vietnamese as well as Chinese merchants especially hard.

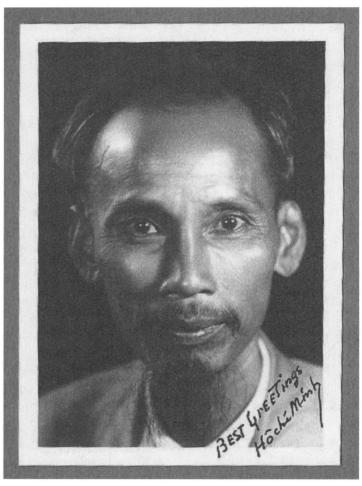

FIGURE 6.2
A signed portrait of Ho Chi Minh in General Gallagher's papers.
Phillip E. Gallagher Papers, U.S. Army Center for Military History

Protests outside the bank's main branch turned violent, resulting in the deaths of six Vietnamese. In retaliation, the Vietminh promptly declared a boycott of the French community, refusing to sell them food and other essential goods. The Chinese army, many of whose officers held the cancelled 500-piaster notes, sided with the Vietminh and briefly held two of the bank's executives under arrest. At this point, Gallagher entered the fray. Calling the

Chinese and French officials together he asked for their permission to try to end the boycott by meeting with Ho. The Chinese acquiesced. In the ensuing meeting Ho pledged to try to lift the boycott. The French took the next step by replacing the ban on the 500-piaster notes with more tolerable restrictions on their circulation.

In the aftermath of the currency crisis General Gallagher began to close down the American advisory mission in Hanoi. The Japanese had been repatriated and the movement of Chinese troops through Haiphong was underway. Gallagher left with the remaining contingent of his staff on December 12, 1945, thereby ending America's first postwar encounter with Vietnam.

As historian Ronald Spector has observed, "General Gallagher's mission to Hanoi must certainly rank among the most difficult assignments of the immediate postwar period."[5] Although he endeavored to stay out of the political intrigue swirling about the city his very presence made involvement of some kind unavoidable. The French, as we have seen, strongly opposed the temporary division of Indochina. When the Americans dismissed those objections, the French perceived sinister motives behind the American decision to allow the Chinese into the north. Colonial officials viewed Gallagher's every move with suspicion. In fulfilling his mission, Gallagher sought to provide humanitarian aid to the French but found it advisable to delay the return of French troops into the north. Lu Han had his own reasons for prolonging the occupation. To the French, of course, it looked as though the Americans and Chinese were colluding to take over their colony.

The French finally reached an agreement with the Chinese in early 1946 that enabled them to return in force to the north. For years afterward, the French blamed the Americans for letting the Chinese army loose in northern Indochina and allowing Ho's forces to gain a foothold there. The French were partly correct. The Americans had divided Indochina for the purposes of taking the surrender as a concession to the Chinese. But in doing so, they did not intend to aid the cause of Vietnamese independence. That is what happened, however, much to the regret of the French and, eventually, the Americans.

JAPAN: SWITZERLAND OF EAST ASIA?

In contrast to the unsettled conditions he left behind in the Philippines, MacArthur was succeeding admirably in Japan. Although SCAP oversaw the whole program of reform in occupied Japan, we will confine our attention to those matters dealing with military policy. The primary task in that category, demilitarization, was well on the way to completion by spring 1946. MacArthur pursued a broader agenda, however. He hoped to make Japan's new status as a disarmed nation permanent. In order to achieve that end he sought sweeping changes in Japan's constitution, the prosecution of Japan's wartime leaders, and, ultimately, a peace treaty that would leave Japan's security under the care of the United Nations. Although his program met with early success, MacArthur eventually encountered resistance from members of his staff and subsequently from the Joint Chiefs, all of whom objected to his vision of Japan as a Far Eastern Switzerland.

The success of MacArthur's program depended on his ability to present Japan to the world as a transformed and repentant nation. The most direct way to demonstrate that Japan was moving in the right direction would be to remove its wartime leaders, including the emperor, from power. MacArthur feared, however, that any attempt to punish Hirohito would produce social upheaval throughout Japan. Moreover, during the early months of the occupation, MacArthur had found it most convenient to rely on Japanese obedience to the emperor to gain compliance with SCAP's directives. As we have seen, MacArthur symbolically demonstrated his willingness to stand by Hirohito, providing he cooperated with the occupation, by having his picture with the emperor released to the press.

MacArthur's conviction that Hirohito was necessary for the success of the occupation dovetailed with an emerging consensus in Washington on the desirability of keeping the emperor on the throne. The argument that had been put forward in the final months of the war, that the emperor was needed to ensure the surrender of Japanese troops, had gained adherents as the surrender proceeded without incident. In the months after Japan's surrender the rapid demobilization of American forces provided an additional incentive for keeping Hirohito on the throne. If MacArthur was using far fewer troops than anticipated, why risk upheaval in Japan by putting Hirohito on trial? Japanese officials did their best to reinforce this thinking by warning of dire consequences should Hirohito be removed. By late autumn the argument for leaving Hirohito in place had gained an aura of irresistibility in Washington. James Byrnes publicly hinted that the United States was contractually bound to keep Hirohito on the throne as long as he carried out his end of the surrender bargain. President Truman privately acknowledged that it made sense to keep the emperor on the throne. Even China Hands like John Carter Vincent reconciled themselves to keeping the emperor in place.[6]

Outside of Washington and GHQ Tokyo, those arguments found fewer adherents. In late December, the Australian government informed Washington that it wanted Hirohito added to the list of the accused awaiting trial for war crimes. Byrnes firmly rejected the proposal. Several days later, MacArthur dramatically weighed in on the matter warning that if Hirohito were put on trial he would need a million men to govern Japan. Given the mood in Washington and Byrnes's previous rejection of Australia's request, MacArthur's intervention was not the eleventh-hour reprieve for Hirohito that the general's admirers and some historians have made it seem. Indeed, as it turned out, MacArthur probably did more to keep Hirohito on the throne several months later when the emperor contemplated abdicating.

As noted, MacArthur's long-range plans for Japan depended on his being able to convince the world that Japan had been transformed and its militarists removed from power and punished. The Allies agreed that those accused of taking Japan into war, should stand trial before an international court created for the purpose of hearing the cases of what were termed "Class A" war criminals. The International Military Tribunal for the Far East, better known as the Tokyo Trials, heard twenty-eight cases beginning in spring 1946 and ending more than two and a half years later in November 1948. Among the most prominent Japanese figures brought before the bar were wartime prime minister general Tojo Hideki and fourteen other high ranking army and navy officers involved in the war in China or the attack on Pearl Harbor. The trials resulted in twenty-eight convictions. Seven of the accused, including Tojo, were sentenced to hang. Defense lawyers as well as several judges who entered dissenting opinions questioned the legitimacy of the trials on several grounds. Some accused the tribunal of applying arbitrary rules of evidence. Others questioned the novel definition of war crimes that allowed government officials to be tried for waging "aggressive war." That criticism formed the basis for the view that the Tokyo Trials amounted to nothing more than victor's justice, a form of vengeance meted out to the vanquished. What government official, critics asked, would wish to have their own conduct judged by the standards being applied to the Japanese defendants?

Several related events strengthened the perception of the tribunal as a kangaroo court. While the Tokyo cases were underway, a separate military court in Manila convicted and executed Generals Homma Masaharu and Yamashita Tomoyuki for crimes committed by their troops in the Philippines. Homma was held responsible for the Bataan Death March, Yamashita for the destruction of Manila in 1945 and the deaths of an estimated 100,000 Filipinos. In neither case did the court show that the generals had direct knowledge of the events in question, nor was it shown that they had ordered or approved of the savage conduct of their troops. The charges appeared particularly tenuous in Yamashita's case since he was more than one hundred miles from Manila when Japanese navy units defied his orders to evacuate the city and launched their bloody assault on Philippine civilians. In both cases, the court ignored possibly exculpatory evidence by asserting that both generals had command responsibility and thus were ultimately responsible for the actions of their men. Yamashita was hanged. Homma died before a firing squad.

Both trials have been criticized as applying standards that none of the officers sitting in judgment would want to meet. In fact, American military courts have been unwilling to apply the concept of command responsibility, the so-called Yamashita precedent, in subsequent cases. MacArthur has come in for special criticism for his role in setting out the unusually broad rules of evidence and for declining to commute the sentences of both officers. Some historians have suggested that the defendants' most serious offense was that of having outshone MacArthur on the battlefield. But MacArthur may also have been influenced by the demands for vengeance emanating from his friends in the newly installed Philippine government. For the most part, MacArthur's biographers, including those favorably inclined toward the general, agree that the Manila trials and executions of Yamashita and Homma were carried out in unseemly haste and with little concern for accepted procedure. MacArthur's denials to the contrary only helped to highlight his part in the miscarriage of justice.

As historian John Dower has noted, victor's justice can mean more than the quest for vengeance by the winners. In the case of Japan it also meant that the victors could exempt from punishment even the most obviously guilty parties. The treatment of General Ishii Shiro and his henchmen is a case in point. Ishii, a bacteriologist, spent the war as the director of the notorious Unit 731 in Japan's biological warfare branch. Stationed in Manchuria, Unit 731 officers freely tested germ warfare agents against Chinese civilians and conducted numerous gruesome experiments on prisoners of war, including vivisections.

Beginning in late 1945, GHQ began granting immunity to Unit 731 scientists in exchange for the results of the field tests and experiments they had conducted in Manchuria. Before long, MacArthur's intelligence section had received a mountain of evidence implicating the members of Unit 731 in scores of the most grisly experiments imaginable. As one American interrogator recalled, "the data came in waves. We could hardly keep up with it."[7] American interrogation of Ishii usually took place in an atmosphere of conviviality. On one occasion MacArthur's head of intelligence (G-2), Major General Charles Willoughby, attended a dinner party at Ishii's house. Willoughby, a strident anti-communist and admirer of Spanish dictator Francisco Franco, apparently admired Ishii. A report from Willoughby's military intelligence section described the Japanese scientist as "pro-American and [someone who] respects the mental culture and physical science of the U.S."[8]

Although the Joint Chiefs and the interagency State-War-Navy Coordinating Committee regarded the information Ishii had spirited out of Manchuria as potentially important in the event of another war, officials in Washington declined to give the Japanese scientists officially documented immunity while the possibility existed that one of the other Allies might raise the issue of germ warfare at the Tokyo Trials. In the meantime, MacArthur's intelligence staff and germ warfare specialists from the United States pored over slides and reports detailing Ishii's grotesque experiments. By 1948, once it became clear that the military tribunal would not bring charges against the Japanese, in part because the Americans withheld a mountain of incriminating evidence, MacArthur received permission to grant Ishii and his team the blanket immunity they desired.[9]

The American partnership with Ishii ranks as one of the more disgraceful episodes of the early postwar era. Civilian and military officials in Tokyo and Washington attempted to justify their actions by asserting that Ishii's records could aid in the development of vaccines and otherwise protect the United States from bacteriological warfare. In order to gain that information, they argued, they needed Ishii's full cooperation. Soviet interest in Ishii and American awareness that the Soviets had captured some of Japan's germ warriors made such logic appear irrefutable. Nevertheless, as historian Sheldon Harris has shown, it is doubtful that the Americans learned anything of value from Unit 731. Ishii's experiments were not only vile, they were also quite crude. In the end, Ishii lived in peaceful retirement collecting a military pension. Many of his associates went on to professional success in postwar Japan's medical and pharmaceutical fields. Ishii and his colleagues survived because they convinced the Americans they had something to trade. Generals Yamashita and Homma were executed because they did not. In the immediate postwar period perceived military necessity trumped the administration of justice. Peace had come to Japan, but American officials were already thinking about the next war.

When it came to meting out justice, the most prominent beneficiary of SCAP's discretionary powers was Hirohito. As we have seen, MacArthur was determined to shield the emperor from prosecution. Hirohito's public renunciation of his divinity on January 1, 1946, was an important step in that process. The emperor's miraculous transfiguration from divine ruler to mere figurehead was followed by an almost equally wondrous conversion of his public image in the United States. Working closely with members of the imperial retinue, Brigadier General Bonner Fellers, MacArthur's military secretary and former head of psychological warfare, set out to reinvent the emperor as a reluctant warrior and the covert leader of wartime Japan's peace faction. Encouraged by Japanese officials, Fellers depicted Hirohito as a virtual prisoner of the militarists. Fellers's revisionist account eventually appeared in the mass circulation *Reader's Digest* in June 1947. By that time, Hirohito, with MacArthur's encouragement, was regularly touring the country and appearing in public at ceremonial functions. Dubbed "Mr. Ah so" in reference to his most common public utterance, the young emperor who once sat astride a white steed in full military dress, had metamorphosed into an almost diffident public servant. Before long Japanese were referring to the former august person as "Ten-chan" the Japanese equivalent of "Emp-baby."[10]

The public relations campaign that transformed the image of the emperor proceeded in tandem with SCAP's plans to formally redefine his constitutional status. As mentioned, SCAP took the initial step reshaping the imperial institution by convincing Hirohito to publicly renounce his divinity, which he did, on January 1. Once the Japanese knew what the emperor was not, the next task was to say more precisely what he was. That redefinition would come through revisions in the Japanese constitution. A Japanese committee set to work on that project but MacArthur's staff found that effort wholly inadequate. Among other problems the Japanese draft allowed the emperor to maintain his prerogatives. Sensing resistance from the Japanese elite,

MacArthur instructed his staff to produce a new constitution from scratch. They did so, taking only seven days to complete the task.

SCAP's improvised "constitutional convention" conducted its work in secret. Neither the State Department's political adviser in Tokyo nor officials in Washington, including MacArthur's immediate superiors on the Joint Chiefs, knew what was taking place. Not surprisingly, the American draft met MacArthur's requirements on the essentials. To begin with, it explicitly reduced the emperor to a symbol of the Japanese people and confined him to ceremonial functions. The American draft also contained a provision required by MacArthur in which the Japanese people renounced war and abolished their armed forces. Over the next several weeks, the draft was shown to the Japanese drafting committee, which succeeded in making only minor changes. The completed draft was made public on March 6 and ratified by the Diet in November.

During the Diet debates over the document, the Japanese included several phrases that were widely seen by both Japanese and SCAP officials to dilute the force Article 9, the section of the new document dealing with the renunciation of war and Japan's right to maintain armed forces. The original American version unequivocally prohibited Japan from keeping military forces or resorting to war in any circumstances. The ratified document qualified Japan's renunciation of war by saying that the nation would not use war to settle international disputes. That, most observers agreed left room for war as a means of national defense. It followed from that interpretation, and MacArthur subsequently concurred, that Japan could support a military establishment, but for purposes of defense only.[11]

The portions of the new document bearing on military matters drew little comment from the Joint Chiefs. One reason for this silence may have been that the navy's wartime planner, Admiral Charles Cooke, had departed Washington to take command of the Seventh Fleet off the coast of China. As we have noted, during the Okinawa campaign, Cooke had raised the possibility of using Japan as a potential makeweight against Russia after the war. On the other hand, even if Cooke had been in a position to renew his earlier recommendation, it is doubtful that the JCS would have been willing to endorse it. Where Japan was concerned, JCS policy was framed in negative terms. The Chiefs opposed any changes in the constitution that would require the deployment of additional forces in Japan. Otherwise, they continued to be guided by the disarmament provisions contained in the Potsdam Proclamation.[12] Although the JCS were growing increasingly concerned about the intentions of the Soviet Union they were just beginning to think about how to address that problem. In the absence of consensus, the wartime view of American postwar strategy persisted. Japan was the enemy to guard against. Toward that end, despite State Department objections, the JCS were vehemently insisting that the United States should claim sovereignty over the Pacific islands captured from Japan. In general, American military planners continued to view the American role in Asia as preclusive, to "keep the rest of the world militarily out of the Pacific," as an earlier statement put it.

That view suited MacArthur. Following ratification of the constitution, the general began to push for the drafting of a peace treaty to end the occupation and restore Japan to the family of nations. MacArthur was on the record as favoring a short occupation, lest America's stewardship of Japan lose its way, as he believed occupations often did. But his timing was almost certainly stimulated by his presidential ambitions. MacArthur's proposed schedule, a conference in the summer and ratification six months afterward, would allow him to make his triumphal return to the United States in time to pick up the Republican nomination for president in 1948.

Politics aside, MacArthur's recommendations for a peace treaty would have been controversial under any circumstances. In broad terms, the general favored an exceedingly liberal and nonpunitive treaty for Japan. Regarding Japan's future security MacArthur recommend that American forces withdraw from Japan without retaining rights for military bases in the main islands. (He made allowances, however, for American bases on Okinawa.) Even more striking, MacArthur called for the newly disarmed Japan to be placed under the protection of the United Nations. MacArthur's endorsement of an early peace conference coincided with the draft of a similarly lenient treaty by a State Department subcommittee. Although the department's draft differed from MacArthur's in several respects, including its call for an extended period of international supervision for Japan, neither plan had a ghost of chance. The State Department draft was actually the work of a small noninfluential group of Japan specialists who could not even win support within their own department. MacArthur's proposal for a disarmed and neutralized Japan provoked immediate opposition in the Pentagon. Riding high from the ratification of the constitution, the Big Chief apparently expected that his international stature would silence potential critics in Washington. If that was his expectation, Macarthur seriously misjudged the situation. Officials in the State and War Departments soundly rejected the idea of an early peace and with it, the vision of a neutral Japan.

By 1947 international conditions worked against acceptance of MacArthur's plan. In March, shortly before MacArthur floated his proposal, President Truman requested aid from Congress to help the Greek and Turkish governments defend against Communist subversion and, in the case of Turkey, Soviet encroachment. The president's request, which became known as the Truman Doctrine, contained language broad enough to suggest that similar aid programs would be developed for other countries under threat. At the same time, full-scale civil war erupted in China. Conditions in Korea, to be discussed below, also underscored the importance for the United States of having a secure friendly Japan under American control.

MacArthur's ideal of a disarmed neutral Japan under United Nations protection was further undermined by his tacit recognition that regional conflict remained likely. His own actions betrayed a lack of faith in the durability of an Asian peace. To begin with, SCAP had shielded Ishii's team from prosecution because it was believed that Unit 731's research might be useful in the event of war. MacArthur's support for U.S. bases on Okinawa also conveyed a tacit recognition that future conflict was possible. Like most advocates of defense preparedness, MacArthur could argue that the American bases would deter war in the region. But those bases could serve multiple purposes, all of which anticipated some unspecified danger. They could be a hedge against a resurgence of Japanese militarism, a forward defense post in the Pacific, a platform for projecting American power onto the Asian mainland, or some combination of the three. Either way, if war remained a possibility, could the United States leave the most dynamic economy in Asia under the protection of the untested United Nations? American admirals and generals were unwilling to trust the United Nations with the protection of the thinly populated central Pacific islands. Would they be willing to trust it with the defense of Japan?

Two of MacArthur's key subordinates were never troubled by those questions. Almost from the start of the occupation, Generals Willoughby and Eichelberger expected that the United States would maintain bases in the home islands of a rearmed Japan. In his capacity as head intelligence officer of the Far Eastern Command, Willoughby, whom MacArthur called his "lovable fascist," operated with the eventual resurrection of the Japanese army in mind. The available evidence indicates, however, that Willoughby acted without MacArthur's awareness of his purposes.

Within months of Japan's surrender, Willoughby was employing high-ranking former Imperial Army officers in a number of schemes with the goal of preserving a corps of key military agencies that could be expanded when needed. These included collection of intelligence on Manchuria, Korea, and China as well as the mapping of possible military strong points within Japan. Some operations served dual purposes that allowed them to take place in the open. For example, the same record keeping necessary for demobilization of Japanese troops allowed Willoughby to keep track of officers and enlisted men who could form the basis of a new army. Willoughby also employed former officers to write official histories of the Imperial Army's conduct in the war. This scholarly endeavor also enabled Willoughby to sustain the nucleus of a general staff system. In undertaking these relatively modest operations, Willoughby and his Japanese conspirators privately admitted that they were influenced by the example of Germany's remilitarization after World War I.[13]

The Eighth Army's General Eichelberger privately declared his opposition to the idea of an unarmed neutral Japan shortly after Macarthur proposed it. Eichelberger argued that the United States, having demilitarized Japan, had an obligation to defend its former enemy. In September 1947, while in Washington, he publicly voiced his support for a lengthy occupation, the establishment of American bases in the home islands, and the gradual reconstruction of Japan's armed forces. Eichelberger's recommendations reflected his personal military convictions based on wartime experience and his assessment of international developments. "Dollar for dollar," he observed "there is no cheaper fighting man in the world than the Japanese. He is already a veteran. His food is simple."[14]

Eichelberger's public criticism of MacArthur's proposals also reflected his personal frustrations with having toiled for MacArthur in near obscurity, in contrast to successful commanders in other theaters. During the war, MacArthur was notoriously stingy in releasing favorable news about his subordinates to the press. Eichelberger believed that MacArthur's jealousy of his subordinates only got worse during the occupation. In several instances, MacArthur declined to recommend or approve the awarding of several medals

Eichelberger believed he deserved. Eichelberger responded to these perceived slights by holding a secret ceremony in which he pathetically awarded the medals to himself. Later, the Eighth Army commander was appalled to learn that MacArthur habitually claimed full responsibility for the occupation's success in his meetings with visiting dignitaries. According to Eichelberger's sources, the Big Chief never acknowledged the Eighth Army's role in the implementation of SCAP policies. Ultimately, Eichelberger became convinced that MacArthur was obstructing his chances for advancement. Shortly after he decided to speak out against MacArthur's peace treaty, Eichelberger hired a literary agent to help him write a memoir that would set the record straight about MacArthur's Pacific campaigns.[15]

Eichelberger and Willoughby were bolstered in the support for rearmament by the work of Harry Kern, foreign editor of *Newsweek* and founder of the American Council on Japan, a group of former diplomats, military officers, businesspeople, and journalists committed to restoring prewar economic ties with the United States and rebuilding Japan as an anti-communist bastion in Asia. Kern's group denounced MacArthur's peace plans and lobbied against many of SCAP's liberal economic reforms as harmful to the restoration of Japan's economic strength. In August 1947, Kern published an article in *Newsweek* in which he openly discussed the growing interest in Japanese rearmament in Washington. Thinking among the Joint Chiefs was also moving in that direction. Although such thoughts still did not constitute workable plans, by early 1947 the Chiefs were referring to Japan as the one country in Asia that could contain what were euphemistically called "our ideological opponents," while the United States and its allies waged an offensive campaign in Europe.[16] The logic of that position left little room for a disarmed neutral Japan.

Given the mounting support for the establishment of U.S. bases in a rearmed Japan, and in light of MacArthur's own contradictory impulses on the subject, it is not surprising that his plan for a disarmed neutral Japan were rejected. Some aspects of his proposal survived, however. Although Japan rearmed, its military establishment never fulfilled the aspirations of those who hoped to see Japan capable of containing the Soviets in Asia. Instead, Japan ultimately created a small, technologically advanced military establishment that met its limited security needs reasonably well. In terms of armament, by the late 1950s, Japan had become an Asian Switzerland. But it was not neutral. MacArthur's desire for a short occupation ending with the creation a neutral

Japan foundered in the Cold War and sank altogether following the outbreak of the Korean War. By the time the occupation officially ended in 1953, Japan was allied to the United States by virtue of a security treaty that granted the Americans extensive base rights in Japan.

KOREA: NATION BUILDING OR SECESSION?

In early 1946, the Truman administration remained firmly committed to a trusteeship for Korea. General Hodge remained just as firmly convinced that trusteeship was an unworkable scheme opposed by nearly all Koreans. In the first months of the occupation he had taken steps that helped make his predictions of failure a self-fulfilling prophecy. Hodge's close cooperation with the Korean Right and his creation of a Korean National Police force that employed large numbers of collaborators placed power in the hands of groups that had the most to lose in any political outcome that empowered the vast majority of impoverished peasants in the countryside.

In Washington, State Department officials still held out hope for some form of trusteeship that would reunite the peninsula. John Carter Vincent urged Secretary of State Byrnes to seek accord with the Russians before the changes occurring on both sides of the thirty-eighth parallel became irreversible. Vincent based his recommendation on the same assumptions that governed his approach to American involvement in China. He reasoned that American power on the mainland was transitory. Delay benefited the Russians. Therefore, if the United States sought a united Korea it was better to seek agreement immediately. Byrnes acted on Vincent's recommendation at the Moscow conference by re-confirming American and Soviet support for a trusteeship.

When they learned of the outcome at Moscow Korean conservatives promptly denounced the trusteeship plan and organized rallies against it. In one instance, General Archer Lerch, the military governor, sat on the platform while Korean politicians blasted the trusteeship proposal. Korean Communists and Leftists also opposed trusteeship but they were temporarily reconciled to the unpopular plan because it aligned them with American and Soviet policy and thus seemed the most likely way to unseat the conservatives. Hodge, who continued to oppose trusteeship, took the Left's compliance as evidence that they were taking direction from Moscow. The Left's support for trusteeship certainly accorded with Soviet desires. It is just as likely, however, that the groups seeking reform in a united Korea realized that the Right's un-compromising approach was leading to a divided peninsula and that the old guard was willing to secede as long as they remained in charge in the south. Once their position was assured, and the Left suppressed, the conservatives would pursue unification on their own terms.

Following the Moscow conference, the dream of a united Korea depended on the outcome of negotiations between American and Soviet representatives from both sides of the thirty-eighth parallel. The Joint Commission, as the conferring body was known, was intended to work out the practical steps to-ward unification of the two occupation zones by creating a provisional gov-ernment. Hodge predicted that the Joint Commission would fail or worse, that it would lead to a Soviet takeover of the south. Byrnes complained about Hodge's attitude to the War Department. Secretary Patterson stood by the general and reiterated Hodge's inaccurate claim that he had received little di-rection from the State Department. By this time Hodge clearly saw himself as battling dangerous forces arrayed against the United States. On April 6, not long before the first meeting of the Joint Commission, the general used his Army Day speech to fire off a screed against critics of the army. "Every right-thinking American," he said "should have the courage to help protect his Army from agitator, anarchist, the foreign guided and inspired termite and the izmites who slander, lie, propagandize—in effect, break down and defame, an American institution designed for the defense and protection of a nation where men are really free." "These termites and izmites," he continued, "within our nation would like to break down our American democracy. They use every insidious vice known to man to conceal their true aims."[17] Hodge did not identify the termites or izmites he had in mind, nor for that matter did he explain what an izmite was, but one suspects that Hodge thought a few of them were boring away at his army from offices in the State Department.

As Hodge predicted, the meetings of the Joint Commission soon broke down. At issue was the question of which Koreans should be consulted. The Soviets insisted that only Koreans who supported trusteeship were eligible. That, of course would disqualify Syngman Rhee and the other conservatives. Hodge, this time with State Department support, argued against punishing Koreans who exercised their right of free speech. Over the course of the next year, the Joint Commission was revived long enough to stir some hope of resolution, only to founder again on this question. By late spring, 1946, the

Truman administration, Byrnes included, was willing to see if they could wait out the Soviets. What Byrnes described as a policy of "patience with firmness" was intended to show the Soviets that the United States was in no hurry to leave the peninsula. While the Americans waited for the Soviets to become more agreeable, Hodge was instructed to reach out to other moderates, including members of the Left and begin the process of economic and social reform in the south.

Hodge grudgingly obliged. By this time, he was beginning to regret his earlier support for the obstreperous Rhee. As he gradually began turning over day-to-day responsibilities to Korean administrators Hodge sought to draw more moderate leaders into working with the military government. In the end it was too little too late. Rhee and the conservative forces were too well entrenched, especially in the National Police, to relinquish control peacefully. Additionally, despite his desire to broaden participation in what was now termed the Interim Government, Hodge's own actions and those of military governor General Lerch actually weakened the conservatives' opponents.

In autumn, workers' complaints about wages and the scarcity of rice mushroomed into a general strike. Peasant uprisings erupted shortly thereafter. These widespread disturbances were suppressed by the National Police and right-wing paramilitary groups with the assistance of American forces. The turmoil convinced Hodge that the Soviets planned to invade the south after the harvest was gathered. He petitioned Washington for permission to build up a "Rightist Youth Army" to help maintain order. When his request was denied Hodge went ahead and subsidized training facilities for an organization called Korean National Youth, which drew its inspiration from a European-educated Korean who professed admiration for the Hitler Youth.

In the midst of the upheaval in the countryside, General Lerch gave opposition parties a scant five days notice that elections for a South Korean Interim Legislative Assembly would be held beginning on October 17. Not surprisingly, given their control of the government apparatus, Rhee and his supporters won an overwhelming victory. Lerch sought to compensate for this outcome by nullifying the results in two districts where fraud was clearly evident and by filling some of the appointive seats in the assembly with moderate and Left leaders. This attempt at correction infuriated Rhee and his followers. Incredibly, they responded by accusing Hodge of seeking to turn the south over to the Communists. When Rhee's accusations failed to halt Hodge's overtures to the more moderate elements in the south, Rhee announced a plan for massive protests and strikes unless the military government abandoned trusteeship and agreed to create an independent South Korea.

In many ways, the events of 1946 represented the fulfillment of decisions made in the early days of the occupation. Hodge had always operated on the assumption that the real reason the XXIV Corps had been sent to Korea was to deny the Soviets complete control of the peninsula. That goal became his priority. Hodge turned to the Japanese and then the Right out of convenience at first. He excluded the Left, however, out of a belief that the numerous local committees were the vanguard of a Soviet effort to take over the south. Once he relied on Rhee and other members of the Right he doomed the trusteeship project for good. Hodge was easily reconciled to that outcome because he had already concluded that conditions in Korea and the changing international setting made trusteeship a long shot at best. It took the Truman administration a lot longer to reach the same conclusion. During 1946 they hoped that a show of American determination would force the Soviets to negotiate. The Right's uncompromising grip on power and the Left's unwillingness to meekly submit foiled that plan. The Soviets continued to support a trusteeship but they were not willing to turn the peninsula over to Rhee and his supporters on the Right. For his part, Rhee would not accept a trusteeship that did not lead to an independent Korea governed by the Right.

Rhee's opposition to trusteeship left the Truman administration with few choices. Most Koreans continued to oppose trusteeship. If Hodge accepted the terms of the Joint Commission and excluded Rhee from participating in a provisional government the Korean Communists would dominate. Moreover, if Hodge jettisoned Rhee he would face massive upheaval in the south. An independent south might be the only way out.

By early 1947, however, policy makers in Washington were catching up with Hodge. The president's announcement of what became known as the Truman Doctrine appeared to summon the United States to the defense of democracy, defined as anti-communism, everywhere. The *New York Times* was quick to point out that Korea faced challenges similar to those of Greece and Turkey. Yet, as the *Times* pointed out, American policy toward Korea was victimized by inconsistency, inattention, and insufficient material support. Korea, noted the editorial, "is at the end of the line for everything. It has received only what has been left over, militarily, economically and diplomatically." Taking note of a recurrence of

GI protests, the newspaper added that "Our troops there are more poorly billeted than anywhere else in occupied lands."[18]

The crystallizing of Cold War attitudes placed Korea in an anomalous state. Army chief of staff Dwight Eisenhower judged that a retreat from Korea would be penny-wise and pound-foolish. It was clear, however, that the United States did not have the resources in hand to maintain the occupation of the south. Nor did Congress seem inclined to provide the means required to do so. Forced to formulate strategy in an atmosphere of budgetary restraint and persistent GI protest, the JCS concluded that militarily Korea was far less important than Western Europe and the Middle East. Nevertheless, the JCS also insisted that Korea had great importance as an ideological battleground. If the United States abandoned the struggle and allowed the Soviets to dominate the peninsula it "would tend to confirm the suspicion that the United States is not really determined to accept the responsibilities of world leadership." *New York Times* columnist Anne O'Hare McCormick made a similar point when she noted that, "The eyes of Asia are on Korea."[19]

Two years after its impulsive decision to occupy part of Korea, the United States was moving toward partitioning the peninsula. Initiated at a moment when Japan's sudden collapse appeared to free American resources for bolder action on the mainland, the Korean occupation had suffered from the rapid contraction of American forces following V-J Day. Unfortunately, the administration's commitment to Korea had grown in almost inverse proportion to the dwindling number of occupation troops. As historian James Matray has argued, there was little likelihood that the United States could coerce the Soviet Union into accepting a government led by Syngman Rhee when it was evident that the Americans could not sustain a sizeable presence on the peninsula.

By mid-1947 the Truman administration was devising a plan to withdraw under the cover of United Nations supervised elections. When the Soviets refused to participate, the United Nations general assembly approved elections for the south alone. In anticipation of the American withdrawal, Hodge recommended a Korean army of six divisions, including headquarters, to be trained and equipped by U.S. advisers within one year. MacArthur overruled Hodge and recommended an increase of the constabulary from 20,000 to 50,000. The War Department accepted MacArthur's program in part because it could be accomplished in time for the elections in spring 1948.

As expected, the Right prevailed and Rhee became president of the Republic of Korea. As the USAFIK prepared to leave the peninsula, army advisers stepped up training of the Korean Constabulary. The Americans started several weapons schools and emphasized defense and internal security. Those seemed like sound choices in light of the conditions prevailing below the thirty-eighth parallel. Following the 1946 autumn uprisings riots, strikes, and violent resistance persisted in the south. The 1948 elections provoked insurrections in several provinces. American forces had succeeded in holding onto a portion of Korea and making it a "bulwark against Communism," as Rhee liked to say. Despite three years of occupation, however, the American quest for stability in the south, to say nothing of democracy, remained unfulfilled.

CHINA: LIMITED INTERVENTION, TOTAL FAILURE

The Truman administration's decision to postpone a peace treaty with Japan while redirecting occupation policy toward rehabilitation of the Japanese economy, and Truman's concurrent acceptance of separate regimes on the Korean peninsula, were reactions to the failure of American efforts to prevent the outbreak of civil war in China.

The resumption of all-out warfare between the Nationalists and Communists in 1947 increased the likelihood that China would return to its prewar state of warlord politics. Such an outcome was not wholly unforeseen by American military strategists. As late as the summer of 1945, army planners had anticipated that China might not emerge from the war intact. That sober assessment was based on an assumption that the war against Japan would continue for months, if not longer. When Japanese resistance collapsed less than a month later it suddenly seemed that the United States would be able to use its military power to produce a favorable outcome on the mainland. After eight years of Japanese blockade, China was finally open to resupply by sea. U.S. shipping and air transports redeployed the Nationalists' American trained divisions into the north where they disembarked at airfields and ports held by fully equipped, battle-hardened U.S. Marines.

The immediate show of force was impressive. American support for Jiang and the Soviet Union's surprising arm's-length treatment of CCP forces in Manchuria drove Mao to the bargaining table and kept him there for the first half of 1946. But Mao was not alone in feeling pressed to negotiate a settlement in China. As Truman quickly learned, the American presence in China was a dwindling asset. Public protest to bring the boys home and domestic pressures to reduce military spending imposed powerful limits on American options in China. The JCS and the civilian heads of the War and Navy Departments argued that the stakes in China were too high to bow to public pressure to withdraw the marines and restrict aid to the Nationalists. Those who opposed American aid to Jiang, such as the State Department's John Carter Vincent, were regarded as Communist dupes or Kremlin agents. General Wedemeyer's characterization of the administration's critics was even more odious. Early in 1946, Wedemeyer told a friend that when Secretary of War Patterson visited Shanghai "I indicated to him that it was my observation in all theaters that radio and press activities appeared to be permeated with Jews and others with radical tendencies." Was this by chance, Wedemeyer asked in a manner that indicated he knew the answer, "or a studied planned penetration by certain exponents of contrary ideologies?"[20]

FIGURE 6.3
General Wedemeyer and Marshall inspect a Chinese guard of honor on Marshall's arrival in Shanghai, December 1945.
Hoover Institution

Although Truman described critics of his China policy as being more loyal to Stalin than to the United States, in calmer moments he concluded that the United States did not have unlimited means to expend in China. The president still desired to see China united and friendly toward the United States. But he and his military advisers believed that Jiang could not unite the country by force. In the event of civil war, American support for the Nationalists would be matched by Soviet aid to the CCP. The ensuing turmoil would only serve Soviet interests by creating a weak, divided China thereby providing the Russians an opportunity to strengthen their position in northeast Asia.

Marshall understood that it would be no easy matter to get the warring parties to compromise. In large measure the success of his strategy depended on the willingness of both groups to heed the desires of the vast majority of Chinese who desperately wanted peace and a chance to rebuild their ravaged country. The prospect of American aid was the carrot that would bring the enemies to the table long enough for them to see the benefits of compromise. That would have to suffice. There was a carrot, but no stick. Jiang quickly recognized that Marshall did not possess the means to goad the Nationalists into compromising with the Communists. The Communists also perceived the inherent contradictions in Marshall's position as mediator. During the course of countless meetings the CCP's negotiators, led by the cosmopolitan Zhou Enlai, came to respect Marshall's personal integrity and his sincere desire to help China. But they also understood that the Truman administration would not cease its support for Jiang's government. For his part, Jiang worried about Marshall's seemingly naïve belief that the Communists could be talked into accepting a subordinate position in a coalition government. But Jiang also believed that in the event of a breakdown in negotiations he could count on continued support from the Truman administration.

In light of American military activities in China it is easy to see why Jiang reached that conclusion. As Commanding General U.S. Forces China Theater, Wedemeyer called for the continuation of the American effort to modernize Jiang's military forces. Convinced that Jiang was the personally honest "benevolent dictator" that China needed, Wedemeyer voiced his criticisms of the mediation effort to Marshall as well as to others more sympathetic to Jiang.[21] Admiral Charles Cooke, the former navy planner and current commander of the Seventh Fleet, also urged the Truman administration to maintain its support for Jiang. As the navy's ranking officer in East

Asia, Cooke seconded Secretary Forrestal's conviction that the marines had to hold on in China. Jiang no doubt knew that he had the support of the top military officers in the theater. Indeed, anyone in China could reach the same conclusion just by observing the amount of U.S. aid pouring into Nationalist-held areas. It was difficult to overlook the vast resources employed in moving Jiang's forces north, the marines stationed along the coast, and the tons of surplus war materiel, including planes and ordnance, being turned over to Jiang's government.

The continued presence of armed Japanese troops working alongside the Americans and Nationalists posed a further obstacle for Marshall. By December 1945 only 30,000 Japanese soldiers had been repatriated from China. The scarcity of shipping accounted for some of the delay in clearing out the Japanese. The primary cause, however, was that the Nationalists relied on the Japanese to hold much of north China for them against the Communists. Japanese officers proved more than willing to work with the Guomindang. Following the formal surrender in Nanking, Japan's supreme commander in China, General Okamura Yasuyi offered to put all his men at Jiang's disposal for the purpose of fighting the Communists. In the western province of Shanxi, former warlord and Jiang ally Yen Hsi-shan worked with the Japanese officer Jono Hiroshi to recruit 15,000 Japanese soldiers to fight against the Communists.[22]

Despite these obstacles, Marshall refused to succumb to the pessimism expressed by veteran China watchers. As Marshall explained to Wedemeyer, he had been given a mission and he planned to carry it out. Toward that end, Marshall relied heavily on the army's experienced China officers. Indeed, despite his role as the president's emissary, the Marshall mission was in many respects a U.S. Army mission. As we have seen, Marshall wrote his own instructions with the aid of General Staff officers in Washington. Before leaving the states he also consulted with the army's China Hands, including his friend and fellow retiree Joseph Stilwell. When he arrived in China he leaned heavily on the talents of Wedemeyer's staff officers. Old habits died hard. As one officer in Washington observed, "General Marshall frequently treats the War Department as if he were still Chief of Staff. . . . It makes a very effective working relationship," he added.[23]

Marshall's reliance on his former subordinates was more than a matter of routine. The success of his mission would depend in large measure on his ability to

FIGURE 6.4
The formidable Rear Admiral Charles M. Cooke, circa 1944.
Naval Historical Center, NH 102845

solve what were essentially military problems. His main task was to negotiate a political settlement between the Nationalists and Communists. But any political arrangement would unravel without a carefully administered truce. Once a truce was in place, the two sides would have to find a way to merge their forces into a national military establishment. These were problems that required technical expertise and staff planning that only the army could provide.

When Marshall arrived in China in December, he immediately dove into the task of bringing the opposing sides into formal negotiations. By February, his efforts had produced agreement on the outlines of a political settlement and support for a truce, the latter to be supervised by the Peiping Executive Headquarters, an office comprised of representatives of the CCP, GMD, and United States. Marshall chose Colonel Henry Byroade, one of the army's China Hands, to oversee the operations of Executive Headquarters and staffed it with officers already in China. To implement the truce in the field, Marshall proposed the creation of three-man teams consisting of one American officer, one Communist, and one Nationalist.

The truce was at best a temporary solution. In order to continue the momentum achieved by these early agreements, Marshall also instructed Wedemeyer's staff to construct a plan for the integration of Communist forces into the Nationalist army. Wedemeyer's men were able to complete this task because they had already prepared a proposal to modernize and reduce the size of Jiang's armies. They adapted that plan to include the Communists, by recommending the creation of army groups compromised of one Nationalist and one Communist army. Command of the groups would alternate: one group would be led by a Nationalist officer, another by a Communist. The plan did not specify the number of army groups because no agreement had been reached on the number of Communist divisions to be melded into the unified military establishment. The proposal did, however, recommend that the Communist units be furnished with equipment comparable to that already supplied to the Nationalists.

The officers who drafted the plan thought it best to delay amalgamation for an unspecified "period of readjustment" but Marshall was determined to push ahead. Much to his consternation, he found that Zhou Enlai was also in favor of delaying the integration of Communist forces into the national army. After some discussion Marshall concluded that Zhou's real concern was that the Communist soldiers would suffer humiliation if they were forced to join the

unified army in their present state. Marshall believed that the Communists ir-
regular units would compare poorly in terms of dress and organization, all of
which would lead to a loss of face. Marshall's remedy was to recommend that
the Americans establish a training camp for the Communists away from
Nationalist-held areas so, as one American put it "there would be no Nationalist Government units in the area to sneer at the Communists first efforts to
organize a modernized force." As Marshall later explained to an appalled
Jiang, the purpose of the camp would be "to prepare the communist officers
concerned for the formal organization of their troops into divisions that could
at least march and parade in an acceptable manner."[24]

As Marshall saw it, amalgamation of China's armed forces depended on the
removal of two obstacles, one operational, and the other symbolic. The operational problem was a purely technical matter involving the reorganization of
Communist forces into standardized units that could be moved to designated
areas. More than organizational conformity was needed to make the merger
go smoothly, however. Appearances had to be taken into account if the two
forces were to shed their separate identities. That is where the matter of face
and avoiding embarrassment came in. It is noteworthy that none of the American officers familiar with the plan expressed the slightest hint of bewilder-
ment at Marshall's reason for creating the training school.

In fact, Marshall's explanation was entirely consistent with the longstanding
habit of American officers in China to rely on the concept of face to understand the often baffling behaviors they encountered in China. In doing so,
they were actually equating Chinese behavior with their own profession's system of values that placed a heavy emphasis on a smart appearance. Attentive-
ness to the symbolic importance of parade ground displays came naturally to
most officers. Indeed, while Marshall was proposing to set up the Communist
training school, one of Wedemeyer's subordinates was searching for musical
instruments to use in a military band he hoped to create for the Nationalists.

Marshall's various proposals, especially the development of truce teams,
were creative attempts to solve China's seemingly intractable problems. Marshall's plan to build a training camp for Communists was another imaginative
and sincere attempt to remove the obstacles standing in the way of amalgamation. In this case, however, it seems clear that Marshall trivialized the real
impediments preventing the merger of China's forces. For the time being,
however, Marshall had reason to believe that he was succeeding.

As part of his comprehensive approach to mediation, Marshall sought to reduce points of contention between the United States and the Soviet Union. When American members of the Executive Headquarters learned that Yen Hsi-shan was employing Japanese troops to defend Taiyuan, they dispatched planes to the city to transport them to the coast where they could be processed for repatriation. Marshall also set May 1 as the closeout date for the China Theater and established a schedule for drawing down the number of marines in north China. Marshall believed that closing the theater and its headquarters and reducing the size of the marine expeditionary force would signal to the Soviets that the United States was not preparing to enlarge its military presence in China. In the case of the marines, Marshall reasoned that there were enough to arouse Soviet suspicions but not enough to deter Soviet encroachment in Manchuria, if that was Moscow's aim.

Although Marshall's recommendations were intended to minimize friction with the Soviets they had the unexpected effect of triggering yet another round in the ongoing rivalry over China between the army and navy. Admiral Cooke thought it better to tie the withdrawal of the marines to developing conditions in China. But he also asserted an independent role for the navy in advising Jiang once the theater was inactivated. Cooke's views alarmed Wedemeyer and convinced him that "The Marines are determined to hold on in China as long as possible." "In fact," Wedemeyer confided to Marshall, "there is much evidence suggesting navy (including marines) want to maintain the largest forces both shore and sea in China area."[25] Cooke, of course, hotly disputed Wedemeyer's contention. In communications with Washington, he declared that the navy desired to withdraw the marines as "rapidly as the situation permits." Privately, however, the admirals insisted on keeping up with the army, which at times they appeared to view as a foreign entity. Admiral John Towers, Commander of the Pacific Fleet, argued that the navy needed to maintain the means to discharge its responsibilities in China lest it "suffer in comparison with the performance of not only well-staffed army units but of British, Chinese, and Russian units."[26] The quarrel eventually came to the attention of Eisenhower and Chief of Naval Operations Admiral Chester Nimitz. Eisenhower accepted Nimitz's defense of Cooke and let the matter drop. Only later did it become clear that Cooke's interpretation of the proviso "as rapidly as the situation permits," was broad enough to keep the marines in China well past the date set by Marshall.

As the army and navy jockeyed for position in postwar China, individual officers also looked to the China market as a refuge from the straightened circumstances awaiting them in the peacetime army. As Colonel Willis Scudder recalled, after the war China "still had the aura of being *the* assignment." Referring to the period immediately after the war, he said that "American officers would come over to China and radio their instructions to their wives: 'Bring the longest, biggest, blackest Cadillac you can'. . . . You could sell it to a Chinese official," he explained, "who would pay in Chinese currency the equivalent of $20,000 to $30,000. You would pay less than $10,000."[27] Even when one allows for some exaggeration, the evidence is clear that officers expected conditions in postwar China to resemble the lush years of the 1920s and 1930s.

Colonel Rothwell Brown, a veteran of the 15th Infantry in prewar China had enjoyed the experience so much that he penned several unpublished articles on the pleasures of hunting in China. After serving as an adviser to a Nationalist armored unit during the war, Brown became a member of one of the truce teams while he tried to land a position in the advisory group. Sizing up the situation from his post in Hanoi, General Gallagher looked forward to a spot in the China MAG as the best insurance against being reduced in rank stateside. Gallagher had also served in the 15th Infantry in China before the war. Thinking about the future he worried that in the postwar scramble for assignments the senior officers in other theaters would be in a better position to take care of their subordinates than Wedemeyer. "It is a well known fact," he wrote, "that the boys who belong to the European [Eisenhower] group are definitely getting all the plums in the States, and Marshall in turn is taking care of his so-called 'white-haired' boys. Next in line and probably most powerful will be the MacArthur group, who are very well known, and, finally, I believe, would come our group." Given the circumstances, Gallagher thought "two or three years out here under the pleasant peacetime conditions would be highly desirable." Referring to his wife, he added, "Leila writes that living conditions in the States are going to be poor at best, and that she personally feels that she would enjoy the comforts of a Chinese home and servants. It should be a nice pre-retirement detail."[28]

In light of the looming civil war, Gallagher's anticipation of "pleasant peacetime conditions" in postwar China seems almost delusional. His expectations become more understandable, however, when one recalls that for most of the 1920s and 1930s, China was plagued by internal warfare. Nevertheless, those were good years for American soldiers, sailors, and marines in China. They ended only after 1937, when Japan invaded China below the Great Wall and drove the Nationalists from the coastal cities. Now that the war was over, cosmopolitan China was open for business again. Internal disorder continued and civil war loomed, but had not that always been the case?

For a brief time American officers did manage to re-create conditions approaching those of the prewar years. Members of the advisory group were joined by their families in comfortable quarters. At first the outbreak of civil war did not affect them. "We were not involved in the war," Colonel Scudder told an incredulous interviewer. "It was almost as if it wasn't there." In the immediate postwar years few people could imagine that the Chinese Communists would expel the Nationalists and evict the Americans from the comforts of their Chinese homes and servants.

Staying on in China was an attractive proposition in terms of service and personal professional interests. But American officers' attitudes were shaped by less parochial interests as well. Wedemeyer and the members of his staff, as well as the many army officers who served in the field with Nationalist troops during the final year of the war, had developed close ties to the officers and men they advised and trained. The success of the American trained divisions gave the Americans reason to believe that with continued support they could build a viable modern army in China. This was not the time to abandon an ally, they argued. Strategic imperatives reinforced personal loyalty. Most American officers regarded the Chinese Communists as the vanguard of Soviet imperialism in China. Even if the CCP could not achieve total victory, the turmoil and national fragmentation caused by a Communist insurgency would benefit the Soviets.

Marshall did not dispute that assessment. He too wanted to facilitate the unification of China under Jiang's leadership. But Marshall believed that even with American assistance the Guomindang would not subdue the Communists. For most of his year in China, Marshall tried to convince the Generalissimo that compromise and the creation of a coalition government was the best way to preserve Jiang's leadership in a unified China. Marshall insisted that the truce and amalgamation of the two armies were important confidence-building steps toward that goal. Jiang remained unconvinced, as did Wedemeyer and General Robert McClure, the head of the liaison system known as the Chinese Combat Command. Zhou Enlai also balked at the prospect of an immediate merger of the troops. Instead, he wanted to see more evidence of Jiang's willingness to share power before the CCP submerged its army into a national force. The omens were mixed. The truce agreement was a positive step, but fighting flared in Jehol. Moreover, the truce did not apply to Manchuria. Both parties stockpiled arms in expectation of a Nationalist move into Manchuria on the heels of a Soviet withdrawal. Despite the uneasiness of the situation, Marshall returned to Washington on March 12 to drum up aid for China's postwar reconstruction. General Gillem filled in for Marshall and tried to complete an agreement that would let the truce teams into Manchuria. When the Soviets began to withdraw on March 13, the Nationalists began their big push to retake Manchuria.

By the time Marshall returned to China at the end of April, the Communists had taken Changchun, a vital railway junction in Manchuria north of Shenyang (Mukden). The Communist victory proved temporary. After a month-long siege Jiang's American trained troops took Siping, seventy miles south of Changchun, but not before the Communists had lost more than 40,000 men. The Communists now seemed amenable to a truce. Zhou told Marshall that they would evacuate Changchun. Jiang agreed to halt the Nationalist advance, but the Guomindang troops pressed on. They entered the city on May 22. Jiang's advisers urged the Generalissimo to follow up that success with a drive on Harbin in the north. Jiang rejected that advice and yielded to Marshall's calls for another truce.

The reasons for that decision are unclear. Jiang appears to have feared that outright defiance of Marshall would jeopardize future support from the United States. On the other hand, he instructed his generals in Manchuria and north China to improve their strategic positions in anticipation of a resumption of fighting. In doing so, Jiang acted on his understanding of the contradictions in Marshall's position. Although Marshall personally strove to behave impartially, Jiang recognized that the Truman administration would continue to support the Nationalists in the event of civil war. For his part, Mao also expected the Americans to take Jiang's side in the event of war. Mao was willing to accept a truce in order to postpone a confrontation the Communists were not ready for, but he remained convinced that the hard road of civil war was the only path to power.

Jiang's confidence was reinforced when he learned in mid-June that Congress had voted additional aid to China. The United States promised to supply through Lend Lease $51.7 million dollars of aid currently en route (in the "pipeline") to China. The Truman administration also pledged to sell China nearly a billion dollars worth of surplus equipment at greatly discounted rates. Jiang's hopes and Mao's suspicions had been realized. By July 1, the civil war was in full swing.

During the summer, Marshall worked tirelessly to stop the fighting. Jiang remained confident, however, that he could subdue his mortal enemies through force. Marshall was convinced otherwise. He was certain that full-scale civil war would draw the Soviets in on the Communists' side. Shortly after Japan's surrender the Russians had provided captured Japanese arms to the Chinese Communists and allowed Mao's troops into Manchuria. But the Soviets had withdrawn their own troops in March and Soviet aid to the Communists remained marginal. Jiang's campaign to crush the Communists compounded a political error with a strategic one by overextending Nationalist supply lines and leaving them vulnerable to attack. In order to save the situation in China and Jiang from himself, Marshall received permission from Truman to impose an embargo on lethal aid to the Nationalists.

The embargo, which remained in place for eight months, was a strong sign of American disapproval of Jiang's policies, but it did not interfere with the flow of supplies already headed for China. Jiang continued to press the attack, convinced as always that the Truman administration would support him against the Communists. This was not an unreasonable assumption. In early September, army and navy staff officers in Washington also believed that the United States would have to stand with Jiang. They recognized that the embargo was imposed to assist Marshall in his negotiations, but they believed that once the secretary of state understood the military implications of the embargo he would reverse Marshall's policy. As the navy's top planner argued "In the event of a declared civil war in China we must have a policy on which, before the people of the US we can justify US intervention & assistance to the [GMD]." The paper that emerged from this process was ultimately judged inadequate. The arguments it made, however, would resurface in later debates over China policy. Chief among these was the assertion that a failure to aid the Nationalists would weaken the confidence of other nations under threat from communism. Within a generation, according to the emerging view, this demoralization could lead to varying degrees of Soviet control over Manchuria, Korea, Southeast Asia, and India.

In order to prevent this from happening, the army prescribed a continuation of material and moral support to the Nationalist government. The navy made similar predictions and also argued for continued material support to the Nationalists. More specifically, the navy called for the indefinite continuation of the marines' mission in north China even though most Japanese troops would be repatriated by December. The public justification for keeping the marines in place would be that for the time being the Nationalists required the assistance of Japanese technical experts. According to the navy's new rationale, the marines would need to stay in north China in order to assure the eventual elimination of Japanese influence from China.

These arguments made little impression on Marshall. With Truman's support he overrode navy objections and insisted on the concentration of marine units in preparation for their departure from China. As Dean Acheson later recalled, it took the president's "crisp instruction to Secretary Forrestal and Admiral Leahy that he wanted General Marshall's recommendations carried out explicitly and promptly" in order to gain the navy's compliance.[29] In late September Marshall made one last effort to negotiate a cease-fire. Nationalist forces were driving on Kalgan, the projected location of the ill-fated training camp for Communist officers. After Jiang agreed to halt operations against the city, Nationalist armies captured it on October 10. Marshall's mission was effectively ended.

In December, the bulk of the marine forces withdrew and a weary Marshall returned to Washington to become the new secretary of state, a development that Jiang could not have found comforting. In China, the fighting soon spread as Jiang sought to capture the Manchurian prize. According to U.S. intelligence reports, the Nationalists were aided in that endeavor by nearly 80,000 unrepatriated Japanese troops. Meanwhile, chastened by his exertions in China, the new secretary began the New Year by taking stock of America's strategic position in East Asia a year and a half after Japan's surrender.

When Marshall returned to Washington he did not wash his hands of the China mess. The new secretary of state still hoped that something could be done to aid the Nationalists. He was, however, unwilling to make an open-ended commitment of American resources to what increasingly looked like a lost cause. In 1947 a series of Communist victories in Manchuria against Jiang's overextended forces confirmed those fears. Domestic politics as well as apprehensiveness about the impact of a Communist victory compelled Marshall to continue aid to the Nationalists. Civil war in Greece and economic crisis in Western Europe were more pressing, but Marshall concluded that in order to win congressional support for the Truman Doctrine and Marshall Plan he would need to placate the Republican friends of Jiang in Congress by seeking aid for the Nationalists as well.

In May 1947, Marshall lifted the arms embargo. But pressure to aid Jiang grew stronger. A month later the JCS strayed into the area of policy by strongly urging the Truman administration to provide the Nationalists with the means to defeat the Communists. Admiral Nimitz followed that recommendation with a call for an update on the situation in China and a report on the specific military actions needed to aid the Nationalists. By the end of June, the JCS recommended the prompt delivery of ammunition and a moratorium on U.S. troop withdrawals. The secretaries of the War and Navy Departments seconded those recommendations. Marshall found the military's reasoning "somewhat impracticable" but he agreed to see what else the United States could do.[30]

Toward that end, Marshall dispatched Albert Wedemeyer to assess conditions in China and, as something of an afterthought, Korea. Wedemeyer's support for Jiang was well known, as were his contacts with prominent Republicans such as Herbert Hoover and Henry Luce. Nevertheless, Marshall no doubt hoped that Wedemeyer would report that Jiang's situation was hopeless and thereby provide the Truman administration with unimpeachable grounds for cutting off aid to the Nationalists. Marshall had reason to be hopeful. Wedemeyer was a Marshall protégé and while his success was the result of his own talent, he could not forget that Marshall had given young Major Wedemeyer the opportunities to demonstrate his ability. Moreover, in 1947, the brass ring seemed tantalizingly within reach. Wedemeyer was widely thought to be a contender for the job of army chief of staff after Eisenhower retired. Marshall's support would be of inestimable value for anyone seeking the army's top spot.

Much to Marshall's and Truman's consternation, Wedemeyer reported back that the United States could save Jiang from himself by sending approximately 10,000 military advisers to help train and direct Nationalist troops. Wedemeyer acknowledged the need for reform in China, but he insisted that military aid took precedence over political reform. Not surprisingly, Marshall and

Truman declined Wedemeyer's invitation to plunge the United States more deeply into China's civil war. Wedemeyer later said that Marshall "virtually told me that if I had any hopes of advancing to the Chief of Staff's job, my report did not enhance that possibility."[31]

Of course, neither Truman nor Marshall welcomed Jiang's failure. They simply believed that in light of the many problems the United States faced, American resources could be more wisely invested elsewhere. Truman blocked the release of Wedemeyer's report and placed restrictions on his testimony to Congress, which only increased the calls for aid to China from Jiang's supporters. Wedemeyer had failed to provide Marshall with the clean break from Jiang he desired. For the next two years, until the Communists drove the Nationalists from the mainland, the United States would continue to provide military advice, arms, and equipment to the Nationalists. This modicum of support would never satisfy the administration's critics, but it would be just enough to persuade Jiang and Mao that direct American intervention was only a matter of time.

NOTES

1. Stephen Rosskamm Shalom, *The United States and the Philippines: A Study of Neocolonialism* (Philadelphia: Institute for the Study of Human Issues, 1981), 20–21. See also H. W. Brands, *Bound to Empire: The United States and the Philippines* (New York: Oxford University Press, 1992), 218–219.

2. "Roxas Claims GIs Aid Reds," *New York Times*, 16 October 1946; Nick Cullather, *Illusions of Influence: The Political Economy of United States-Philippines Relations, 1942–1960* (Stanford, CA: Stanford University Press, 1994), 51; Benedict J. Kerkvliet, *The Huk Rebellion: A Study of Peasant Revolt in the Philippines* (Berkeley: University of California Press, 1977), 150–151.

3. James F. Schnabel, *The History of the Joint Chiefs of Staff: The Joint Chiefs of Staff and National Policy. Volume 1: 1945–1947* (Wilmington, DE: Michael Glazier, Inc., 1979), 341–346; Cullather, *Illusions of Influence*, 54–59; Shalom, *United States and the Philippines*, 59–67; Lawrence M. Greenberg, *The Hukbalahap Insurrection: A Case Study of a Successful Anti-Insurgency Operation in the Philippines, 1946–1955* (Washington, DC: U.S. Army Center of Military History, 1987), 99.

4. Brig. General Philip Gallagher to Maj. General Robert McClure, 20 September 1945, Philip E. Gallagher Papers, U.S. Army Center for Military History, Washington, D.C.

5. Ronald Spector, *Advice and Support: The Early Years, 1941–1960. The United States Army in Vietnam* (Washington, DC: Center of Military History, 1983), 72.

6. Hal Brands, "Who Saved the Emperor? The MacArthur Myth and U.S. Policy toward Hirohito and the Japanese Imperial Institution, 1942–1946," *Pacific Historical Review* 75 (May 2006), 271–305.

7. Daniel Barenblatt, *A Plague Upon Humanity: The Hidden History of Japan's Biological Warfare Program* (New York: HarperCollins, 2004), 207.

8. Eiji Takemae, *Inside GHQ: The Allied Occupation of Japan and its Legacy* (New York: Continuum, 2002), 255.

9. On Unit 731 and the cover up, see Sheldon Harris, *Factories of Death: Japanese Biological Warfare 1932–45 and the American Cover-Up* (London: Routledge, 1994) as well as the books by Barenblatt and Takemae cited above.

10. John Hunter Boyle, *Modern Japan: The American Nexus* (Fort Worth, TX: Harcourt Brace Jovanovich, 1993), 323; Haruou Iguchi, "The First Revisionists: Bonner Fellers, Herbert Hoover, and Hirohito's Struggle to Surrender," in Marc Gallicchio, ed. *The Unpredictability of the Past: Memories of the Asia-Pacific War in U.S.–East Asian Relations* (Durham, NC: Duke University Press, 2007); John W. Dower, *Embracing Defeat: Japan in the Wake of World War II* (New York: W. W. Norton & Co., 1999), 277–339.

11. Richard B. Finn, *Winners in Peace: MacArthur, Yoshida and Postwar Japan* (Berkeley: University of California Press, 1992), 114–117; D. Clayton James, *The Years of Macarthur, Volume III: Triumph and Disaster, 1945–1964* (Boston: Houghton Mifflin Company, 1985), 343.

12. "Reform of the Japanese Governmental System," JCS Memorandum for SWNCC, 18 December 1945, *FRUS, 1946*, 7: 102–103.

13. John Welfield, *An Empire in Eclipse: Japan in the Postwar American Alliance System* (London: Athlone Press, 1988), 65–70.

14. Meirion and Susie Harries, *Sheathing the Sword: The Demilitarization of Japan* (New York: Macmillan, 1987), 231.

15. Paul Chwialkowski, *In Caesar's Shadow: The Life of General Robert Eichelberger* (Westport, CT: Greenwood Press, 1993), 158–162.

16. Memorandum by the Joint Chiefs of Staff to the State-War-Navy Coordinating Committee, and Appendices, 12 May 1947, *FRUS, 1947*, 1: 734–750; Michael

Schaller, *The American Occupation of Japan: The Origins of the Cold War in Asia* (New York: Oxford University Press, 1985), 90.

17. "Fast demobilization Invites War, Hurts Prestige, Eichelberger Says," *New York Times*, 7 April 1946, 28.

18. "Help for Korea," *New York Times*, 19 March 1947, 24.

19. "The Two-Zone Test on the Korean Peninsula," *New York Times*, 26 February 1947, 24. The JCS are quoted in James I. Matray, *The Reluctant Crusade: American Foreign Policy in Korea, 1941–1950* (Honolulu: University of Hawaii Press, 1985), 114. On continuing GI protests as well as the relationship between the Truman Doctrine and Korea, see William Stueck, *Rethinking the Korean War: A New Diplomatic and Strategic History* (Princeton, NJ: Princeton University Press, 2002), 48–55, n43; and Matray, 108.

20. Wedemeyer to Brigadier General C. T. Lanham, 12 February 1946, Folder U.S.-3, Box 3-A, Albert C. Wedemeyer Papers, Hoover Institution, Stanford, California. Wedemeyer also alleged that criticism of United States–China policy was also instigated by "the old Stilwell crowd." Wedemeyer to Patrick Hurley, 24 December 1945, Folder 3-E, Hurley File, Albert C. Wedemeyer Papers.

21. Marc S. Gallicchio, *The Cold War Begins in Asia: American East Asian Policy and the Fall of the Japanese Empire* (New York: Columbia University Press, 1988), 141.

22. The CCP also recruited the Japanese. Accurate figures are unavailable but the authors conclude there were far fewer Japanese working with the Communists than with the Nationalists. Donald Gillin and Charles Etter, "Staying On: Japanese Soldiers and Civilians in China, 1945–1949," *Journal of Asian Studies*, 42 (May 1983), 497–518.

23. Lawrence Lincoln to Wedemeyer, 12 February 1946, Marshall folder, Box 3-F, Wedemeyer Papers, Hoover Institute.

24. All quotes from Marc Gallicchio, "About Face: General Marshall's Plans for the Amalgamation of Communist and Nationalist Armies in China," in Larry I. Bland, ed. *George C. Marshall's Mediation Mission to China, December 1945–January 1947* (Lexington, VA: George C. Marshall Foundation, 1998), 391–407.

25. For this quarrel see Memorandum for the Record, 27 February 1946; Memorandum for the Record, 11 March 1946; Admiral Chester Nimitz to General Eisenhower, 4 April 1946, enclosing Nimitz to Admiral John Towers, n.d.; all in P&O 484 TS, Policy and Operations, 1946–1948, RG 319, Modern Military Records

Branch, National Archives, College Park, Maryland; and Larry I. Bland, editor *The Papers of George Catlett Marshall* 5, *"The Finest Soldier": January 1, 1945–January 7, 1947* (Baltimore, MD: Johns Hopkins University Press, 2003), 326, n.1.

26. Towers to the Chief of Naval Operations, 9 May 1946, folder C-2 (4), Box 158, OP30, Operations, Naval Historical Center, Washington Navy Yard, Washington, DC.

27. Interview with Colonel White and Colonel Willis Scudder, 7 June 1983, Willis B. Scudder Papers, Military History Institute, Carlisle Barracks, Carlisle, Pennsylvania.

28. Gallagher to General Robert McClure, 26 October 1945, Philip Gallagher Papers, Center for Military History.

29. Edward J. Marolda, "The U.S. Navy and the Loss of China, 1945–1950," Bland, ed., *Marshall's Mediation Mission*, 412.

30. Schnabel, *The Joint Chiefs of Staff and National Policy, 1945–1947*, 447–455.

31. Robert Hertzstein, *Henry R. Luce, Time, and the American Crusade in Asia* (Cambridge, MA: Cambridge University Press, 2005), 89.

7

Conclusion: No Peace for Asia

A year after Japan surrendered the *Newsweek* correspondent Harold Isaacs declared that a traveler in Asia could go from the Korean peninsula through China to the tip of Indonesia and rarely be out of the sound of gunfire.[1] Those conditions worsened the following year as civil war and revolution erupted throughout the region. The volatile conditions in Asia posed a new challenge for the United States at a time when most Americans expected to be able to return to peacetime pursuits and enjoy the fruits of their hard won victories over Germany and Japan. American officials were not completely surprised by the turmoil that followed Japan's defeat, but they remained uncertain of how to respond to the unsettled conditions in Asia. Did the changes sweeping over the continent threaten American security? Did the anticolonialism and civil strife jeopardize America's postwar plans for the region? Did the conflict spreading throughout the mainland create new opportunities for Soviet expansion?

Consideration of these questions took place under rapidly changing circumstances. As we have seen, American power in the region reached its zenith in September 1945, and swiftly ebbed after that. A month after Japan's surrender, 40,000 marines landed in north China, creating a larger American military presence in that country than existed during the entire war. The same month the combat ready XXIV Corps under Lieutenant General John Hodge occupied Korea below the thirty-eighth parallel. Across the Korea Strait, an

American force consisting of approximately 460,000 troops occupied Japan. Within weeks, however, American congressmen began receiving angry letters demanding the return of loved ones stationed in the far-flung reaches of Japan's former empire. The rapid pace of demobilization continued over the next two years. By 1947 the armed forces consisted of one and a half million men and women, down from the wartime high of twelve million. America's armed forces did not demobilize, Harry Truman recalled, they "disintegrated."

The mounting dissatisfaction of the American public and the public disagreements between American officials reflected a genuine uncertainty about the peacetime purposes of American military power. But the growing concern over American policy also owed much to the surprising suddenness with which the decisions to send troops onto the Asian mainland were made. Despite nearly four years of total war in the Pacific, the decisions that led to an unprecedented American military presence in Asia were made only weeks before Japan's surrender.

During the next two years, American military and political officials struggled with the consequences of those decisions as they sought to build a stable democratic Japan, a non-communist China allied to the United States, and a newly independent Korea free from internal turmoil and great power manipulation. Americans also hoped that the example of Philippine independence would serve as a model for the creation of an independent non-communist Vietnam. Instead, French obduracy led to the Vietminh insurgency. The Philippine government's protection of entrenched interests provoked a rebellion among the peasants of central Luzon. In South Korea an authoritarian government took power and held onto it by brutally suppressing all opposition. Japan seemed a haven of tranquility in the midst of turmoil. Looming over all was the problem of China.

Seismic forces were at work in Asia at the end of the war. The civil conflict that roiled Asia was the consequence of vast inequalities and social dislocation rooted in hundreds of years of exploitation by imperialists and indigenous elites. Japan's bid to dominate Asia was the latest chapter in that saga. In banishing the older imperialists, however, Japan had shattered the myth of white supremacy and nourished nationalist aspirations throughout the region. Japan's defeat reopened the question of who would rule Asia. The surrender touched off a frenzy of expectation and opportunist maneuvering by the great powers seeking to reclaim lost empires or create new ones. The end of the war also created new opportunities for revolutionary nationalists to challenge the power of traditional elites and foreign overlords.

In the waning days of the war, the United States joined the scramble for Asia. Distance from the mainland placed the United States at a disadvantage. Difficulty in obtaining shipping and unavoidable delays in mounting troops for unexpected deployments in China and Korea posed additional problems. Britain and Nationalist China faced similar obstacles. In the aftermath of Japan's surrender, the Truman administration found it necessary to prolong the life of the Japanese empire rather than see Vietnamese, Koreans, or Chinese Communists enhance their claims to legitimacy by taking the surrender of Japanese troops. The scramble for Asia did not occur in a vacuum. Japan retained considerable power by virtue of the vast territory still controlled by its unconquered troops. Worries that Japanese troops might continue to resist the emperor's order to surrender were compounded by concerns that Japanese troops might surrender to the wrong people. General Order Number One provided the means through which the United States, Britain, and China sought to employ Japan's military forces for their own purposes.

From the start, the task of taking the surrender of Japanese troops was a political as well as military operation. American forces performed the military aspects of that mission with skill and efficiency. The repatriation of millions of Japanese soldiers and civilians to Japan, the evacuation of hundreds of thousands of Korean and Chinese forced laborers from Japan, and the transportation of 500,000 Nationalist Chinese troops north were monumental undertakings. Those accomplishments appear even more impressive when one considers that they occurred while the United States brought home millions of GIs from Europe and the Pacific. American forces displayed a remarkable capacity for solving the technical problems involved in moving large numbers of people great distances. They were less successful, however, in producing remedies for the political turmoil that followed in the aftermath of Japan's surrender.

In retrospect it seems clear that it was never within the ability of American military forces to achieve the orderly transfers of power that their presence in Korea, China, and Vietnam were intended to secure. The deck was stacked against them. The Americans arrived late and left early. American soldiers and marines were a momentary presence in an area where change had been underway for decades. Understaffed and ill-prepared for their missions, the hastily inserted American forces were incapable of achieving the ambitious political goals of their evolving missions.

At times the Americans added to their difficulties through their own actions. The decision to use the sixteenth parallel in Indochina as the boundary between the Chinese and British occupations was one such case. American policy supported a resumption of French rule. Nevertheless, the temporary partition of the country for purposes of the surrender inadvertently gave the Vietnamese revolution valuable breathing space in which to develop. In the Philippines and Korea American commanders consciously relied on entrenched elites to provide an orderly transfer of power from Japanese rule. Hodge believed that excluding the Korean Left from participation in the military government was in keeping with his real mission, the blocking of Soviet influence on the peninsula. In both cases, the Americans left those seeking radical change little recourse except resistance. In Korea opposition to the return of the old order took the form of strikes, riots, and armed uprisings in the countryside. In the Philippines, the Huks resorted to armed rebellion after being excluded from the electoral process.

In China, incipient civil war made the process of taking the Japanese surrender overtly political. The Americans transported Nationalist troops and landed marines in the north for the ostensible purpose of taking the surrender of Japanese troops. The Nationalists, it could be argued, were fulfilling the responsibilities expected of them in General Order Number One. But the marines were in China to prevent the Communists from expanding into the north. In either case, the Chinese Communists could not be expected to sit idly by while Jiang regained control over the territory he had yielded to the Japanese. That placed the marines in the middle. Like Hodge, Wedemeyer concluded that his instructions were inherently contradictory. He could not transport Nationalist troops, disarm the Japanese, and avoid involvement in China's fratricidal war. The marines expressed the same understanding of their role when they asked "Who are we supposed to be neutral against?"

Japan was an exception to the turmoil that greeted Americans elsewhere. There, after much planning and preparation, American occupation forces arrived in large numbers. The movement of American troops into the home islands occurred earlier than expected, but unlike the deployments in China and Korea, the occupation was a fulfillment of American plans, not a departure. More important for the success of the occupation was that unlike China,

Korea, or Vietnam, the authority of the prewar Japanese government remained intact.[2] In the long run, the decision to conduct the occupation
through the existing government gave Japanese authorities considerable opportunity to blunt or obstruct SCAP's reforms. In the short run, however, reliance on the government, including the emperor, smoothed the way for the
occupation.

Two years after Japan's surrender the United States abandoned its more
ambitious goals on the mainland in recognition of the limits of its power.
Japan was once again the key to American strategy. The navy appeared willing
to concede the contest over China to the army. By early 1947 the admirals were
moving away from their infatuation with China. Instead they looked to
Japan's Yokosuka naval base as their new home in the western Pacific. Navy
plans envisioned the offshore islands as bases from which to launch offensive
operations against the Soviet Union in the event of war. This emphasis on
Japan amounted to a return to earlier thinking about American postwar security in East Asia. As early as May 1945, Admiral Cooke had warned that conditions in China might require the United States to rehabilitate Japan. That
summer, on the eve of the Potsdam Conference, General Lincoln's Strategy
and Policy Group had concluded that a divided China and enlarged Soviet
presence in Manchuria would not threaten America's vital interests so long as
the United States controlled Japan.

In keeping with its reassessment of ends and means, The Truman administration gingerly tried to disengage from its commitment to Nationalist China
and sought to avoid being drawn further into that country's civil war. American forces withdrew from Korea and placed that country's political future in
the care of the United Nations. Efforts to revive Japan's struggling economy
and ensure that country's cooperation with the United States replaced earlier
plans to project American power onto the mainland. With trouble brewing
elsewhere, a defensive position anchored on the offshore island chain promised to offer the most economical protection of American security.

Still, the American presence lingered on the mainland. Military Advisory
Groups in China and South Korea and a small marine contingent at Tsingtao
betrayed the administration's ambivalent attitude toward its new offshore policy. The administration's support for the South Korean government and continued congressional endorsement of Jiang Jieshi's Nationalist regime further
frustrated any attempts at a clean break from the mainland. For the moment,

however, the situation seemed manageable. More critical problems elsewhere, in Europe and the Middle East, claimed the administration's attention and resources. Few Americans could imagine that within three years the United States would become France's chief source of aid in a war against the Vietminh or that the United States would be thrust once more into the middle of the Chinese civil war while American troops battled to a deadly stalemate on the Korean peninsula.

NOTES

1. Harold R. Isaacs, *No Peace for Asia* (Cambridge: MIT Press, 1967), 1. This is a reprint of the 1947 edition with a new introduction by the author.

2. Ronald H. Spector, "After Hiroshima: Allied Military Occupations and the fate of Japan's Empire, 1945–1947," *Journal of Military History* 69 (October 2005), 1135–1136.

Selected Bibliography

The following is an abbreviated list of the works I found most useful in writing this book. It is offered as a guide for further research and is not a comprehensive list of works cited in the end notes. Individual manuscript collections and repositories are cited in the endnotes.

BACKGROUND, SURVEYS, AND ESSENTIAL WORKS

Readers should begin with Ronald H. Spector, *In the Ruins of Empire: The Japanese Surrender and the Battle for Postwar Asia* (New York: Random House, 2007). Spector's book became available as I was making the final revisions on this manuscript. However, he previewed some of his arguments in "After Hiroshima: Allied Military Occupations and the Fate of Japan's Empire, 1945–1947," *Journal of Military History* 69 (October 2005), 1121–1136. In the earlier article and the book, Spector gives equal time to British operations in Southeast Asia and presents a truly international perspective on the aftermath of the war. For an early vivid account of these events by a veteran journalist see Harold R. Isaacs, *No Peace for Asia* (Cambridge: MIT Press, 1967). Isaacs's warning about the consequences of the great powers' failure to accommodate the forces of Asian nationalism was originally published in 1947.

For the diplomatic background see Akira Iriye, *The Cold War in Asia: A Historical Introduction* (Englewood Cliffs, NJ: Prentice Hall, 1974). Melvyn P. Leffler, *A Preponderance of Power: National Security, the Truman Administration, and the Cold War* (Stanford, CA: Stanford University Press, 1992) is a magisterial look at American policy making in the early Cold War.

Readers can begin their own research with several readily available primary sources. The United States Department of State, *Foreign Relations of the United States*, commonly referred to as FRUS, is the official diplomatic record of the United States. Most of the volumes, including those for the Truman years, have been made available online courtesy of the University of Wisconsin Digital Collections at the following web address: http://digicoll.library.wisc.edu/FRUS/. I also benefited from using *The Historical New York Times*, a searchable database published by ProQuest Historical Newspapers.

CHAPTER ONE

My discussion of unconditional surrender and the end of the war with Japan draws on my own research but it also leans heavily on the following works. Brian Loring Villa, "The U.S. Army, Unconditional Surrender, and the Potsdam Proclamation," *Journal of American History* 63 (June 1976), 66–92, remains one of the best studies of the unconditional surrender policy. As the title indicates, Michael D. Pearlman, *Unconditional Surrender, Demobilization, and the Atomic Bomb* (Fort Leavenworth, KS: Combat Studies Institute, U.S. Army Command and General Staff College, 1996)[1] carefully reconstructs the connection between manpower issues and national policy. Other important works are Charles F. Brower, "The Joint Chiefs of Staff and National Policy: American Strategy and the War with Japan, 1943–1945," Ph.D. dissertation, University of Pennsylvania, 1987; Keith Eiler, *Mobilizing America: Robert P. Patterson and the War Effort, 1940–1945* (Ithaca, NY: Cornell University Press, 1997); Mark A. Stoler, *Allies and Adversaries: The Joint Chiefs of Staff, the Grand Alliance, and U.S. Strategy in World War II* (Chapel Hill: University of North Carolina Press, 2000). Richard B. Frank, *Downfall: The End of the Imperial Japanese Empire* (New York: Random House, 1999) is a compelling and comprehensive look at final months of the war. For a highly readable survey that highlights the hopelessness of Japan's situation see Thomas Zeiler, *Unconditional Defeat: Japan, America, and the End of World War II* (Wilmington, DE: Scholarly Resources, 2004). Much ink has been spilled in the debate over the decision to use the atomic bombs and their impact on the end of the war. The works I found most useful, in addition to Frank, *Downfall*, are Edward J. Drea, *MacArthur's Ultra: Codebreaking and the War Against Japan, 1942–1945*

(Lawrence: University Press of Kansas, 1992); Robert James Maddox, *Weapons for Victory: The Hiroshima Decision Fifty Years Later* (Columbia: University of Missouri Press, 1995) and Robert P. Newman, *Truman and the Hiroshima Cult* (East Lansing: Michigan State University Press, 1995). Douglas J. MacEachin, *The Final Months of the War with Japan: Signals Intelligence, U.S. Invasion Planning, and the A-Bomb* (Central Intelligence Agency: Center for the Study of Intelligence, 1998), contains facsimiles of many of the planning documents for the invasion.

For the Republican perspective on unconditional surrender see Gary Dean Best, *Herbert Hoover: The Post-Presidential Years, 1933–1964* (Stanford, CA: Hoover Institution Press, 1983); and Robert E. Hertzstein, *Henry R. Luce, Time, and the American Crusade in Asia* (Cambridge, MA: Cambridge University Press, 2005). Mountbatten's views can be followed in John Terraine, *The Life and Times of Lord Mountbatten* (London: Hutchinson, 1968); and Philip Ziegler, ed. *Personal Diary of Admiral the Lord Louis Mountbatten, Supreme Allied Commander, South-East Asia, 1943–1946* (London: Collins, 1988) in addition to Spector, *In the Ruins of Empire.*

CHAPTER TWO

For the Soviet campaign against Japan begin with David Glantz, *August Storm: the Soviet Strategic Offensive in Manchuria* (Fort Leavenworth, KS: Combat Studies Institute, U.S. Army Command and General Staff College, 1983).[2] Glantz is the leading authority on AUGUST STORM and much else about the Soviet Army in World War II. Tsuyoshi Hasegawa, *Stalin, Truman, and the Surrender of Japan* (Cambridge, MA: Belknap Press of Harvard University Press, 2005) is good on Stalin's diplomatic maneuvering but unpersuasive in its argument that Soviet entry would have been sufficient to compel Japan's surrender. The final acts of the war are analyzed in two important scholarly articles; Barton J. Bernstein, "The Perils and Politics of Surrender: Ending the War with Japan and Avoiding a Third Atomic Bomb," *Pacific Historical Review* 66 (February 1977), 1–25; and Sadao Asada, "The Shock of the Atomic Bomb and Japan's Decision to Surrender—A Reconsideration," *Pacific Historical Review* 67 (November 1998), 477–512, reprinted with minor changes in Asada, *Culture Shock and Japanese-American Relations: Historical Essays* (Columbia: University of Missouri Press, 2007). The making of General Order Number One is covered in Marc S. Gallicchio, *The Cold War Begins in Asia: American East Asian*

Policy and the Fall of the Japanese Empire (New York: Columbia University Press, 1988); and Judith Munro Leighton, "The Tokyo Surrender: A Diplomatic Marathon in Washington, August 10–14, 1945," *Pacific Historical Review* 65 (August 1996), 455–474. MacArthur's eleventh-hour maneuvers are described in D. Clayton James, *The Years of MacArthur* II, *1941–1945* (Boston: Houghton Mifflin Company, 1975), and Frank, *Downfall.* On the surrenders see Samuel Eliot Morison, *U.S. Naval Operations in World War II.* Volume 14, *Victory in the Pacific* (Boston: Houghton Mifflin Company, 1960); and Louis Allen, *The End of the War in Asia* (London: Hart-Davis MacGibbon, 1976). For Mountbatten and SEAC operations see the works cited above and John Ehrman, *Grand Strategy. 6: October 1944–August 1945* (London: Her Majesty's Stationery Office, 1956).

CHAPTER THREE

The following works were especially helpful in preparing the biographical sketches of MacArthur, Hodge, and Wedemeyer: James, *The Years of MacArthur.* Volumes 1–3 (Boston: Houghton Mifflin, 1970–1985); Michael Schaller, *Douglas MacArthur: The Far Eastern General* (New York: Oxford University Press, 1989) debunks the myth, propagated by the general and his supporters, that MacArthur possessed a superior understanding of Asian affairs. There is no full biography of Hodge but see Michael C. Sandusky, *America's Parallel* (Alexandria, VA: Old Dominion Press, 1983), which is a briskly written work critical of Hodge's conduct. Although primarily about Korea, this overlooked gem deals with many of the political and military issues raised by Japan's surrender. Albert C. Wedemeyer, *Wedemeyer Reports!* (New York: Holt, 1958) and Keith E. Eiler, ed. *Wedemeyer on War and Peace* (Stanford, CA: Hoover Institution Press, 1987) tell the general's story from his point of view. Eiler has collected and published some of Wedemeyer's most significant reports and memoranda. William Stueck, *The Wedemeyer Mission: American Politics and Foreign Policy during the Cold War* (Athens: University of Georgia Press, 1984) is a more critical but fair analysis of the general. The situation at the State Department is well covered in Robert L. Messer, *The End of an Alliance: James F. Byrnes, Roosevelt, Truman, and the Origins of the Cold War* (Chapel Hill: University of North Carolina Press, 1982); Robert L. Beisner, *Dean Acheson: A Life in the Cold War* (New York: Oxford University Press, 2006); and Gary May, *China Scapegoat: The Diplomatic Ordeal of John Carter Vincent* (Washington, DC: New Republic Books, 1979).

The following works nicely explain political conditions in the Philippines and American policy toward the islands from liberation to independence: H. W. Brands, *Bound to Empire: The United States and the Philippines* (New York: Oxford University Press, 1992); Nick Cullather, *Illusions of Influence: The Political Economy of United States–Philippines Relations, 1942–1960* (Stanford, CA: Stanford University Press, 1994); Benedict J. Kerkvliet, *The Huk Rebellion: A Study of Peasant Revolt in the Philippines* (Berkeley: University of California Press, 1977); Stephen Rosskamm Shalom, *The United States and the Philippines: A Study of Neocolonialism* (Philadelphia: Institute for the Study of Human Issues, 1981). These works are critical of MacArthur's and the Philippine elite's treatment of the Huks, but so is Major Lawrence M. Greenberg, *The Hukbalahap Insurrection: A Case Study of a Successful Anti-Insurgency Operation in the Philippines, 1946–1955* (Washington, DC: U.S. Army Center of Military History, 1987).

The details regarding the disarmament of Japan and the repatriation of Japanese troops can be found in two official histories, Douglas MacArthur, *Reports of General MacArthur, Supreme Commander for the Allied Powers*, 2 volumes (Washington, DC: U.S. Government Printing Office, 1966); and Charles R. Smith, *Securing the Surrender: Marines in the Occupation of Japan* (Washington, DC: Marine Corps Historical Center, 1997) as well as James, *Years of MacArthur*.

Official histories stress the inadequacy of preparation for the occupation of Korea. Independent scholarly studies agree but to varying degrees they find fault with Hodge's decisions to favor the Right. See James F. Schnabel, United States Army in the Korean War series, *Policy and Direction, the First Year* (Washington, DC: U.S. Army Center of Military History, 1972), Robert K. Sawyer, *United States Military Advisory Group to the Republic of Korea* (Washington, DC: Office of the Chief of Military History, Dept. of the Army, 1955). Bruce Cumings, *The Origins of the Korean War: Liberation and the Emergence of Separate Regimes, 1945–1947* (Princeton, NJ: Princeton University Press, 1981) provides the most authoritative and detailed analysis of the political and social conditions that the Americans found so vexatious. In addition to Sandusky, *America's Parallel*, I also relied heavily on James I. Matray, *The Reluctant Crusade: American Foreign Policy in Korea* (Honolulu: University of Hawaii Press, 1985) and William Stueck, *Rethinking the Korean War: A New Diplomatic and Strategic History* (Princeton, NJ: Princeton

University Press, 2002), both of which are particularly helpful in explaining American policy.

Postwar military operations in China are well covered in official histories. See James F. Schnabel, *The Joint Chiefs of Staff and National Policy, Volume I: 1945–1947* (Wilmington, DE: Michael Glazier, Inc., 1979) and Benis M. Frank and Henry I. Saw, Jr., *History of U.S. Marine Corps Operations in World War II, Volume V: Victory and Occupation* (Washington, DC: Historical Branch, G-3 Division, Headquarters, U.S. Marine Corps, 1968). Two memoirs, E. B. Sledge, *China Marine* (Tuscaloosa: University of Alabama Press, 2002) and the unpublished manuscript by Henry Aplington II, *Sunset in the East: A North China Memoir, 1945–1947,* colorfully describe conditions in north China from the perspective of an enlisted man and an officer. Warren I. Cohen, *America's Response to China: A History of Sino-American Relations* (New York: Columbia University Press, 2000, 4th edition) is a delight to read and does the best job of placing U.S. policy in historical context. Vincent's battles with the Pentagon are covered in May, *China Scapegoat* and Gallicchio, *The Cold War Begins in Asia.* Odd Arne Westad, *Cold War and Revolution: Soviet-American Rivalry and the Origins of the Chinese Civil War, 1944–1946* (New York: Columbia University Press, 1993); Westad, *Decisive Encounters: The Chinese Civil War, 1946–1950:* (Stanford, CA: Stanford University Press, 2003); and Chen Jian, *Mao's China and the Cold War* (Chapel Hill: University of North Carolina Press, 2001) have done much to improve our understanding of Mao's and Stalin's policies in the immediate postwar period.

The literature on U.S. involvement in Indochina is voluminous. The best account of General Gallagher's mission is in Ronald H. Spector, *The United States Army in Vietnam, The Early Years, 1941–1960: Advice and Support* (Washington, DC: Center of Military History 1983). For understanding the situation on both sides of the sixteenth parallel I found the following very helpful: Mark Philip Bradley, *Imagining Vietnam and America: the Making of Postcolonial Vietnam, 1919–1950* (Chapel Hill: University of North Carolina Press, 2000); Peter Dennis, *Troubled Days of Peace: Mountbatten and Southeast Asia Command, 1945–1946* (New York: St. Martin's Press, 1987); Lloyd C. Gardner, *Approaching Vietnam: From World War II Through Dienbienphu, 1941–1954* (New York: W. W. Norton & Co., 1988); John T. McAlister, *Vietnam: Origins of a Revolution* (Garden City, New York: Doubleday and Company, 1971).

CHAPTER FOUR

The domestic turmoil that greeted Truman is vividly described in Robert J. Donovan, *Conflict and Crisis: The Presidency of Harry S. Truman, 1945–1948* (New York: W. W. Norton, 1977). My discussion of postwar military politics leaned heavily on Ernest R. May, "Cold War and Defense," in Keith Neilson and Ronald G. Haycock, eds., *The Cold War and Defense* (New York: Praeger, 1990); James, *Years of MacArthur*; Walter Millis, ed., *The Forrestal Diaries* (New York: Viking Press, 1951); Schnabel, *The Joint Chiefs of Staff and National Policy, Volume I: 1945–1947*; and Leffler, *A Preponderance of Power*. The official history of the demobilization controversy by John C. Sparrow, *History of Personnel Demobilization in the United States Army* (Washington, DC: Center of Military History, United States Army, 1951, facsimile, 1990) describes the protestors as unknowing Communist dupes. More balanced assessments are available in Jack Stokes Ballard, *The Shock of Peace: Military and Economic Demobilization in World War II* (Washington, DC: University Press of America, 1983) and R. Alton Lee, "The Army 'Mutiny' of 1946," *Journal of American History* 53 (December 1966), 555–571. On the Doolittle Board see Mark R. Grandstaff, "Making the Military American: Advertising, Reform, and the Demise of an Antistanding Military Tradition, 1945–1955," *Journal of Military History* 60 (April 1966); and Eiler, *Mobilizing America*.

For the decisions leading up to the Marshall Mission and much else regarding China in the postwar period, see the works cited in the previous chapter as well as the many excellent articles by an international group of scholars in Larry I. Bland, ed. *George C. Marshall's Mediation Mission to China, December 1945–January 1947* (Lexington, VA: George C. Marshall Foundation, 1998). Ernest R. May's short incisive *The Truman Administration and China, 1945–1949* (Philadelphia: J. B. Lippincott, 1975) analyzes the choices available to Truman and highlights Marshall's influence on China policy.

CHAPTER FIVE

My discussion of the status of the various occupation armies and their interactions with local inhabitants was constructed from the coverage in the *New York Times;* the unpublished history "United States Army Forces in Korea, XXIV Corps," (G-2 Historical Section) cited in the endnotes, as well as the following: Matray, *Reluctant Crusade*; John Hunter Boyle, *Modern Japan: The American Nexus* (Fort Worth, TX: Harcourt Brace Jovanovich, 1993); John W.

Dower, *Embracing Defeat: Japan in the Wake of World War II* (New York: W. W. Norton & Co., 1999); James, *MacArthur*, III; Holly Sanders, "Prostitution and Indentured Servitude in Modern Japan," Ph.D. dissertation, Princeton University, 2005; Nicholas Evans Sarantakes, *Keystone: The American Occupation of Okinawa and U.S.–Japanese Relations* (College Station: Texas A&M University, 2000); Mark Wilkinson, "A Shanghai Perspective on the Marshall Mission," in Bland, ed., *Marshall's Mediation Mission to China*; Cullather, *Illusions of Influence*; and Wurfel, "American Implementation of Philippine Independence."

For integration of the military the official history is Morris J. MacGregor, Jr., *Integration of the Armed Forces, 1940–1965* (Washington, DC: Center of Military History, United States Army, 1981). Bernard C. Nalty, *Strength for the Fight: A History of Black Americans in the Military* (New York: Free Press, 1986) and Sherie Mershon and Steven Schlossman, *Foxholes and Color Lines: Desegregating the U.S. Armed Forces* (Baltimore, MD: Johns Hopkins University Press, 1998) are also good on postwar policy. The following were particularly helpful with reference to the occupation forces in the Pacific and East Asia: Hal M. Friedman, *Creating an American Lake: United States Imperialism and Strategic Security in the Pacific Basin, 1945–1947* (Westport, CT: Greenwood Press, 2001); Yukiko Koshiro, *Trans-Pacific Racisms and the U.S. Occupation of Japan* (New York: Columbia University Press, 1999); John Curtis Perry, *Beneath the Eagle's Wings: Americans in Occupied Japan* (New York: Dodd Mead, 1980); Sarantakes, *Keystone*.

CHAPTER SIX

For the sections on the Philippines and Indochina see the sources cited in chapter 3. For the final gasp of the Korean trusteeship idea and the development of the South Korean armed forces see the works on Korea cited in chapter 3.

John Hunter Boyle, *Modern Japan: The American Nexus* provides a highly readable introduction to the American occupation of Japan including most of the subjects discussed in chapter 6. For the treatment of the emperor, the war crimes tribunals, the Japanese constitution, and MacArthur's recommendations I found the following helpful: Hal Brands, "Who Saved the Emperor? The MacArthur Myth and U.S. Policy toward Hirohito and the Japanese Imperial Institution, 1942–1946," *Pacific Historical Review* (May 2006), 75:2,

271–305; Dower, *Embracing Defeat*; Richard B. Finn, *Winners in Peace: MacArthur, Yoshida, and Postwar Japan* (Berkeley: University of California Press, 1992); James, *Years of MacArthur*; Eiji Takemae, *Inside GHQ: The Allied Occupation of Japan and Its Legacy* (New York: Continuum, 2002). The appalling story of Unit 731 is told in Daniel Barenblatt, *A Plague Upon Humanity: The Hidden History of Japan's Biological Warfare Program* (New York: Perennial, 2004); and Sheldon Harris, *Factories of Death: Japanese Biological Warfare 1932–1945 and the American Cover-Up* (London: Routledge, 1994). On Japanese rearmament see Meirion and Susie Harries, *Sheathing the Sword: The Demilitarization of Japan* (New York: Macmillan, 1987); Paul Chwialkowski, *In Caesar's Shadow: The Life of General Robert Eichelberger* (Westport, CT: Greenwood Press, 1993); John Welfield, *An Empire in Eclipse: Japan in the Postwar American Alliance System* (London: Athlone Press, 1988).

Marshall's communications and reports during his mission to China can be followed in Larry I. Bland and Sharon Ritenour Stevens, editors, *The Papers of George Catlett Marshall* 5, *"The Finest Soldier": January 1, 1945–January 7, 1947* (Baltimore, MD: Johns Hopkins University Press, 2003). For how different interested parties viewed Marshall's mission see Bland, ed., *Marshall's Mediation Mission*; Schnabel, *The Joint Chiefs of Staff and National Policy*; and Hertzstein, *Henry R. Luce*. The Nationalists' use of Japanese troops is examined in Donald Gillin and Charles Etter, "Staying On: Japanese Soldiers and Civilians in China, 1945–1949," *Journal of Asian Studies* 42 (May 1983), 497–518. China expert Arthur Waldron takes an interesting counterfactual look at Jiang's military strategy in "China Without Tears: If Chiang Kai-shek Hadn't Gambled in 1946," in Robert Cowley, ed., *What If?: The World's Most Foremost Military Historians Imagine What Might Have Been* (New York: G. P. Putnam & Sons, 1999). Stueck, *The Wedemeyer Mission* ably examines the origins and consequences of the general's controversial mission.

NOTES

1. Pearlman's study is also available online through the Combined Arms Research Library Digital Research Library at http://www.cgsc.army.mil/carl/contentdm/home.htm.

2. Glantz's study is also available online through the Combined Arms Research Library Digital Research Library at http://www.cgsc.army.mil/carl/contentdm/home.htm.

Index

About the Author

Marc Gallicchio is professor of History at Villanova University and has twice been a Fulbright Visiting Lecturer in Japan. He is the author of *The Cold War Begins in Asia: U.S. East Asian Policy and the Fall of the Japanese Empire* (1988); *The African American Encounter with Japan and China: Black Internationalism in Asia, 1895–1945*, which won the Society for Historians of American Foreign Relations' Robert H. Ferrell Book Prize; and editor of *The Unpredictability of the Past: Memories of the Asia-Pacific War in U.S.–East Asian Relations* (2007).